THE YORKS

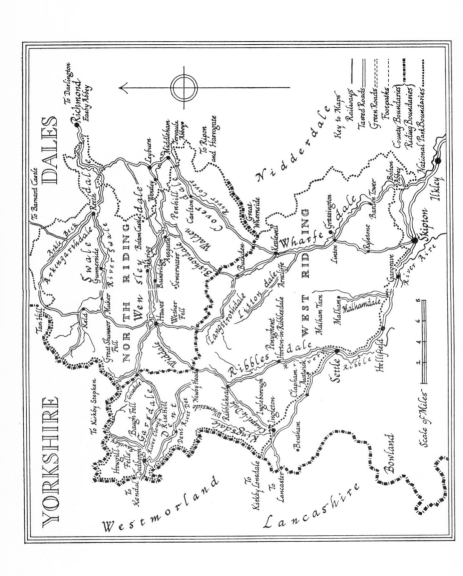

THE YORKSHIRE DALES

Marie Hartley and Joan Ingilby

Illustrated by
Marie Hartley

SMITH SETTLE

First published in 1956 by
J M Dent & Sons Ltd

This new edition published in 1991 by
Smith Settle Ltd
Ilkley Road
Otley
LS21 3JP

ISBN 1 870071 72 7

Printed and bound by
SMITH SETTLE
Ilkley Road, Otley, West Yorkshire LS21 3JP

INTRODUCTION TO THE 1991 EDITION

By and large only a few changes have overtaken the facts in this book. The appearance of the landscape of the Yorkshire Dales in general remains the same, but with new practices and the introduction of tractors and labour-saving equipment since 1950, farming has brought subtle changes. For instance occasional large buildings have replaced the small stone barns, of which many are now redundant. Walls are not always kept up, and the meadows have lost their flowers. Various schemes are on foot to rectify these trends. Besides all this, new houses and bungalows have been built and ruins renovated for the influx of newcomers to the Dales. Tourism too has escalated in volume, and large car parks, sometimes combined with National Park Information Centres, have been made.

We also see, on the outskirts of small towns, industrial estates with individual workshops. Low Mill at Askrigg opened in 1976 as a residential young people's centre. Whernside Manor in Dentdale is no longer a private house, but after being a caving centre is now occupied by an army unit for adventure training. The Georgian Theatre in Richmond re-opened permanently in 1962. The dairy for cheese-making in Coverdale has closed, but a few new cheese-making establishments have been started. The Settle-Carlisle Line after threats of closure has been saved, but does not have the close relationship with local life described in this book. Museums at Richmond, Reeth, Aysgarth, Hawes, Settle and Skipton preserve many relics of past ways of life in the Dales, keeping their memory fresh. The new sports of hang-gliding and mountain bicycling have arrived. But walking, aided by a network of youth hostels, remains the most popular pastime, and tracks on the Pennine Way and elsewhere have had to be repaired at great cost. The popularity of the Yorkshire Dales causes problems and to some extent has diluted its special character.

MH and JL, 1991

ACKNOWLEDGMENTS

THIS book has been made possible by the co-operation of many people, of whom we cannot hope to thank all by name. We wish to thank the archivists and librarians who have made available the documents in their charge, in particular at the Public Record Office, the Institute of Historical Research, Chatsworth House, the North Riding Record Office, Leeds Reference Library, York Minster Library, St Anthony's Hall, York, the library of the Yorkshire Archaeological Society, Skipton Public Library, and the Public Library and the Cartwright Hall, Bradford.

We should like to thank Mr H. L. Bradfer-Lawrence, Mr T. Lord, Mrs M. S. Radcliffe, and Mr G. B. Harker, who have given access to papers in their possession, also Miss N. NcNeill O'Farrell of London, Mrs G. Metcalfe recently of Austwick, Mr B. L. Gee of Settle Limes Ltd, Mr H. B. Miller of Middleham, Mr T. Gill of Reeth, Rev. B. W. Simpson of Thornton-in-Lonsdale, Mr W. S. Worthington of Ingleton, Mr J. Capstick of Dent, Mr J. Scott of Aysgarth, and Mr J. M. Taylor of Horton-in-Ribblesdale station, together with other station-masters of the Settle to Carlisle line, who have given information. Mr R. M. Chapman of Askrigg has kindly read the manuscript. The brief history of the Swaledale lead-mines is based on a collection of papers purchased in 1948 from Mrs E. R. Fawcett. We thank the many who have sped us on our way with hospitality, and those who have shown us their houses or the public buildings or business premises in their charge.

Thanks are due and permission is acknowledged to reproduce plans based on large-scale plans in the keeping of the following societies and offices: Bolton Priory from the Thoresby Society, Jervaulx Abbey from the Yorkshire Archaeological Society, Coverham Abbey and Bolton and Middleham Castles from the Victoria County Histories (North Riding), Richmond Castle and Easby Abbey from the official guides issued by H.M. Stationery Office.

CONTENTS

CONTENTS

ILLUSTRATIONS

NOTE. The key included in the endpaper map applies to all maps which precede sections.

I

THE YORKSHIRE DALES

BETWEEN THE Peak District and the Roman Wall lies a massif of the Pennines that we speak of as the Yorkshire Dales. By this is meant the pastoral hill country of the North and West Ridings, adjoining but apart from industrial Yorkshire and Lancashire. This book covers the central mass, the Craven Dales in the West Riding and the dales of Richmondshire in the North: the area, with some additions, of the Yorkshire Dales National Park that covers 680 square miles.

Of the rural landscapes of England the Yorkshire Dales are to many 'beloved over all.' Where else in England is to be found so large and unspoilt a tract of country with so many high grass-covered hills, so many peopled valleys, so many crystal-clear rivers? The main peaks rise to a little over 2,000 feet above sea level, and from 400 feet to 1,000 feet the dales are inhabited not densely but with a village here, a hamlet there. In these thousands of acres scarcely a blemish is visible.

Each valley plays its own variations on the same theme of hill, dale, and river. Swaledale is narrow, steep-sided, grand, and wild; Wensleydale is broad, wooded, and gracious; Wharfedale is long, winding, and consistently lovely. In Malhamdale a miniature scene contains great cliffs of rock; in Ribblesdale vast rolling lands billow between mountains. We find Dent a hidden oasis, Chapel-le-Dale slung between peaks, and many side dales, secret fastnesses far flung into the hills.

Except for a small territory, the Howgill Fells, in the north-west corner of Yorkshire, the dales belong to one geological age, the Carboniferous, so that the variations on the theme are played in one key—the same rock structure: Great Scar Limestone many hundreds of feet thick, topped by layers of Yoredale Rocks, and capped by millstone grit. The whole rests on ancient rocks—the Pre-Cambrian, the Ordovician, and the Silurian; the latter, as we shall see, composes the Howgills, and all three are exposed here and there in the deep gills on the west of the territory. Bordering the dales on the east is a mass of millstone grit, and the most striking point of demarcation between it and limestone is near Bolton Abbey.

We might presuppose monotony, but not a bit of it. Those upheavals of the earth's surface, the Craven Faults and the Dent Fault, which bound the area on the south and west respectively, have given us the wonders of limestone cliff and scar scenery. Nor do the dales of the West Riding altogether resemble those of the North; the first are pure limestone land and the second are mixed. This is because the whole structure tilts slightly down-hill to the north-east. In Craven, except for the peaks such as Ingleborough and Whernside, the Yoredale Rocks have been worn away altogether by aeons of weathering, and the Great Scar Lime-stone, covering the surface, forms the white walls of Wharfedale, Kilnsey Crag, Malham Cove, and Gordale Scar. In Wensleydale in the North Riding the Great Scar Limestone lies far down below, only seen here and there, and it is buried completely in Swaledale. In these dales the Yoredale Rocks predominate, with their alternating layers of sandstones, shales, and limestones (different from the Great Scar), and give us typical terraced effects.

Lastly, modifying the shape of the dales, came the Ice Age, which we are told ended some 10,000 years ago. Ice covered most of the dales, with only the highest peaks looming above it; and glaciers moving down each valley scooped out the sides and left behind debris that we call moraine, drift, and alluvium. The drift fills out what would otherwise be emaciated slopes, such as the flanks of Ingleborough; the moraines make the turbulent hump-backed contours of the valley floors, as in Upper Ribbles-dale and Wensleydale; and alluvium in the valley bottom gives a fertile soil for rich grass land.

The glaciers left behind them lakes, of which Malham Tarn and Semerwater have survived. The one-time presence of many others can be seen in the flat stretches of valley, for example near Kilnsey. Often lakes were formed in the side valleys by the damming up of the outlets to the main dale by glacial debris. Almost invariably we approach branch dales over a rough tract of country that is glacial moraine; hence the secret, hidden character of many.

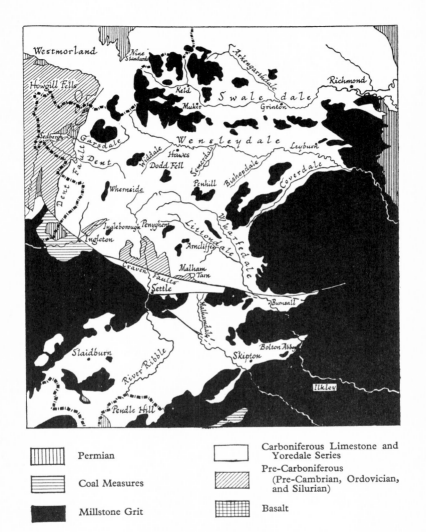

Geological Map of the Yorkshire Dales

Permian

Coal Measures

Millstone Grit

Carboniferous Limestone and
Yoredale Series

Pre-Carboniferous
(Pre-Cambrian, Ordovician,
and Silurian)

Basalt

The limestone wonders of Craven lead us on to the caves and pot-holes, the underground phenomena of the Great Scar Limestone, for extent and interest nowhere to be rivalled in England. Some caves, for instance the Victoria Cave near Settle, were inhabited, and provide remarkable glimpses into a remote past; and the rocky entrances to others once made landmarks used to define boundaries. Since the Rev. John Hutton wrote his adventures in *A Tour to the Caves* in the eighteenth century, the subterranean channels of Gaping Gill, Long Churn, Alum Pot, Ingleborough Cave, White Scar Cavern, and dozens of others have attracted explorers (the spelaeologists), attained international fame, and acquired a literature of their own.

The weather, be it dowly, snizy, or maguey,[1] is a part of dales life, and at all times not a conventional but an absorbing topic. The climate shapes the dales as it shapes the life of the people. The farther we penetrate into the hills the bleaker it becomes. Compared with that of the Plain of York it is wetter and colder, but compared with that of the Lake District it is colder but far drier.   Smog is unknown; but springs are late and autumns early. In the dales the difference between the seasons is emphasized: winter is indrawn and quiescent, summer free and animated.

Rocks, soil, and climate give a variety of vegetation and wild life: heather grows on the millstone grit caps, rough grasses on the glacial drift, a close greensward on the limestone land.   Everywhere, especially in May and June, flowers accompany every walk: the flowery meads before haytime, the flora of woods, of limestone clints, and of an arctic climate on the high rock faces of the hills. Over the moors curlew, snipe, gulls, and green and golden plover call from March to September; redstarts, owls, and tits haunt the woods, and heron, wagtails, and duck the rivers.   Otters are sometimes seen, badgers rarely; foxes, the killers of lambs, are kept down; and since 1955 the rabbit has largely gone.   Trout and grayling, which are mostly preserved for the fishing associations, give sport in the rivers.

We see the dales at a certain moment in time and think of their green hills and valleys as permanent.   Yet each dale and village has its own long story.   Some have castles and abbeys: Richmond, Middleham, Bolton, and Skipton Castles, and Easby, Jervaulx, Coverham, and Bolton Abbeys.   Each has its own life—life in

---

[1] Three dialect words meaning respectively dull, raw, misty.

Littondale

the West Riding dales, which are nearer to industry, differs from that in the North—and each has a continuity that has been affected but not broken by changing social conditions.

Armed with present-day knowledge, we look back to the arrival of the first men, Mesolithic men, who as hunters penetrated a country of wooded hills and swampy valleys, the haunt of deer and wild boar, after the Ice Age. Pygmy flints and a harpoon in the Victoria Cave reveal their presence. As we explore the dales we shall occasionally find a stone circle or a tumulus of the next group, Bronze Age men. Lastly in prehistoric times came the villages and hill-forts of the Iron Age.

The Iron Age men and women, the Brigantes, had to contend with the invasion of the Romans and their 350 years of occupation. In the dales they appear to have been the remnants of a once proud people. The climate then was poor; they suffered from arthritis and lived a Swiss Family Robinson kind of existence. Their tumbledown round huts and the little crofts of their villages are traceable on many dry limestone plateaus. A three-holed bone pipe, a kind of primitive recorder, accurately tuned, has been found in Malhamdale, and it illuminates our meagre knowledge of the lives of these people.

We look back to the men who founded the present-day villages: the Angles, who coming up the river valleys had first choice of sites, the Danes, who filled in the gaps, and the Norsemen, who coming from the west found the heads of the dales to their liking. Briefly, place-names ending with 'ton,' 'ham,' and 'ley' point to Anglian settlement, those with 'by' and 'thorp' to Danish, and 'thwaite,' 'wick,' 'sett,' and other terminations to Norse.

These peoples plotted the area of the townships, a deceptive name meaning the territory round a village, and an important division of land in the dales. Whereas in the south the area of the ecclesiastical parish is all-important, in the north it is often too large to make a compact unit. Several townships usually make up a parish, and each one, with its village, is a nucleus round which life revolves. The township (often called a civil parish nowadays) was originally the unit of agricultural life, with its open fields, wastes, and commons shared by the inhabitants. It used also to be the administrative area for the local constabulary and the poor-law, and it still is the territory presided over by the parish council. Ask any dalesman the boundaries of his township and he will tell you them at once.

After the Norman Conquest Domesday Book gives us a tantalizingly blurred image of the dales. Most villages, except those at the dale heads, are to be found in it. Some, as we shall see, are lost. 'There are moors there,' says an entry under one of them, Crooksby in Bishopdale, giving a rare hint of the terrain. Although several others would exist, churches are only mentioned at Spennithorne, Long Preston, and one in Lower Swaledale.

Almost without exception the villages of Domesday Book were surrounded by the arable land of the Open Field System, and, owing to the hilly terrain, the strips of cultivated land, the feature of this system, were here arranged in terraces, called ranes. Grassed over now, the ranes are distinguishable from natural ridges by their straight lines, and may be seen on all sides, particularly west of Bolton Castle in Wensleydale and round Conistone in Wharfedale. The ranes formed strips cultivated by ploughs drawn by teams of oxen; and we shall often refer to them. Tithe suits in the ecclesiastical courts, manorial records, and lawsuits picture the growing of corn up to the mid seventeenth century and sometimes into the eighteenth, where now we should never think of visualizing corn fields.

In those times the boundaries of Yorkshire on the west were ill defined. The country from Austwick to Sedbergh lay in 'Lanesdale,' a colony rather than a part of the county; and not until 1131, when Henry I gave Nigel de Aubigny a portion of Lonsdale, which included these places, did the wapentake of Ewecross, now the western corner of Yorkshire, come into being.

After the Conquest we see medieval England in the dales dominated by the monks in their monasteries and the lords in their castles. The Scropes, the Cliffords, the Percys, the FitzHughs, and the Mowbrays gave huge tracts of land to the religious houses. In almost every village chapels existed where priests daily said mass for the souls of the dead. The monks developed their sheepfarming on the moors and their vaccaries—cow runs or 'kye gates' —with regulated pasturage on the hillsides.

Then, people lived on manors as bordars or free men, earning their tenancies by labour or by paying small rents and following their lords and the Wardens of the Marches to fight on the Borders. The menace of the Scots, at its greatest in the unhappy fourteenth century, culminated in 1513, when 'warlike wights' rode out from Craven and Richmondshire to Flodden Field.   In spite of the ravages of the plague, Elizabethan times were an important period of development.

Most of the foundations if not the fabrics of the churches in the dales date from the Middle Ages.   Although as a whole they compare unfavourably with those in other districts of Yorkshire, nevertheless at least a dozen contain individual features of intense interest.   In Wharfedale we shall see the rood-loft at Hubberholme and the nave of the priory church at Bolton, now the parish church, with its Early English west front and wall-arcading.   In Swaledale, Easby church has fascinating early frescoes; in Wensleydale, Spennithorne and Wensley contain many rich details.

In Craven, noted for its lack of good church architecture, Kirkby Malham is outstanding as an almost perfect example of a Perpendicular church.   Skipton shows many features, not least the Clifford tombs, and Long Preston, with Jacobean woodwork, belongs mostly to the Decorated period.   Both Hubberholme and Horton-in-Ribblesdale attract by their appearance of great age. Other churches not to be missed are Sedbergh, Giggleswick, Grinton, Burnsall, and Linton-in-Craven.

Feudalism lasted a long time, long after the Dissolution of the Monasteries and up to the Civil War.   The Pilgrimage of Grace and the Rising of the North arose as much to preserve the old framework of economic as of religious life.   All over the dales people were tenants on large estates, holding to their farms by their 'ancient birthright of title.'   Briefly, this 'tenant right' consisted of minute rents, fines on the deaths of tenants and their lords, and possession descending from father to son (or daughter); in Richmondshire it included the obligation of military service on the Borders.   Often rents were handed over in churches; the men of Langstrothdale paid theirs to the Percys in the porch of Hubberholme.   In the seventeenth century, when the system was abandoned, many disputes clouded the adjustment to rents as we know them.

For long people here and there paid those strange rents once commuted for labour services.   The boon hen, on which Lady Anne Clifford and the tenant who had paid it dined, is a famous example, and broad-headed arrows, roses, pounds of pepper, gloves, also smoke and plough silver were paid to the Scropes at Thornton Rust in Wensleydale in 1616.

The deer, inseparably linked with feudalism, largely disappeared with it. They were valuable not only for sport, but as food for the castle households and dependants. Neither fields of corn nor meadows might be fenced off against them; but people were allowed to drive them out with 'little dogs,' and they sometimes sat up at night to thus protect their crops. A number of deer survived up to early Stuart times in remote dales, such as Cotterdale, Raydale, and Arkengarthdale in the New Forest; in the 1620's the deer disappeared from Wharfedale, hunted to their deaths by the Yorkes of Gouthwaite in a bitter feud with the Cliffords. In Swaledale, where the deer had been carefully protected by the Whartons, they vanished about 1725. Undoubtedly the felling of woods, by diminishing their feeding and breeding grounds, aided their disappearance. In modern times herds of deer were kept in Bolton Park in Wensleydale, in the Deer Park at Bolton Abbey, and at Buckden in Wharfedale; but these have all gone.

Out of the ashes of feudalism rose the yeomen, who had lived on their farms generation after generation. Enjoying prosperous times in the general interchange of property of the seventeenth century, they bought their lands, and, mostly towards the end of the century, built their solid houses to be found in all the dales, especially round Settle, where they are enriched by a wealth of architectural detail.

These houses, with door-heads carved with the date of building and the initials of the yeoman and his wife, make one of the features of the dales. In most cases it is safe to assume that they have been built on the site of an older house, and those with tiny round-headed windows almost invariably stand on the site of a monastic grange.

Some of the names of the yeomen, going back to the seventeenth century, and a few to the fourteenth, survive to this day. Once large families of many sons, who often figure in old records, ensured that the same names were carried on from generation to generation, and up to the Industrial Revolution many people still lived in places from which they took their names, as the Ellertons at Ellerton in Swaledale. The names still indicate to which dale people belong. Clans such as the Metcalfes and Aldersons hail

Penyghent

from Wensleydale and Swaledale respectively; Sedgwicks and Capsticks come from Dent, Redmaynes and Kidds from Ingleton, Demaines and Listers from Wharfedale, and so on. In Tudor times a good many people—Willans, Hodgsons, and Masons—seem to have moved from the west (Dent) into Wensleydale.

The eighteenth century saw the development of industrial ventures—the lead-mines, the knitting industry, the cotton and woollen mills. A large labouring class that does not exist nowadays lived in small cottages in yards in the villages or on small holdings on the hillsides. The important Keighley to Kendal and Richmond to Lancaster turnpikes, and others, improved travel and communications. Westwards through Wensleydale on the Richmond to Lancaster road were carried 'corn, butter, cattle, bacon, and potatoes,' and eastwards 'grocery goods, liquor, timber, and mahogany.' Every large village enjoyed its complement of craftsmen, physicians, and attorneys; and the Georgian houses of these people may be picked out in village and market town.

In the next century decline followed the Industrial Revolution and the importation of foreign lead; the industries failed, the corn mills ceased to work, and the craftsmen to ply their various trades. The search for employment drove people to Lancashire and Durham and sent many to Australia or across the 'girt Dub,' as they called the Atlantic Ocean, to America. Farming and the beginnings of a tourist industry were left. Introduced in the previous century, Methodism, by filling a need, became firmly established. In spite of, or perhaps because of, the coming of the railways, the population in remote places declined. In many lonely gills and dales ruined houses, owl-haunted and pregnant with memories, will be seen on our travels.

Finally, we look back over the last fifty years to the appearance of motor transport, that together with the First World War ineluctably broke down the insularity of the dales. Many of the fairs and feast celebrations, partly jolly country amusements, partly drinking orgies, ended. We see the closure of railway lines, whose arrival not long before had been greeted with excited enthusiasm, and the National Grid system of electricity spreading to all the dales. Populations rise in market towns and on the southern border, but in remote valleys, especially in Upper Wharfedale and the dales of the North Riding, the fall continues.

Farming remains as the main source of livelihood and the chief factor in shaping the face of the country. No one can remember the building of the walls for the enclosures of the last century, but in a long lifetime a man can have witnessed the change from scythes to mowing machines, the replacement of horses by tractors, the slump of the 1930's, and the wartime and continuing post-war wave of prosperity.

Though cattle may well predominate on those in the valleys, and sheep on those on the hills, the farms are usually mixed, and small enough to be run by the farmer and his family. It is almost essential to be born in the dales to succeed on one. Small box-like barns in the North Riding and large barns of great beauty in the West are scattered about the fields rather than near the farm-house, that often in a village looks no different from any other house. Breeds of sheep—Swaledale, Wensleydale, Dalesbred, Rough Fell—suiting the different types of ground and herbage have been evolved, and the native Shorthorn and the introduced Friesians and Ayrshires are attested T.T. cattle. 'I'm cow proud,' explains the valley farmer. 'He's got a hill eye,' says the wife of a sheep man.

What strikes us nowadays is the neatness, cleanliness, and extreme quiet of the villages of the dales. Yet in spite of depletion in numbers they are lively and have resources for most needs. Although it has lost many communal activities, village life is still gregarious. On winter nights dances and badminton for the young, whist drives for the middle-aged, educational classes for all, clubs for the men, Women's Institute meetings for the women, keep up a constant series of 'stirs,' as they say in Swaledale.

Formerly sporting events, the hunts of every district, the horse-races, foot-races, cock-fights, bull-baiting, and hound trails, filled a large place in dales life. Their place has been taken to-day by football, grouse shooting on the moors, agricultural and flower shows, and sports from large events with motor-cycle races, horse trotting, and bookies to children's sports and fancy-dress parades on village greens.

In the dales people are individuals, sometimes bristling with local pride, deeply rooted to their home land. Many tales emphasize the strength and stature of past dalesmen; for example, one man walking home overnight from Liverpool to Howgill, near Sedbergh, eighty miles, had to rest at Kirkby Lonsdale, not for himself but for his dog. They ate hugely, and were often 'all legs and wings.' Perhaps oatcake and porridge, once the staple diet, made from oats ground at the mills, nourished bone and muscle. People lived and still live to great ages, sometimes to over a hundred.

The dalesman (the name was coined over the last hundred years) speaks a dialect derived largely from the Norse and, alas, in process of dying out. It is a foreign language to the uninitiated, and, except where the two begin to merge in Craven, it bears no resemblance to the speech of the people of the West Riding industrial towns. For example, where the West Riding man says 'stooan' the dalesman says 'steean.' It has a large vocabulary of its own words, such as kitle (smock), stee (ladder), twitchbell (earwig), bumble kite (blackberry), and many 'sikelike' words; the Yorkshire Dialect Society and the important linguistic atlas mapped by Professor H. Orton of Leeds University record pronunciation and manifold expressions.

In October 1954 the Yorkshire Dales were designated as a National Park; and the Pennine Way, a signposted path for the walker over the hills, is planned. The dalesman is a natural host, usually courteous and helpful. Visitors have been welcomed to the dales for many years, and if more are to come good relationships will be preserved if three simple rules are followed—shut gates, leave no litter, and avoid hay fields. Also, if wild flowers are to survive to be enjoyed, no single plant should be uprooted.

We have small country hotels, boarding-houses, rooms, and youth hostels to cater for holiday-makers; and a local speciality, Wensleydale cheese, that takes its name from the one dale but is also made in others.

In Elizabethen times Camden and Leland described Craven and Richmondshire with all the freshness of new discovery. Eighteenth-century tourists set down impressions of their travels there, and Whitaker wrote his great historical works on the eve of social changes. Following them came Harry Speight, Edmund Bogg, Halliwell Sutcliffe, J. S. Fletcher, Willie Riley, Ella Pontefract, and others writing to-day. To their work we add our contribution to the appreciation of the dales.

II

WHARFEDALE

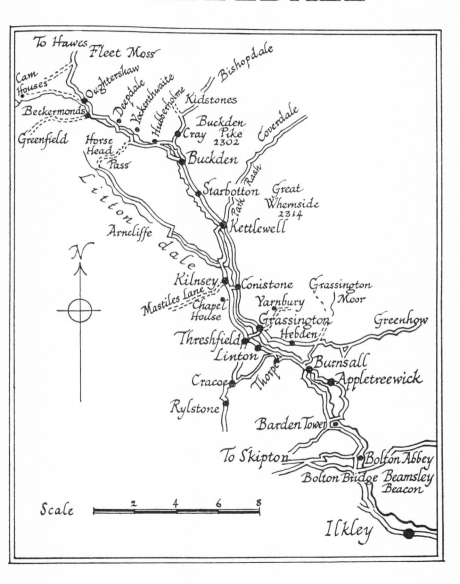

To Hawes · Fleet Moss · Bishopdale
Cam Houses · Oughtershaw · Deepdale · Yockenthwaite · Hubberholme · Kidstones · Coverdale
Beckermonds · Buckden Pike 2302 · Cray
Greenfield · Horse Head Pass · Buckden
Litton dale · Starbotton · Park Rash · Great Whernside 2314
Arncliffe · Kettlewell
N
Kilnsey · Conistone · Grassington Moor
Mastiles Lane · Yarnbury · Greenhow
Chapel House · Grassington
Threshfield · Hebden
Linton · Burnsall
Cracoe · Thorpe · Appletreewick
Rylstone · Barden Tower
To Skipton · Bolton Abbey
Bolton Bridge · Beamsley Beacon
Scale 2 4 6 8
Ilkley

1. BOLTON BRIDGE TO BARDEN

O N 17TH FEBRUARY 1698 the Earl of Burlington's steward wrote from Bolton Bridge in Craven to a landowner in Wensleydale. He proposed a meeting on the Kidstones Pass thirty miles away at the head of Wharfedale, but suggested that they wait 'until the days are longer, the Season warmer, and the Moors more passable.'

When spring came and the steward set out up the dale he saw the familiar vistas that we enjoy with some surface changes. He rode along white dusty tracks through a more rustic scene than that of to-day, with no walls on the commons, woods clothing many hillsides, deer in the parks, small cottages with ling thatches in the villages, and the wheels of corn mills turning by the becks.

He passed Bolton Priory, ruinous and neglected, Barden Tower, restored by Lady Anne Clifford forty years before, crossed the new bridge at Barden for Appletreewick and Burnsall and over Linton Bridge for Conistone; saw Kilnsey Crag, or Kilnsey Scar as it was then called, across the valley; continued to Kettlewell, where, if it was Thursday, stalls would be set up for market-day, and through Starbotton and Buckden and up the Rakes reached Kidstone Causey on the boundary between Wharfedale and Wensleydale.

With the addition of Langstrothdale west of Buckden and the valley between Ilkley and Bolton Bridge the steward traversed Upper Wharfedale, the area we propose to describe, a country-side of hill and dale and winding river of inspiration to poet and artist, a limestone land where sunshine intensifies the brilliancy of white walls against emerald meadows, where storms veil a land-scape that is light in key; whose beauty rests on the silvan rocky charms of river scenes, on the magic view of a distant dale head, on woods and pastures bright with rare flowers, and on grey villages at the foot of steep hillsides.

Before starting out from Bolton Bridge to follow in the wake of the steward, we shall see, if we first climb Beamsley Beacon two and a half miles to the east, on the one hand Ilkley and Addingham, dense centres of population that we are about to leave behind, and,

on the other, fertile valleys and foot-hills and the lower reaches of
the dale that lies before us.

Approaching the bridge along what was once the coach road
from Skipton to Knaresborough over Blubberhouses Moor, we pass
Beamsley Hospital, alms-houses for old women founded in 1593
by Lady Anne Clifford's mother, as a tablet over the entrance
explains. The tiny round chapel and cottages in cloister-like
seclusion off the busy main road are an architectural curiosity.

A bridge at Bolton is mentioned as early as 1318 (Saxton's map
shows one there), and Bolton Bridge was washed away in a flood
on 17th September 1673. The house east of it was once the Red
Lion Inn; and a priest ministered at a chapel here, for on the beam
of a cottage alongside was once a pious inscription.

Bridgefield, a sixty-acre pasture, stretches away from the bridge
towards Bolton Abbey.[1]   Originally it was one of the open arable
fields of Bolton, well fenced at great expense by the hunting
Cliffords to keep out the deer. Here it is believed that Prince
Rupert, bound for Marston Moor, quartered his troops and
trampled down the corn. In the eighteenth century the field was
famous for the fattening of stock, and it is still a rich pasture. At
the village end is the great tithe barn, rebuilt on the site of an
older barn, and now used as a storehouse for the estate.

At the Devonshire Arms Hotel near by we turn off for Bolton
Abbey and Upper Wharfedale. In 1792 Lord Torrington on his
northern tour stayed at the Devonshire Arms, then called the
Burlington Arms. He found excellent lodging for the night and
paid 4s. 2½d., a sum that included mutton chops, salad, cold veal
pie, and hay and corn for his horse. Here guides could be hired
to conduct parties through the woods. In modern times the
hotel is one of the best known in the county.

Imagine the name Bolton without the suffix 'Abbey.' It at
once merges into all the other numerous Boltons derived from the
Old English _bōðl_, a building, that with 'ton' merely denotes a
village. But Bolton Abbey means to most people in the West
Riding a pause in living, a sparkling, idyllic pause; it means
summer afternoons by a rippling river, green pastures, and the
priory ruins casting over their environment an extraordinary
peace; it means a landscape of natural grace, shaped by man over

---

[1] The monastic ruins at Bolton are those of a priory and should be so called;
by long usage the village has come to be named Bolton Abbey.

The ruins casting over their environment an extraordinary peace

many centuries; it means a blend of historic and legendary romance, and a neighbourhood with the bloom of a place of popular resort.

Before the Norman Conquest Bolton-in-Craven occupied the position of importance that Skipton later held. It was the centre of one of the extensive possessions of the Saxon Earl Edwin, whose manor-house probably stood on or near the site of the priory. This large estate included nineteen hamlets, one of which was Skipton, and other places as far afield as Hellifield and Malham. After 1086 William gave the estate to a Norman, Robert Romilly, who moved his manor-house from Bolton to Skipton, thus establishing Skipton as the head of the fee or honour for later lords. There, as we know, the castle was built.

In 1120 Robert's daughter, Cecily Romilly, together with her husband, William Meschin, established a cell of Augustinian canons at Embsay, near Bolton; and Alice, one of her three daughters, who married a nephew of King David of Scotland, gave Bolton to the canons, who moved there from Embsay in 1155.

The Honour of Skipton remained in the possession of the Romillys until it ended in the female line and came into the hands of the Crown. In 1311, when the castle was granted to Robert Clifford, this family's long association with Skipton began. At the Dissolution in 1542 Bolton was sold to Henry Clifford, Earl of Cumberland, who at the same time obtained Langstrothdale by marriage with a Percy. In 1635 the only child and heiress of the last earl, Lady Elizabeth Clifford, married Richard Boyle, second Earl of Cork and first Earl of Burlington. The last descendant of this family was Charlotte Elizabeth, who in 1748 married the fourth Duke of Devonshire.

Romillys, Cliffords, Percys, names that breathe of power and great events, dominated Craven for centuries and are inseparable from the lore and legend of Wharfedale. Legend ascribes the gift of the site of Bolton to the canons to the sorrow of Alice Romilly for the loss of her son, the Boy of Egremont, who was drowned at the Strid. Wordsworth tells the poignant story in *The Force of Prayer*. It is not based on fact, as 'the boy' signed some of the foundation deeds of the priory; but he may well have met his death jumping the Strid.

Alice, by giving rights in Bolton 'in wood and plain, in waters, meadows, and pastures,' made possible the building of the priory near the Wharfe. It requires an effort to picture the site crowded with buildings and quick with that blend of religious and commercial life distinctive of monasticism. Yet here the canons lived for almost four hundred years, sometimes in debt, sometimes reprimanded for laxity, sometimes overburdened with guests. They developed their many estates, traded in wool, bred horses, mined lead and iron, eventually waxed rich, and were destroyed.

The Earls of Burlington and the Dukes of Devonshire were absentee landlords of these estates valuable for their mineral and sporting rights; yet to them we owe that 'rural carelessness' that still makes the present-day charm of Bolton. The archway spanning the road, built as an aqueduct to the corn mill, was a conceit of an Earl of Burlington. Even the waterfall, tumbling down the cliff on the east bank of the river, is artificial. Many of the farmhouses—Park House, Stank Farm, and the Arches—reflect estate architecture. The Strid Cottage was designed by Sir Joseph Paxton, and John Harper, a York architect, worked at Bolton in the early nineteenth century under 'the Bachelor Duke.' A distinct resemblance between this countryside and the park land of Chatsworth, the Derbyshire home of the Devonshires, testifies to the subtle effect of the influence of the hand of man.

When the may blossom scents the air and the gnarled ash by the chancel shows not a touch of green, or when the woods and the bracken of the Deer Park flame with colour, these are the times to visit Bolton. All the summer days groups of people stray in many directions: through rustic gates to the ruins, into the present-day parish church that was the nave of the priory church, across stepping-stones to the woods at Storiths and Hazlewood, past the Cavendish Pavilion to the black stony chasms of the Strid.

Ruskin has recorded the profound influence of the melancholy beauty of Bolton Priory on the art of Turner. Here Landseer, wearing a maroon velvet shooting-coat, made sketches from which he painted his 'Bolton Abbey in Olden Time,' exhibited at the Royal Academy in 1834 and now at Chatsworth. This picture made known and popularized the place. But of all the pictures painted here that by Thomas Girtin best conveys the serenity of Bolton. It shows the ruins against a late evening sky with the light reflected on to the river in the foreground.

The priory would not appear the same without the rustic rectory near it. The old part of this building housed Bolton Free School, founded under the will of the Hon. Robert Boyle in 1697, as an inscription on the porch records. Fee-paying boarders were admitted, and the homely regulations stipulated that the children of Dissenters need not attend the church services and that the 'scholars be kept as much as can be from climbing the abbey walls, fruit trees, and from the danger of the river. And that such children as come a mile or more, to be loosed a little sooner in winter time that they may get home ere it be dark.' In 1864 Bolton parish was separated from Skipton; and some ten years later the school building was converted into a rectory.

The Rev. William Carr, incumbent of Bolton for fifty-four years, who died aged 80 in 1843, lived at the Arches Farm. He it was who bred the Craven Heifer in 1807. This huge beast weighed 150 stone and was sold for £200. On the Arches Farm are Parson's Meadow and the Duke's Barn; in the latter the heifer was kept in a stall with an extra wide door still to be seen. This barn is partially cruck-built, with a ling thatch covered with corrugated-iron sheeting.

Footpaths and drives lead to Barden, three miles up the river, footpaths roofed with canopies of branches and foliage, and drives along which wagonettes plied until the last war. In past times, even as early as 1838 when a small guide-book, *Gleanings in Craven*, by Frederic Montagu, recorded them, the view-points along the drives were given names. On the east side of the river there were the Oak, Clifford, and Strid Seats, and Boyle Ford Seat, and similarly in the Valley of Desolation Law Seat, Buck Rake Seat, and the Devonshire Seat. On the west side is the Hawkstone, a rocky promontory on the path between the Strid and Barden.

Across the wooden bridge from the Cavendish Pavilion, where meals may be obtained, Park House stands at the foot of the Deer Park, where deer were kept up to the First World War, and farther up the river the Valley of Desolation strikes off to the moors. The name of the latter, given to it after the damage wrought by a severe storm in 1826, typifies the romanticism of Bolton; its real name is Posforth Gill. A woodreeve in the early eighteenth century recounted other destruction in this and other gills by the cutting of trees for building, fencing, lead-mines, and Grassington smelt mill.

So on this side of the river we reach Barden Bridge. Narrow and humpbacked and slung between steep hillsides it crosses a swiftly running reach of the Wharfe. If we had to make a choice we should choose Barden as the loveliest of the dale bridges.

Above it Barden Tower stands boldly on a knoll above the river. Within recent years the scene has changed: the wood alongside the road has been cut down, and with it the overhanging wayside tree that used to frame the familiar group of ruin and retainers' house. None the less the tower, if with less charm, remains as a monument to feudalism and the Cliffords.

Occupying what was originally the site of the chief hunting lodge of the Cliffords of Skipton Castle in the Forest of Barden, the tower was built in about 1485 by Henry Lord Clifford, known as the Shepherd Lord because he was brought up in seclusion as a shepherd.   The estates of his father, Butcher Clifford, killed at Towton in the Wars of the Roses, were confiscated by the Yorkists, and not until the Shepherd Lord was thirty were they restored to him.   At times journeying to Cumberland or London, but mostly enjoying simple pursuits at Barden, Henry Clifford is a figure round which to weave stories.   He led Craven men to Flodden Field in 1513, and he died ten years later.

When in 1657 the tower came into the hands of Lady Anne Clifford, though it was never legally hers and in fact belonged to the Countess of Cork, she forthwith began extensive repairs and rebuilding.   Indomitable, dominating, and pious, the figure of Lady Anne Clifford emerges vividly from the past.   Gray, the poet, after visiting her tomb in Appleby church in Westmorland, wrote an epitaph on her:

> Now clean, now hideous, mellow now, now gruff,
> She swept, she hiss'd, she ripened and grew rough,
> At Broom,[1] Pendragon, Appleby, and Brough.

Though attempts were made to retain it, after Lady Anne's death Barden reverted to its rightful owner, the Earl of Burlington. Even so he had to write to his steward: 'Keep firm the tenants of Barden from playing tricky.'   The tower, however, fell into disuse. When Whitaker saw it in 1774 it was whole, but shortly afterwards it was stripped of its roof.   Until 1872 cottages stood in the field below it.

None of the ancient houses with their ling-thatched roofs remains: Littlegate farmhouse at Drebley is not thatched but it is cruck-built.   Doubtless if they looked picturesque, their interiors were low and dark.

However, several thatched barns in the neighbourhood still convey an idea of the old buildings of the dales.   Counting the Duke's Barn at Bolton, four barns are cruck-built: Bombey Barn, a mile due north of Barden and now in ruins, and Corn Barn and another barn at Drebley.   A fifth, Barden Scale, stood not far from the junction of the Embsay road near Barden Tower, but was moved piecemeal and re-erected at Shibden Hall Museum at Halifax a few years ago.   On the other side of the river Watergate Barn above Barden Bridge and a barn on

[1] Brougham in Westmorland.

Howgill Farm are ling-thatched, but neither of these is cruck-built. A number of barns built on the estate in the 1740's cost from £15 to £18.

Nowadays Barden, like Bolton, means to most people a romantic ruin rather than a modern community. In the early eighteenth century there were twenty-seven tenants at Barden, who had to do suit and service at 'ye Court and Corn Mill of ye Countess Juliana at Barden, and such boons and service as should be paid and performed.' Feudalism has gone; but several families—Listers, Demaines, Moons—who were tenants under the Cliffords still remain. Unfortunately some of these old names so long connected with the district are in process of dying out, but it is to be hoped that the notable courtesy and dignity of these people of the communities of Bolton and Barden will continue.

2. APPLETREEWICK TO GRASSINGTON

A s IF A skilful hand had planned each division to sharpen
and hold interest, Wharfedale separates into parts like a
book into chapters. The divisions, however, are natural,
made by the curves of the valley as we advance plunging farther
and farther into the high hills. At Barden we begin a new
chapter, the stretch of valley between it and Grassington, seven
miles away. Two roads start off at either side of the river, that on
the right leading through Appletreewick and Burnsall.

Strung along a sun-warmed hillside, Appletreewick lies between
bleak brown moorland and the banks of the Wharfe; and the
houses dispose themselves graciously along its hilly street, backed
in the one direction by Thorpe Fell and in the other by Simon's
Seat. Much of the village's story weaves round old families—the
Youngs, Cravens, Prestons, and Yorkes—whose houses still lend
to the street and the neighbourhood the dignity of the yeomen:
Low Hall at the foot, Monks Hall in the middle, High Hall at the
top, and Percival Hall out on the hills to the north-east.

At the time of the Domesday survey Appletreewick was a small
place that, like the Manor of Bolton, was transferred to the Romillys.
But after several changes it was bought in 1300 by the prior and
canons of Bolton, who during their 240 years of ownership
established the village as a centre of trade. They mined for lead,
developed a cloth trade, and held a great four-day fair. Monks
Hall is on the site of their grange; restored in 1697, it has an
unusual door-head possibly of fifteenth-century date.

After the Dissolution the manor passed through many hands,
and at length in 1653 it was bought by Sir John Yorke of Gouthwaite in Nidderdale; and the younger sons of the family lived at
Percival Hall. This house, for long used as a farmhouse, was
considerably restored by Sir William Milner in the 1930's, and,
standing above terraced gardens, it is now a show-place.

Though there was an earlier house on the site, High Hall or Elm

Tree House was built by the Craven family. William Craven, born at Appletreewick in 1548 in a cottage now converted into a chapel of ease, is the Dick Whittington of Wharfedale. Apprenticed to a mercer in London, he became Sheriff of London in 1600 and Lord Mayor in 1610. High Hall retains its original plan with a hall and minstrels' gallery, and has fine oak panelling, an oak staircase, elaborate plaster work, and a window with 720 leaded lights. After the Cravens the Youngs lived here until 1857. The ancient elm on the roadside at the entrance gate was felled a few years ago.

Low Hall, on the other hand, is a comparatively modern house altered in 1868 by William and Robert Procter. But its yeomen owners were the Prestons. In 1597 Thomas Preston bought the property, of which he was tenant, from George, Earl of Cumberland. The house itself was built in 1658 and the farm buildings in 1690. These, some of which were once cottages, show a wealth of architectural detail: mullioned windows with carved lintels, doorways with masons' marks, stone troughs, and oak-pegged doors.

Those to whom the use of stone gives pleasure will find much to see here and in the street and down the lanes of the village.

In early Stuart times a prolonged feud between Francis, Earl of Cumberland, and Sir John Yorke, the grandson of the Sir John who bought the manor, colours the story of Appletreewick. The quarrel concerned the deer jealously guarded by the Cliffords, who employed many keepers and who hunted where they pleased in the forests and chases of Skipton, Barden, and Bolton. On the other hand, Sir John claimed free warren over his lands as originally granted to the canons, and with him were allied other landowners such as the Claphams of Beamsley and the Tennants of Chapel House near Kilnsey.

The long and bitter feud, punctuated by many lawsuits, was in effect symptomatic of the slow extinction of feudalism. The deer offered a tempting source of food, and were poached by 'notorious deer stealers, men of mean estate and worse condition and such as live idly in this Dalish country.' George Clapham told how his grandfather opposed a great hunting party of the earl's coming on to his land, and he himself confessed that once his servants went out because 'his wyfe did long for a peece of venison.'

From 1606 to 1622 the marauders, either led or encouraged by

Sir John Yorke, hunted from one end of the dales to the other, in Langstrothdale, up Littondale, into Ribblesdale, in the Forest of Elsoe, in Washburndale, and in Nidderdale. Armed with guns and crossbows and accompanied by either greyhounds or blood-hounds and sometimes 'drawing dogs,' they met at night, often in the townfields of the villages and hamlets. They killed many deer, some of them well known, such as one called Broad Head. In 1621 Sir John's men came to blows with the earl's men, who as usual had attended Appletreewick Fair to buy sheep; it marked the end of the feud, for by then almost all the deer had been destroyed.

Nowadays no fair is held at Appletreewick. It ceased about the middle of the last century and is remembered only in place-names: Sheep Fair Hill and Onion Lane where onions were sold. Craftsmen, lead-miners, and workers in small neighbouring cotton mills have gone; and many newcomers, week-end cottagers, and retired people fill out the village's diminished population. It is a lovable place, perhaps the most expressive in Wharfedale of native charm.

In the one and a half miles between Appletreewick and Burnsall the road first runs alongside Woodhouse Kail, an easily ascended little hill that offers an attractive view; next, in the fields to the west, is Woodhouse Manor, in monastic times the property of the priory of Marton-in-Cleveland, and afterwards of the Cliffords, who were followed by yeomen owners. It is one of Yorkshire's lost villages, of which only the manor-house, now a farmhouse, and its barns remain.

A little farther on the few scattered houses of Hartlington—the hall, mill, and former inn—make up a place that, like Appletree-wick and Burnsall, was mentioned in Domesday Book, and that at one time passed by marriage to Sir Thomas Metcalfe of Nappa Hall in Wensleydale. Hartlington Hall was built in 1894 by Colonel R. H. Dawson and was occupied in the Second World War by the boys of Leeds Grammar School.

From this side of the valley we reach Burnsall Bridge, but from the road on the west side of the river the bridge, houses, and church tower of Burnsall, framed by trees and seen against a background of hill, compose a ready-made picture. Beautifully situated at a river crossing and alongside a bend of the Wharfe, it is an easy place to visit, and with riverside and moorland walks has been for many years, and still is, a holiday resort. The Red Lion Hotel, once the Bridge End Inn, caters for the motorist; and Burnsall Sports, held in August, make a popular event.

Burnsall was an early centre of Christianity, as the hogbacks and fragments of Anglo-Danish crosses preserved in the church bear witness. The early font, too, that dates from about 1150, is particularly fine. Burnsall's ancient and extensive parish once included Conistone, near Kilnsey; Rylstone was taken out of it in 1876; and at that date, by allotting one to Rylstone, the two medieties of the rectory were abolished.

The churches of Wharfedale were remarkable for the divided livings, that is medieties, once existing at Burnsall, Linton, and Kettlewell. They originated from the places having two manors and two lords who had the right of presentation to the living. It was a complicated arrangement, for the two rectors needed two houses and two stalls and often had two pulpits in the churches.

Though he was born at Appletreewick, Sir William Craven devoted his charitable bequests to Burnsall. In the early seventeenth century he bore the charges for a restoration of the church, he rebuilt the bridge, and founded and endowed the grammar-school.

You might mistake the grammar-school building next to the church for a house unless you chance to pass on a summer's day, when the scholars in shorts or bright cotton frocks play in front of it and their childish voices ring out over the village street. As a school its record is undistinguished; girls were admitted about 1860 and it became an elementary school in 1876. But the building, graceful, elegant, and well proportioned, is one of the most attractive examples of domestic architecture in the Yorkshire Dales.

From Burnsall a choice of two ways leads to Grassington, the direct through Hebden, the circuitous by Threshfield. That by Hebden joins the Pateley Bridge to Grassington road that has come over Greenhow Hill, a road famous as the route of the monks of Fountains from their Wharfedale granges to the abbey, and as an eighteenth-century turnpike busy with the traffic of carting lead. Hebden itself was once a miners' village, the mines being reached up Hebden Gill.

Along the roundabout route to Grassington lies Thorpe-sub-Montem in the parish of Burnsall. If you wish to see Thorpe, tucked between the limestone knolls of Kail Hill and Elbolton, you leave the main road and by narrow lanes drop down to this secret hidden village of only fifty-three inhabitants, a hundred years ago a place busy as a centre of cobblers' shops, now a sleepy hollow where the lanes end in green tracks on to the fell. Thorpe never seems to change; the old ruined houses with blocked-up windows turn blank eyes year by year to the same scene. The Georgian manor-house was in fact gutted by fire on 13th October 1939, but, except for the interior panelling that was destroyed, it has been repaired and looks none the worse.

The reef-knolls, between two of which Thorpe shelters, make a remarkable feature in the broad stretch of valley where the Wharfe turns northwards and there is the opening southwards to Skipton. Skelterton, Carden, Butterhaw, Stebden, Elbolton, and Kail Hill, as they are called, are green conical hills composed of fossiliferous limestone; of them all Elbolton is the most interesting. In it is Navvy Noddle Hole, one of the inhabited caves of Craven excavated several times since 1888, in which lead has been mined. Across the valley from these knolls a similar hill, called Swinden, has been quarried for limestone since 1902.

From Thorpe through Linton and Threshfield to Grassington the map on page 15 best explains the confusion of roads. South of the main road the ridges of the ancient arable fields of Thorpe and Linton are plainly seen; and a new feature here is the Linton Camp of the National Camp Corporation opened on 10th July 1940. It is rented by Bradford Education Authority as a school for delicate children.

Hidden in trees and approached by a network of side roads, the houses of Linton surround a green that slopes down to a beck crossed by three bridges, clapper, pack-horse, and modern road bridge. The elaborate building of Fountaine's Hospital, with a cupola and side wings, dominates the village. The hospital was built by Richard Fountaine as alms-houses in 1721, and it still provides homes for six or seven old men and women. So sequestered is the village that we feel to be trespassing. A red post office van is being washed in the beck, a carpet cleaned in a garden; trout dart in the water in the shadow of a bridge, and perhaps it is springtime with snowdrops in bloom. On the green a column topped by an astrolobe denotes that Linton was judged the loveliest village in the North in a competition sponsored by the *News Chronicle* in 1949.

Here at the house called White Abbey lived Halliwell Sutcliffe, romantic novelist; here live Dr Arthur Raistrick, archaeologist, geologist, and authority on the early history of the dales, Mr G. B. Drayson, Member of Parliament for Skipton Division, and at Linton Falls Mr James Gregson, dramatist and producer.

Half a mile away from the village, close to the Wharfe, are Linton church, Linton mills, the Tin Bridge over to Grassington, and Threshfield School.   Linton church, reached along a cul-de-sac, is interesting and ancient.   The mill, which makes artificial silk and employs many operatives from Lancashire, has been used for wool and cotton, and in the late eighteenth century was connected with a large wool-combing house in Skipton.

Threshfield School, a grammar-school now turned primary, was founded under the will of the Rev. Matthew Hewitt who died in 1674.   It counts the historian, Dr Thomas Dunham Whitaker, amongst its pupils.   Though heavier in style than Burnsall's school building, Threshfield School is none the less a fine example of seventeenth-century architecture; and it has one of the most delightful ghosts, Pam the fiddler, who holds a school there and plays to his scholars.

The village of Threshfield stands at a meeting of roads and on the main route up Wharfedale from Skipton.   Many of its houses lie back from the traffic behind a little public garden.   Threshfield colliery, out on the moors to the west, was worked for centuries, though troubled by water.   'Whoever has a mind to treat for the same may apply to Thomas Dean of Linton,' reads a colliery notice of two hundred years ago.   At Ling Hall in the village lived the Ibbotsons, the famous makers of besoms, sold far and wide throughout many dales.

To reach Grassington we must cross Grassington Bridge, or Linton Bridge as it should properly be called.   A stone bridge replaced a wooden one in 1603, and not until 1784 was it enlarged to its present width.   It gives us a glimpse of the curving Wharfe in green meadows with Grass Wood in the distance.   A steep hill brings us to a terrace of houses and blocks of shops that herald Grassington.

Grassington's main street never fails to surprise and please.   It opens out into a small cobbled market-place, narrows between houses, hotels, cafés, and shops, and with alleys branching from it climbs to Town Head.   The congested plan resembles that of

Grassington Bridge

other dale villages with an industrial background, in the case of Grassington the lead-mining industry developed in the eighteenth and nineteenth centuries. Round this centre have grown up houses built after the railway was brought to the village from Skipton in 1902, and council house estates have also been built in the inter-war years. The Yorkshire Dales Railway, as it was called, was closed for passenger traffic in 1930.

In the last war many evacuees came and settled here; and a little more of the village's individual character was submerged. Grassington, with familiar old shops and some new—china, iron-mongers', and antique shops—appears prosperous. It is still a visitors' centre, a little metropolis for Upper Wharfedale. A new secondary modern school attended by children who come from as far afield as Beamsley in the one direction and Oughtershaw in the other was opened in July 1955.

To be sought out amongst the buildings are reminders of Grassington's story: Grassington House in the square is an early nineteenth-century building, once occupied by the Alcocks, bankers and promoters of the Grassington to Pateley turnpike road; at the head of Gars Lane are two cottages that mark the site of the theatre opened by Thomas Airey in the first years of the last century, and near by is a fine early barn in front of which John Wesley is said to have preached; and on the western outskirts of the village is the Old Hall that, incorporating twelfth-century details in its structure, is one of the most ancient inhabited houses in England.

These are fragments from a comparatively recent past.   But if you go from Town Head by Chapel Street and make a way to the pastures called Lea Green you will find an earlier Grassington, in an Iron Age village occupied from about 200 B.C. to A.D. 400.   As you walk amongst the square fields, divided by grassed-over stone balks, hut circles in little crofts, sunken roads, and dew-ponds, you can usually find a flint scraper or a fragment of a flint knife thrown up in molehills; but the best collection of these finds is to be seen at the Craven Museum at Skipton.   Lea Green is one of the most interesting prehistoric sites in England, and here and round Kilnsey were the most thickly populated neighbourhoods in the dales in the Iron Age.

Not far from Lea Green is to be seen a different facet of past life.   At Yarnbury up the moor road due north from Town Head is a group of buildings sheltered by trees, once the headquarters of Grassington Moor lead-mines.   From farther on at the top of the hill the mining field lies spread out before us, a shallow valley with across it an extensive sloping hillside covered with little thrown-out heaps, the debris from the mines of Colebeck, Moss, Sara, Peru, Chatsworth, Beaver, Turf Pits, and many others, all worked by shafts and levels, not by hushes.   Far across the gill are the smelt mill with its double flues, and farther over the dams on Blea Beck that fed many mines by an elaborate system of watercourses round the hillsides.

Though few early records exist, mining here is ancient, and was expanded when miners were brought from Derbyshire in the reign of James I.   The mines were worked by the Cliffords, the Earls of Cork and Burlington, and by the Dukes of Devonshire, who in the last century extensively developed them and each year raised lead worth thousands of pounds.

Here ancient laws regulated mining.   Adventurers renting ground paid a fifth of the product to the royalty owners who provided a smelt mill, and they leased areas of ground marked by stones inscribed with the initials of the lessees, stones that can sometimes still be found on the moor.   Contracts for working the veins were settled by Dutch auction; and a Bar Master and Barmoot Court tried any disputes that arose.

Once Grassington Moor provided an outing for visitors.   In 1838 Frederic Montagu wrote: 'I strongly recommend the uninitiated to visit the mines,' and he went on to describe a Dutch auction: 'The scene is peculiarly striking—the pale face, and contemplative cast of countenance of the miner in his earth-coloured garments, with his arms enfolded over his bosom, and broad hat bent over his forehead, would not make a bad subject for the pencil.'   In 1869 the Rev. Baily J. Harker, whose book *Rambles in Upper Wharfedale* publicized the dale, recommended to tourists a journey underground, 'though,' he said, 'the descent may frighten them a little.   The bottoms of some of the shafts are reached by ladders and others by ropes.'

The mines closed down towards the end of the last century; and all the activity to be seen at Yarnbury now is the lorries and riddling plants of one or two modern mining adventurers who work on the tailings, the spoil heaps, still productive of barytes and lead ore.

3. GRASS WOOD TO OUGHTERSHAW

A~T~ GRASSINGTON a further division of Wharfedale begins. Not only does the valley take a bend from a north-west to a northerly direction but the scene changes its character. The millstone grit hitherto close at hand, sometimes thrust across the valley, sometimes on the hilltops at either side, recedes; and far away to the limits of the dale and beyond stretches the pure limestone country of the Yorkshire Dales. Onwards we shall follow a crystal-clear river flowing over smooth rocks, pass the great bastion of Kilnsey Crag, and see grey walls blue-shadowed or almost pure white in the sun.

A mile from Grassington the road up the dale runs through Grass Wood that clothes a rocky hillside and is adjoined by Bastow Wood. Although it is private property—it was part of the Bolton Abbey estate until sold to timber merchants in 1955— public footpaths cross it, and at all times of year it is worth visiting.

Grass Wood, as well as the limestone crags and pastures around it, is botanically famous. It is here that a large number of uncommon and interesting plants may be found amidst almost a carpet of lily of the valley (*Convallaria majalis*). Various orchids are present, including the helleborine (*Epipactis atrorubens*), the fly orchid (*Ophrys insectifera*), and the twayblade (*Listera ovata*), which is abundant. The delightful little bird's-eye primrose (*Primula farinosa*), a rare milkwort (*Polygala amara*), and the blue moor-grass (*Sesleria caerulea*) occur in the pastures above the wood, whilst on some cliffs the Jacob's ladder (*Polemonium caeruleum*) grows in surprising profusion. In spite of the area's renown, it is to be hoped that all the species will continue to thrive without being picked or destroyed by thoughtless individuals.

Besides Grass Wood there were once Kilnsey Wood and the wood called Threshfield Rise, which between them covered a large part of the valley hereabouts. Originally they formed part of the

commons and wastes of their respective townships, where people
had rights of wood and pasturage, and in them, especially in
Kilnsey Wood, the deer usually bred and grazed.

Kilnsey Wood, vestiges of which can be seen opposite Grass
Wood, was destroyed in the latter half of the seventeenth century
by indiscriminate cutting down and rooting up of trees by various
local people, such as the Wades, who held it in common.

So we reach Conistone and Kilnsey facing each other across the
valley and separated by acres of flat, green meadow land, once a
great post-glacial lake.   Behind the one village are the two limestone knolls of Wassa and Conistone Pie, and behind the other is
the crag, so that both clusters of grey houses blend with the scene:
more harmonious groupings would be hard to find.   The villages
are of early foundation, and at Conistone in particular the ridges
of the two large open arable fields of the township show up plainly
on the slopes on either side.   Kilnsey Field, south-west of the
village, can be seen from a little way up Mastiles Lane.   Both too
have superb backgrounds of wild moorland; and whilst Conistone
claims the church, Kilnsey has the monastic associations.

When in about 1156 Alice Romilly gave Kilnsey to the monks of
Fountains Abbey the village grew, and eventually it became the
headquarters of the abbey's property in Wharfedale, Littondale,
and Malhamdale.   There were eight principal houses, a chapel,
great barns, and corn and fulling mills.   It was the centre for the
manor courts, for the washing and clipping of sheep, and for the
collection of clips from other granges.   Transit for wagons was
granted the monks through many nearby places, and what is now
Mastiles Lane connected the village with the Malham and Lake
District granges of the monks.   It was an altogether different
Kilnsey from the one we see to-day.

After the Dissolution the Yorkes of Gouthwaite, the same
family that hunted the deer, bought the manor and later sold the
farms and mills to former tenants of the abbey—the Wards,
Settles, Kyds, Rainers, and Leylands.   The Tennants bought
Chapel House, and the Wades eventually bought much monastic
property, and in 1648 built their fine hall at Kilnsey.

Amongst the houses of the village, so dwarfed by the nearness of
the crag, are the Tennant Arms Hotel by the roadside, and behind,
with its back to the steep hillside, the hall, now used as a barn.
As a farmer's wife told us, it was built to last and 'not blown up as

The houses . . . dwarfed by the nearness of the crag

they are nowadays.' The small building in front of it was the porter's lodge.

Chapel House, not far away, is a Georgian house on an old site, and it once supposedly had two ghosts, a lady dressed in brown clothes and a medieval head-dress, and a coach and four heard at midnight.

The crag establishes Kilnsey as a natural centre for events in the dale. Three lamb sales in the autumn, and in early September a large show that has developed from the old Kilnsey Feast, are held in the flat fields. For show day a temporary encampment of marquees assembles; at one end sheep-dog trials are in progress, and far away at the other three men engage in a walling competition. Near them farmers parade cattle or lean over pens of Dalesbred sheep. In the centre a ring for flat races, horse trotting, and galloping races is so large that figures on the far side of it are dwarfed. Bookies shout as at any race-meeting, and thousands of people from industrial towns eclipse by their numbers the men and women of Wharfedale and neighbouring dales. The crag races, competed for by local men and noted runners from the Lake District, make the high light of the day.

Three miles up the dale beyond the turn to Littondale, Kettlewell comes into sight huddled at the foot of the deep cleft up which Park Rash leads to Coverdale between Great Whernside and Tor Mere. We are nearing the head of the dale where the bold sombre masses of Great Whernside and its neighbour Buckden Pike, the fifth and sixth highest hills in Yorkshire, divide the northern bounds of Wharfedale from Nidderdale, Coverdale, and Wensleydale, majestic barriers that cut off from each other not only dales but the North and the West Ridings.

We cross to the village by a fine stone bridge. In 1457 the monks of Fountains paid 2s. 8d. for work on Kettlewell Bridge, then no doubt a wooden structure. The village, rather more bosky than some dale villages, spreads along either side of a beck and straggles up into the gill. Hotels—the Racehorses, the Blue Bell by the bridge, and the King's Head near the church—proclaim it a centre for visitors.

Kettlewell can show a long and full story. Settled by Ketil, who had an Irish-Norse name, it is mentioned in Domesday Book and had an early market. It was once of more importance than Grassington, and gave its name, Kettlewelldale, to one of the bailiwicks of the Forest of Skipton. The canons of Coverham Abbey and Bolton Priory, the monks of Fountains Abbey, and great lords bargained for property here. The manor was divided; half belonged to Coverham Abbey and half came to the Nevilles of Middleham Castle. In 1410 the Nevilles enclosed a deer park, called Scale Park, now farm land traversed by the road up Park Rash to Coverdale. As part of the Lordship of Middleham, it came to the Crown and was eventually sold to the yeomen.

All manner of incidents happened at Kettlewell over the centuries. For instance, in 1218 the parson was found dead in the fields, and suspicion fell on Ralf the Marshall who had seduced his mistress and taken her to Skipton. In Elizabethan times the fact that the parson kept an inn in his house 'for honest resort' was not surprising, since he was only paid £5 a year. In 1616 a violent dispute focused on the corn mill that stood across the beck from the present post office. The miller, objecting to a new owner, gathered with him a large crowd and for two days and nights laid siege to the mill. They captured it, and after holding it for five weeks were thrown out by the justices of the peace.

In 1838 there were at Kettlewell lead-mines, a cotton mill, five inns, a beerhouse, three schools, and a surgeon, three blacksmiths, two joiners, two shoemakers, and a tailor. Nowadays the market square opposite the King's Head appears no different on Thursdays from any other day, and the grinding of the water-wheels of the corn mill and smelt mill is hushed.

We talked with Mr Christopher Wiseman, a member of a local family who were carriers. 'Distance was distance i' them days,' he said. He remembers the early morning starts with horses and wagon for Skipton, the band contests at Hardraw Scar in Wensleydale, red-letter days in his youth, and the change-over to motor transport in the 1920's. 'I've been many a mile fast and slow,' he remarked.

From Kettlewell to Starbotton steep unbroken ridges of hill hem in the valley; and on the lower slopes above the road the terraces of arable land where barley, oats, flax, and hemp were once grown show up plainly. For centuries the flooding of the Wharfe caused damage to corn and hay, and besides recurring floods a violent and terrible thunderstorm on 8th June 1686 devastated both Kettlewell and Starbotton.

The road twists and turns through Starbotton past the inn, the Fox and Hounds, past a Quaker burial-ground, and past fine barns with outshutts and large porch doors. At the back is the hall, now divided into cottages, once the home of the Symondsons who entertained Lady Anne Clifford on one of her journeys; and in the gill are the ruins of a smelt mill. From the green-walled lane abruptly scaling the hillside you can climb Buckden Pike, or cross Tor Mere into Walden, or circle the top of Scale Park to reach the head of Coverdale.

Two miles from Starbotton, Buckden is a place at which to call a halt, a centre for the exploration of the head of the dale, and a terminus of traffic, nowadays of buses, in old days of the mail-coach. In the years of the movement of population from the dales to Lancashire many people returning for holidays reached Buckden by coach and walked on to Wensleydale and Swaledale. At the foot of Buckden Gill and facing a little green, the village stands at the last of the turning-points of Wharfedale, where Langstrothdale branches off westwards and where the main road continues northwards through Cray and up the Kidstones Pass to Wensleydale.

Until 1947, when the estate was sold, the village had belonged to one family after another; and some estate cottage architecture, the Georgian hall in its grounds, and the high walls of kitchen gardens proclaim single ownership rather than the more usual dale village medley of houses built at all times by all manner of people.   The hall, Buckden House, is now a Methodist Guild Holiday Home.

Like Bainbridge in Wensleydale, Buckden was established by feudal lords in Norman times as the headquarters of a forest.   In this case the lords were the Percys of Northumberland and the forest was Langstrothdale Chase.   The name of the village means the valley of bucks, and the Buck Inn, with a deer figuring on the signboard, emphasizes the original nature of the country.   Until the estate was sold a herd of fallow deer grazed in the woods across the river.   To walk through these ornamental woods, to climb the hillsides on paths through bracken, and suddenly to come upon deer grazing in a glade was a pleasure that has gone.

Up the Rakes along the lower edge of the Pike what was part of a Roman road from Ilkley to Bainbridge is plainly to be seen, and it may be followed as a green track across ledges of fell to where beyond Cray this ancient road joins the Kidstone Pass and leaves it again to continue as the Stake Pass to Wensleydale.

It was to these heights that we started out from Bolton Bridge with the Earl of Burlington's steward who was meeting a land-owner to settle a lead-mining boundary dispute.   It was neither the first nor the last dispute there; for the mines of Buckden and Bishopdale Gavel, adjoining but in different ridings, were rich. As early as 1369 the workmen of Robert Neville of Middleham had been imprisoned for stealing lead from the Wharfedale mines of Henry Percy, Earl of Northumberland.

At Cray the White Lion welcomes travellers either breasting the hill or coming down to Wharfedale.   In former days the steep pass was regarded by motorists as a dangerous hill; and even now, when modern cars make light of it, a snowstorm can render it slippery and dangerous.   In wet weather becks rush down the huge slopes of the fells on either hand.   Foaming white torrents pour down clefts, plunge into amphitheatres of rock; spray blows like smoke, springs gush out, streams run helter-skelter down to Cray, and with a roar dash and splash over many falls.

One mid-October day as we leant over Buckden Bridge on the way to Langstrothdale, a kingfisher, a flash of luminous blue, shot out from under the arch. A watery sun shone between clouds to light up the yellows and russets of sycamores. There was the smell of sheep-dip, and no sound other than the ring of hammer on stone as a labourer repaired a wall knocked down by flood waters. The brown river ran swiftly; but two days before it had swept down as a mad rushing torrent overflowing on to the fields: rushes plastered on to walls showed its force and height.

The bridge was the subject of a broadsheet published in 1750 and headed: 'A Bridge is built in yonder Dale, and on this Bridge there hangs a Tale.' It related how there had been no suitable bridge at Buckden by which to reach Birks Mill, a lead smelt mill on Water Beck above the Deer Park on the west side of the valley, and that a candidate for a parliamentary election promised a bridge for votes. At the same time £200 allowed by the county to rebuild Hubberholme Bridge, washed down by floods, was used to build Buckden Bridge, which was afterwards commonly called the Election Bridge.

The last division of Wharfedale, Langstrothdale, awaits us. Each as we have explored it has seemed of surpassing beauty, and this the last reach of the Wharfe is a fitting climax to the whole dale. Through much of it only a few yards of smooth turf separate river and road. The river, scarcely more than a beck, hurries from shallow pools to small waterfalls in its water-worn limestone bed; and hamlets, sheltered by sycamores, are grouped near gills or on the hillsides, steep hillsides strewn with rocks and streaked with bracken and ancient woodland. Where the valley narrows at the entrance to Langstrothdale is Hubberholme.

Hubberholme church is a place of pilgrimage for many people. We cross the bridge with, on one side, the George Inn, formerly the vicarage, and on the other the church in what used to be called Chapel. Picnic birds flutter at the gate to the churchyard; sheep and lambs graze between the headstones; the squat tower seems reefed against storms.

In the interior the rough unplastered walls, the pews by Thompson of Kilburn, the blue hassocks and kneelers, and the round iron candelabra accentuate the medieval atmosphere that

Hubberholme at the entrance to Langstrothdale

Hubberholme's rood-loft gives. After the edict to destroy rood-lofts was issued in the York Diocese in 1571, this one, only dated thirteen years earlier, survived because of the remoteness of the place. But isolation caused difficulties of a less happy kind and the parson and parishioners were often in trouble, and often having to journey to York to settle disputes.

In early times, when the Percys were patrons of Hubberholme, sometimes three priests, including a monk of Sawley Abbey, officiated there, but burials took place at Arncliffe church, the mother church of the parish in which Hubberholme was a chapel of ease. The Corpse Way started from Buckden to cross the hills to Litton and Arncliffe, and many difficulties were experienced in floods and snow. In the latter half of the fifteenth century the people of Langstrothdale complained, and described how a party of four bearers had the corpse they were carrying swept from their grasp by the swollen Wharfe, and another of eight bearers had almost perished in deep snow. Probably from that time the funeral processions ceased.

In the seventeenth century instead of a plenitude of priests there was a scarcity, especially during the Commonwealth. Incumbents came and went in rapid succession, and the farmers of the tithes neglected to pay them their stipend of £5 a year. At one time the inhabitants settled the troubles by bringing in their own man.

From 1807 to 1833 the Rev. Thomas Lindley, incumbent of Halton Gill, crossed over the Horse Head Pass to take the service each Sunday; and the story has been handed down of the sexton watching for the minister on his white horse, and when he saw him ringing the bell for the service. The writer of a diary wrote on 1st January 1830: 'Met old Mr Lindley coming to preach for 6s. at Hubberholme, and advised him to have a curate, but he was deaf to that. Much snow on Horsehead.' The diarist was referring to the New Year's Day letting of the Poor Pasture, a ceremony preceded by a church service for which the vicar was and still is paid 6s.

Men of the Bronze and Iron Ages dwelt in Langstrothdale, as witness the stone circle by the river a little west of Yockenthwaite and the tumbledown huts and overgrown crofts and fields up Deepdale Gill. Hubberholme, Raisgill, Yockenthwaite, Deepdale, and Oughtershaw were named by the Norsemen. They became lodges in the forest and are now sheep and cattle farms.

Ruined houses testify to the greatly diminished population: there were nine tenants at Deepdale and eight at Yockenthwaite in 1613 compared with the two or three farms and cottages of the present day. Formerly a now forgotten cross-country route from Newcastle to Lancaster passed through the dale; along this way came George Fox and converted James Tennant of Scar House above Hubberholme to the Quaker faith. In early Stuart times the yeomen families were Tennants, Lodges, Slingers, and Jaqueses, that were followed by Parkers, Fosters, Beresfords, and Hirds. Of these only Beresfords and Hirds remain; and since the last war a good deal of change of tenancy and ownership of farms has taken place.

Continuing up the dale, we pass Yockenthwaite's pack-horse bridge, the dove-grey of the stone-work standing out against a massive clump of sycamores, and Deepdale with fine trees and an elaborate door-head on one of the farmhouses.

The road mounts alongside the ever-narrowing river and drops down to Beckermonds, its appearance changed by the loss of the tall ash-trees blown down one by one in recent years. Here at this meeting of the waters Greenfield and Oughtershaw Becks join to become the Wharfe; and a tarred road that eventually turns into a track past Greenfield and across the fells to Ribblesdale branches off.

At Oughtershaw, the last cluster of houses in the dale, we think of the Woodds who built the little church, the hall, and the two farms of Nether Gill and Swarth Gill, the last farms in the dale. Cam Houses, farther on near the first springs of the Wharfe, keeps a close contact with the dale but is in fact in Horton-in-Ribblesdale township. Out here amongst wild wastes of moorland we have reached the watershed where a narrow ribbon of road mounts to Wensleydale.

III

LITTONDALE

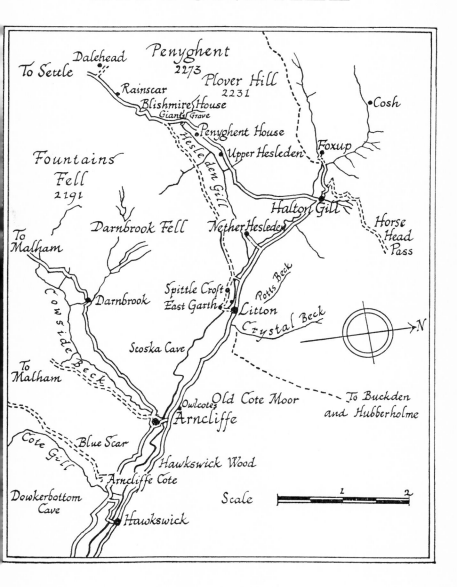

To Settle · Dalehead · Rainscar · Blishmire House · Giant's Grave · Penyghent House · Upper Hesleden · Foxup · Cosh · Penyghent 2273 · Plover Hill 2231 · Hesleden Gill · Fountains Fell 2191 · To Malham · Darnbrook Fell · Nether Hesleden · Halton Gill · Horse Head Pass · Cowside Beck · Darnbrook · Spittle Croft · East Garth · Potts Beck · Litton · Crystal Beck · N · To Malham · Scoska Cave · Old Cote Moor · To Buckden and Hubberholme · Cote Gill · Blue Scar · Owlcotes · Arncliffe · Hawkswick Wood · Arncliffe Cote · Dowkerbottom Cave · Hawkswick · Scale · 1 · 2

III

LITTONDALE

WATERED by the River Skirfare, screened from inquisitive eyes by the folds of the hills, Littondale branches off Wharfedale, and striking up into the Pennines reaches the watershed in the short space of eight miles. Penyghent and Greenfield Knot girdle it at the head, and ranges of flat-topped hills, deeply cleft by Hesleden and Cowside Gills, bound it. At the foot of the dale's steep sides are the villages of Hawkswick, Arncliffe, Litton, and Halton Gill, and the hamlet of Foxup.

From Wharfedale two roads on either side of the Skirfare run into the dale, Wordsworth's 'Amerdale' and Kingsley's 'Vendale'; and two other roads, riding over the hills like the white wakes of boats breasting huge rollers, reach more directly into the centre of the valley, one from Malham by Darnbrook Farm, and the other from Settle and Stainforth to Halton Gill. Besides these, ancient tracks, once used by monks and packmen, cross the hills into the dale from Langstrothdale, Malhamdale, and Ribblesdale. Yet although the many routes give access for a summer invasion of visitors, the tracks are hilly, the roads narrow, and buses infrequent.

Of all the routes those over the hills give the best views of the U-shaped valley scooped out by glacier action, of the dark huddle of roofs of a village, of the woods round Arncliffe, and of the limestone scars along the hillsides. In early spring, when the grass is bitten close and wasting snow streaks the fellsides, the pastures of Littondale take on a colour unlike that of any other dale—a pale tawny, shot with olive-green and brushed with the burnt orange of bracken, against which the white of walls and scars shines out.

Secluded the valley may be, yet it gives out a sensation of great age that springs from long occupation by man. The Giant's Grave below Penyghent is the burial-place of Bronze Age man. On the tops of the hills, in particular Blue Scar, Iron Age huts and fields extend for several miles, and Dowkerbottom Cave was inhabited up to the third and fourth century A.D.   Well-marked terraces of arable strip cultivation round all the villages speak of the townfields of places of Anglian foundation.   Both Arncliffe and Hawkswick figure in Domesday Book, and Litton is there as a berewick of Giggleswick when the connection lay with Ribblesdale rather than with Wharfedale.

As with other dale country after the Conquest, Littondale became a hunting forest that, stretching from Owlcotes above Arncliffe to the dale head, belonged to the great estates of the Percys of Northumberland.   Richard Percy gave the forest to the monks of Fountains except for certain sheep pasturage already granted to Sawley Abbey.   Their properties added to by other benefactors, Fountains soon turned the dale into a highly organized sheep-run with granges at Arncliffe and Hawkswick Cotes, Owlcotes, Litton, Hesleden, Foxup, and Cosh.

After the Dissolution the Cliffords of Skipton Castle, by purchase and marriage with the Percys, acquired almost all the dale, that was still valued for its stock of deer and game.   The forest was the scene of several of the marauding raids by confederates of the Yorkes of Appletreewick.   We picture one of them on a June day in 1607 when the deer-stealers with three or four brace of greyhounds met at 'Haltongill Feild,' and finding some thirty deer grazing there drove them on to Penyghent, then on to Malham Moor, where they killed two hinds and 'cawsed other two to breake their necks from the toppe of a great Rocke.'

Apart from a few lead-mines at its foot and a cotton mill at Arncliffe, Littondale was not invaded by industries.   Its population has diminished from 563 in 1801 to 266 in 1951, and there are now only 70 houses in the dale.   In spite of some dependence on the outer world, for doctors, schooling, and food-stuffs, Littondale is a remote self-contained community of farming families only sparsely intermixed with townspeople in holiday cottages.

One March day we took the gated road from Wharfedale between river and fell to Hawkswick.   On the slopes above us the once cultivated ranes of the townfield of the village plainly show up, with above them an Iron Age village site, and above that the deeply trodden paths leading up over the scars to the high pastures.

Superficially unaltered for many years, Hawkswick's grey houses and barns that open on to the village street, and the small crofts behind, fit admirably this landscape of limestone, scrub, and close-bitten turf. We saw a lofty barn with ancient oak-pegged doors, a big yew-tree in a small walled garden, and a seventeenth-century building full of hens in batteries. A stone's-throw away the river is spanned by a bridge under which dippers skim the water.

A farmer to whom we spoke said: 'There ought to have been no villages built i' Littondale.' Farmsteads spaced out along the narrow valley would have divided the land better than farms with their lands inconveniently mixed together, grouped in the villages. Everywhere on the cold March day at the end of a long hard winter sheep were gathered together, dark blobs on fields with hay strewn under the walls. Our farmer had opened all the gates of his pastures so that the strong sheep could go away up to the top while the weak ones stayed down. As in other limestone country where the soil is often shallow and the pastures poor, the sheep must frequently be moved to fresh land, and in some cases they must be wintered out of the dale.

Across the valley from Hawkswick the Cotes, the farms, which were granges of Fountains, lie on either side of Cote Gill. Hawks-wick Cote's farmhouse is old, carefully restored, and has modern buildings; Arncliffe Cote's house on the other hand is not so old— an ancient house used as an outbuilding stands in a garth below it —but it has fine old barns. Here washings and clippings of the abbey's flocks pastured on the extensive commons above took place. Each grange had its own arable field near at hand; and no doubt a smithy existed in Smithy Croft at Arncliffe Cote.

Most people enter Littondale on this, the south side, by the road that crosses flat, treeless pasture and meadow with the furrowed face of Blue Scar on their left. Distant trees mark habitation and the overwrapping hills of the dale draw near. We approach Arncliffe by an avenue of sycamores, past the hall in park land, and enter the large green.

Houses almost completely surround the green—the small houses of the one-time craftsmen, statesmen, and graziers of Littondale. Here is a Georgian house with a good doorway, here and there whitewashed houses, and at the far end the Falcon Hotel; but the large sycamore and other trees felled in the early 1950's no longer lend shade, nor except for the post office are shops visible, although Arncliffe has a village shop near the church.

The overwrapping hills of the dale draw near

Roads meeting at a stone pump of mid nineteenth-century date, criss-cross the green. A cattle lorry is parked there; but few people come and go. Steep hills with prominent cairns standing up on the south side enclose the scene. We hear blasting far away in Ribblesdale. At midday children in brightly coloured jerseys rush into the picture; and even more colourfully clad youths and girls, who have come over the hills from Malham, suddenly appear.

A genuine country inn, the Falcon is kept by a local man, Marmaduke Miller. Staying there, you may fish for trout in the four and a half miles of river that belong to the inn, or walk to the lonely Darnbrook Farm or up Cowside Beck in search of rare flowers. Or you may admire the pictures of M'duke Miller, wood-engraver and water-colourist as well as innkeeper.

It is of an abundant flora that we think in Littondale, of *Dryas octopetala*, *Draba verna*, *Primula farinosa*, *Geranium sanguineum*, and in Arncliffe Wood lily of the valley. Once during a short stay we picked without special effort over 70 varieties; and the Rev. W. A. Shuffrey collected over 300, some of which are listed in *Littondale Past and Present*. Here as elsewhere we mourn the lady's slipper orchis, uprooted and destroyed in the last century.

North of the village and green, Arncliffe Bridge carries the road up the dale over the river. From the bridge in its leafy hollow we look on the one side to Bridge End, a house with a lawn sloping to the water and associated with the visits of Charles Kingsley, and on the other to where the river swirls below the church tower, ancient and rugged like that at Hubberholme. Enclosed in a bower of trees with snowdrops and aconites at their feet in the spring, the river constantly murmurs over its pebbly bed.

Except for the tower the church was restored in Victorian times. It is the mother church of a parish that includes Hubberholme and Halton Gill; and many episodes stand out in its story, particularly disputes with Hubberholme over dues, upkeep, the right of appointment of incumbents, and stipends from the tithes. The tithes were given to University College, Oxford, by Henry Percy in 1443, and of the many men from that college who have been vicars, three served Arncliffe for over fifty years—Arthur Colcotes and Miles Tennant in the seventeenth and eighteenth centuries, and Archdeacon Boyd in the last. At the present time the vicar and his wife farm the glebe.

Continuing across the bridge we soon reach Owlcotes by the roadside, a farmhouse that typifies the architectural grace and skill of the seventeenth-century builders of the dales, as do the fine barns dotted along the way to Litton.

Litton is well named from the Old English *Hlȳdan-tūn*, the village on a torrent. Several of its houses that straggle along the road between Crystal Beck and Pots Beck or down green lanes towards the river have dated door-heads. Next to the Queen's Arms, Manor Cottage, with the inscription 'HTG 1707,' is on the site of the manor-house. The Queen's Arms replaced the old inn in 1842, when a bridge was built over the river a little farther up the dale. Here at Litton the post office and joiner's workshop seem the focal point.

Across the Skirfare, in what is called Old Litton, many buildings are falling into ruin; one in particular, the Old School, is little altered from when it was built in 1695. A waterfall, briefly called Foss, pours out of a cave to fall down the hillside. Farther on is Spittle Croft, once a house, perhaps on the site of a hospice of the monks on the green road that can still be followed on foot to join the Halton Gill to Settle road near the Giant's Grave.

Beyond Litton the dale narrows; the hills draw close; and for two miles up to Hesleden Bridge the Skirfare disappears underground, a fact that has saved the dale from being made into a reservoir. Suddenly a cleft in the hills reveals a view of Penyghent far away poised as it were between earth and sky; then the rift snaps to again.

At the foot of the wooded gill stands Netherhesleden Farm.

Here and at Upper Hesleden the Fawcetts were the yeomen after the Dissolution, and one of the two dated door-heads is inscribed 'TFA 1748.' At the present day members of the Ingleby family, who came into the dale from West End near Blubberhouses some 90 years ago, farm Netherhesleden and Litton Brow Farms, that between them cover some 1,100 acres. The farms carry 70 or 80 Friesian cattle and 620 Dalesbred sheep in summer, and the elaborate new buildings and modern appliances prove the well-being of the hill farmer who has drawn on government subsidies. That many Littondale farmers have taken advantage of these may be seen from new buildings and the activity in remote hamlets.

The dale road runs on, even more narrow; trees become more sparse; the lower slopes of the hills are burnished with bracken and scored with water channels. At first sight the last village in the dale, Halton Gill, a little dark cluster of buildings and trees set in a nook at the foot of a gill, looks like an oasis at the world's end; yet it lies only ten miles by a tarred if hilly gated road from Settle.

All the houses except one date from the seventeenth century. The hall, with a two storeyed porch, was built by the Dawsons in 1641. At the far end of the village is the little school and church under one roof with a large ash and yews in the walled enclosure in front of it. Over the school door the date and initials 'WF 1626' remind us of the dalesman, William Fawcett, a prosperous wool merchant of Norwich, who had it built. At present fifteen children, only five of whom are girls, attend the school.

As at Arncliffe the parsons stand out individually. For instance, the Rev. Miles Wilson, incumbent from 1737 to 1777, kept a private school as well as teaching at the village one. He wrote a tract called *The Man in the Moon* in which was related the adventures of a Horton-in-Ribblesdale cobbler, Israel Jobson, who erecting a ladder on Penyghent reached the moon, but soon came down again because dissatisfied with the food!

Following him the Rev. Thomas Lindley, a bachelor, taciturn in his later days, served the cure until 1847, and from 1807 until his eightieth year he either walked or rode over the Horse Head Pass on most Sundays to take the service at Hubberholme.

We called on Miss Knowles, aged 84, the last member of her family in the dale. Many of the Knowleses fought at Flodden Field, and were tenants under the monks. Our friend sat by the hearth in a high-backed horse-hair chair with a canopy and many brass tacks against a background of a dresser filled with pewter dishes handed down from her yeoman ancestors. She died in 1955. A Tristram Knowles living at Arncliffe Cote in 1579 had with his father occupied the tenement for 120 years. These two men had seen six generations of Cliffords and nine sovereigns of England.

At a crude wooden signpost marked 'Hawes' the Horse Head Pass starts to zigzag across the fellside and from each turn to give glimpses down below of the village and Foxup, the last hamlet. That March day the north wind blew; the track crossed the gill by a huge snow bridge, and the gate on to the high pastures was wedged open in a drift. Ingleborough and the hills of many dales came into view. Gone are the packmen on their cross-country route from Lancashire to Northumberland, but the pass still makes a droving road, a fine route for walkers, and sometimes a trial hill for motor-cycles.

If at Halton Gill the air is edged with sharp winds from the fell-tops, at Foxup it blows sweet with the constant splashing of water on rock. Here Foxup Beck and Cosh Beck meet to become the Skirfare. The first of these in the last few hundred yards of its course runs under four little bridges. One of these leads to Bridge Farm that in 1954 was rebuilt, the dated stone, 'MMK 1686,' commemorating the Knowles being replaced by one with the inscription 'MCD 1954,' representing the owners, the Dawsons of Langcliffe Hall in Ribblesdale.

The name Foxup means fox's valley, and lying at 1,200 feet above sea level the meadow land of the three farms looks snatched from the surrounding wastes of rush and bent. It gives the impression of being the most ancient of all the settlements of Littondale, largely because of four old ruined houses, and an ancient barn with a wide, blocked-up arch in a meadow at the west end of the hamlet.

Two miles from Halton Gill, reached by a wet track from the first bridge at Foxup, is the outside farm of Cosh, 1,450 feet above sea level. The 'Grenefeld Coche' of the monks, it was occupied until 1953, since when the house has been deserted and the land farmed from High Birkwith, four miles over the fell in Ribblesdale. Once this wild place, certainly the most remote dwelling in the dales, had three houses and self-sufficient inhabitants spinning and

Foxup

weaving cloth for their own clothes.   For many years it was rented by Askrigg farmers short of pasture, and a driving road leads to Beckermonds less than two miles away.

Robert Campbell, who died at Arncliffe aged 85 in 1955, lived as hind at Cosh 50 years before.   He remembered that he drove with a horse and cart once a month to Settle and could buy all the provisions he required for three gold sovereigns.   He farmed 18 acres of meadow land that yielded a light crop of hay, kept two cows and a horse, grazed 500 sheep and summered another 700. In winter the sheep were sometimes driven to lower country over hard-frozen snow.

Between Foxup and Hesleden on the slopes of the Berghs (pronounced bark), called variously Far, High, Low, and Hesleden Berghs, can be seen the numerous remains of Iron Age villages. The population on this now uninhabited side of the valley must once have been considerable.

The road to Settle from Halton Gill crosses Hesleden Bergh, and sweeps round to climb up and away as if bound for a harbour in space.   At the top the gale meets the traveller with a roar.   In two miles first Upper Hesleden and then Penyghent House a mile farther on come into view above the deep gill. Penyghent looms up close at hand, its summit scattered with millstone grit boulders, its sides rent by the waters of many springs. The eye ranges over moorland brown and treeless save for the islands of meadow land round the two farms.

Nowadays isolation no longer means lack of modern amenities. At Penyghent House the farmer has harnessed a small waterfall to generate electricity, and thus enjoys the conveniences of an electric milking-machine, a washing-machine, a cooker, and the entertainment of television. The farm is large, with 900 lambing ewes, 40 head of cattle in winter, and 11 milking cows.

Across high pastures we continue past the Giant's Grave, past two more farms, Blishmire and Rainscar, and see Dalehead, a gamekeeper's whitewashed house on the right on a track to Horton. Dalehead was once a pack-horse baiting inn, and near it was a meeting-place for the rebels in the Pilgrimage of Grace. A gate bars the road ahead and through it on the grass verge on the left is a large stone, the base of Ulfgil Cross, a boundary stone of the monks of Fountains. Beyond it lie Ribblesdale and Settle.

IV

UPPER AIREDALE

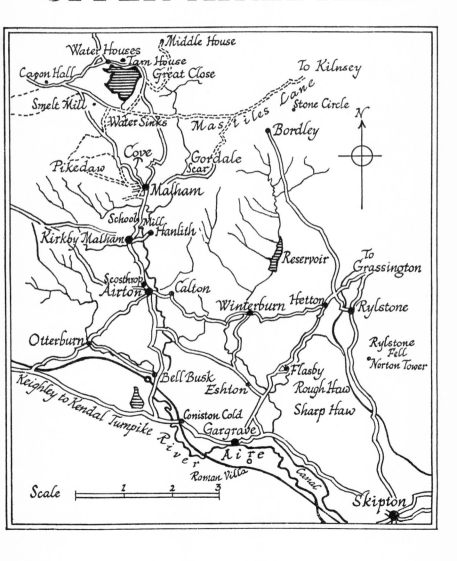

1. SKIPTON TO CALTON

WHEN in 1747 John Wesley contemplated the possibility, which never materialized, of being appointed schoolmaster at Skipton Grammar School, he wrote in a letter: 'Skipton-in-Craven lies in a little vale, so pent up between two hills that it is scarcely accessible on any side; so that you can expect little company from without and within there is none at all.'

Since Wesley's day the picture is altogether different, and a deal of company comes to Skipton from without. Mostly it is company passing through this the market town for Wharfedale and Upper Airedale, and the jumping-off point for the exploration of Craven by walker and motorist alike; and in the long story of the place it is of comings and goings and of the passage of people that we think.

But first, to see to best advantage the town in Wesley's 'little vale,' walk to the top of the High Street, turn up to the castle on its rock; enter the gatehouse topped with the stone letters spelling DESORMAIS; cross the courtyard almost roofed over by its yew-tree, mount worn stone steps up to the leads; and from there look out to a crowded scene pressed between the two hills at the side of the valley of the Aire.

We see the town spread fanwise, with the church and the High Street and the slate roofs of rows of houses glimpsed amongst many trees, and from side to side green hills hemming in most of our view. Yet westwards Pendle Hill stands up boldly. In that direction we look towards the opening called the Aire Gap, the easiest of the ways through the Pennines; and if we examine the view closer we find that the hills dip here and there to hint at other routes between them. To and fro across these rifts have come men and women from prehistoric times to the twentieth century. In fact, we stand at a point where we may picture passing before our eyes a pageant of the peopling of Craven.

First came Mesolithic man on sporadic visits; next the metal traders of the Bronze Age used the Aire Gap as a route between Ireland and Denmark, and some of these people settled here and there in Malhamdale and Wharfedale; here, too, the Brigantes retreated from the Romans and lived in villages now in ruins on the hills of the dales.   The Romans themselves carried across the gap their great military highway from York to Ribchester, and also made a road known later as Queen Street, northwards to Settle and Upper Ribblesdale.

The next arrivals, the Angles, coming up the Aire, cleared the land in the valleys, cultivated arable fields, and founded many of the villages we know to-day.   In the ninth and tenth centuries Danes and Norsemen approaching by way of East Yorkshire and Ireland respectively settled in their turn, and in the Middle Ages people journeying from castle to castle and from abbey to abbey came past Skipton on their way to and from Lancaster, York, and Richmond.

By pack-horse lane, by turnpike, canal, and rail, travellers and traders have made use of these rifts; as to-day roads from Harrogate, Wharfedale, Lancaster, the industrial West Riding, and industrial Lancashire traverse them to meet at Skipton.

In the light of this it seems strange that we see a pleasant but comparatively small town of some 13,207 inhabitants, and pick out amongst its buildings only a few mill chimneys, and beyond them green fields instead of black houses on the slopes of the hills.   A market charter for market and fairs was granted to Skipton in 1203; the canal was made to the town from Bradford in 1773 and continued to Liverpool forty-three years later; the railway arrived in 1847; and the mills of five or six large firms, including John Dewhurst & Sons, makers of the mercerized thread called Sylko, were built in the last century.   Yet Skipton has remained predominantly a centre for agriculture.   Once it was a great corn market; now it has an important auction mart for stock.

The reason for this is to be found not at the mart, the railway station, or the mills whose backs overlook the canal with its muddy towpath, coal barges, and mercantile atmosphere, but at the opposite end of the town at the castle with its estate, and other estates in this pleasant vale preserved to this day for agriculture.

The building of the first Norman stronghold at Skipton raised the status of what was then a tiny hamlet to a place of relative importance, an importance that continued to grow after Robert Clifford had been granted the estate in 1311.   The castle remained the principal seat of the Cliffords (later the Earls of Cumberland) until the death of Lady Anne Clifford in 1676; and the influence of this powerful family and their descendants on Skipton has been incalculable.

Skipton became the centre of a wide district with, in 1323, nine farms in a forest that covered some 1,500 acres between Wharfe and Aire; and the honour was divided into three parts, Airedale, Malhamdale, and Kettlewelldale, each with its own bailiff.

After the Dissolution of the Monasteries it was said that the first Earl of Cumberland, who had bought the Bolton Abbey property, could ride from Skipton to Brough in Westmorland on his own land. Six of the Lords Clifford died before they were forty, most of them on the battle-field. Of them all the two best known are Butcher Clifford, who having murdered the Earl of Rutland forfeited his life and estates in the Wars of the Roses, and his son, Henry, 'the Shepherd Lord,' who, brought up in secret as a shepherd, regained his property after the victory of the Lancastrians in 1485. It was Henry's son who was created the first Earl of Cumberland.

Lady Anne Clifford, Countess of Dorset, Pembroke, and Montgomery, is famous for her stubborn character and for her prolonged and successful fight for her inheritance of the Clifford estates. From the castle roof we have seen the family motto, 'Desormais' (henceforth), on the back and front of the parapet of the gatehouse built by Lady Anne after the damage caused during the siege of the castle in the Civil War; and down below us in the church amongst the Clifford monuments is the magnificent table-tomb displaying heraldic shields put up by Lady Anne to her father.

From the castle can be seen Cock Hill, a knoll marked by a few trees on its summit, from which the cannons of the Parliamentarians are supposed to have fired at the castle. The three years of partial siege were years of alarm and dismay for the townspeople, who hid their valuables under the floors of their houses, often heard the Royalists sally out at night, and saw the gatehouse, so it is said, hung about with sacks of wool like the tower of Bradford church.

From an inventory taken in 1644 during the siege and after the death of the last earl we picture the castle: the bell of the 'great ancient clock' striking in the Great Hall and the several chambers hung with tapestries depicting biblical scenes, and in the gallery, amongst other objects, 'one shovell board table'; or see the trunk

The gatehouse, Skipton Castle

of child-bed linen in 'my Ladyes Chamber,' and amongst the sheets and cushions '1 fayre green velvet mantle lined with taffety laced about with a gold lace and fringed with a deep gold fringe'; picture the kitchen with its huge fire-place, still there, where deer were baked whole; but in the stables the many horses with names such as Fennick, Shaftoe, Bradford, and Parke were 'all plundred.'

Again from the leads of the castle we see part of the High Street, a wide bustling busy street packed with parked cars on its cobbled borders, enclosed by three-storeyed shop buildings dominated by the public library, and amongst the buildings an inn here, a garage there, red telephone kiosks, television aerials, and an isolated block of shops, Middle Row, that makes behind it narrow Sheep Street. In autumn the avenue of limes on the cobbles harmonizes and lends a little colour to the grey street; for the more garish modern shops are out of sight at the industrial end of the town. Or from the leads at the back of the castle we look far down to three waterways, all of which originate from Eller Beck and are fed from dams in the woods. The one nearest the castle —the site of the moat—is Springs Canal once used for shipping limestone from a quarry on the estate, the middle one is Eller Beck itself, whose waters are used by Dewhursts, and the third, the mill-race for the old corn mill.

Perhaps because of the late rebuilding Skipton has a more cheerful aspect and less of medieval gloom than most castles. From Lady Anne the inheritance descended to the Tufton family, of whom Lord Hothfield continued to own much of Skipton and the castle until 1955, when the estate was sold to a trust as an investment.

It is time to leave our roof-top view and to go down and walk round the moat, or explore some of the yards that lead off the High Street like those at Kendal; or to visit the public library that houses the Craven Museum; and away from the centre of traffic seek out the Ermysted Grammar School founded in the fifteenth century, or the Middle School for Girls that has been in existence since 1879 when it received funds from the Petyt Trust.

The grammar-school at Skipton originated as a chantry school established by Peter Toller some time before his death in 1492, and it was one of the schools that survived the attack on the chantries. But when in 1548 William Ermysted, a Craven man, founded a grammar-school in Skipton, the small income from the chantry school was added to his endowment, and so the two became united. In spite of being closed for four years in the eighteenth century, it weathered the costly lawsuits symptomatic of the corruption of the times; and now housed in fine new buildings it caters for the educational needs of a widely scattered population.

The merit of the Craven Museum lies in the fact that it is a repository for local finds. Here amongst the well-arranged exhibits is visible proof of much of the story of Craven: minerals found there, finds from Elbolton Cave, the spearhead from Malham Moor, Iron Age pottery, and an Iron Age sickle from Grassington, Roman coins, glass bracelets, Samian ware, collections of bygone domestic utensils and farm implements, and prints of the town and surrounding places.

Skipton possesses a national treasure in the Petyt Library founded by Sylvester Petyt. Sylvester and his brother William were born at Storiths near Bolton Abbey in the seventeenth century. William studied law, published books; and as Keeper of the Records of the Tower of London saved multitudes of documents from destruction through neglect. Sylvester, a lawyer, became Principal of Barnard's Inn, acted as trustee for his brother's

*C

estate, and left much of his own fortune to trustees for the benefit of local charities.

Partly collected by Sylvester himself, and added to by books from his brother's library, by friends, and by old scholars of Skipton Grammar School, the library consists of about 5,000 items, largely political and religious, and ranging in date from 1497 to 1716. The *Nuremberg Chronicle*, illustrated with woodcuts, is the oldest book, and a collection of Civil War tracts the most rare. In fact of some 287 items either only one other copy or no other copy exists in England. Many are curiosities, such as a book on *Food* by William Muffett, dated 1655; only a very few, for example, *Spiritual Thrift* by Elizabeth Warren, are by women; and here too are the books written by William Petyt himself.

Although some of the books were strictly for the use of the school, the majority were available to the townspeople. Never housed properly as Sylvester wished, the library has suffered from neglect; it was for years kept in the church, and several times was in danger of being sold. In this century the books have come to the public library, and aided by a generous donation they are being catalogued and rebound.

One September day we found many shops closed for two days of the September holidays. Outside the library a notice-board advertised winter courses from 'Hand Embroidery' to 'Boiler House Practice' and 'Old Time Dancing' to 'Car Maintenance.' We found a café open. A youthful waitress with corn-coloured hair spoke of the September break and said: 'And they give the children a week too. I have four. Four sons.' Her remarks seemed like a peep-hole into present-day life, and opened up a vista of wars, many children born, and wives at work.

One of the oldest routes out of Skipton is that leading to Wharfedale by way of Rylstone, the medieval route north. The road runs between the low fells of the neighbourhood, on our right the sprawling mass of Rylstone Fell and on our left the rough country of what was the Forest of Elsoe, with Sharp Haw Beacon and Flasby Fell standing out. The sight of the little pointed beacon, made familiar by its distinctive shape, marks for many travellers the approach to the dales.

The few houses of Rylstone group themselves in trees round a pond, and the church, away from the road and seen against the fells, has one of the finest positions of any church in the dales.

Here instead of the Cliffords we find the Nortons. These power-ful families quarrelled over the deer; and in a lawsuit of Eliza-bethan times a witness described how he had seen 'old Lady Clifford, mother of my lord Cumberland that now is, hound her greyhounds within the said grounds of Rilston, and chase deer and have them away at her leisure.'

In 1532, when Sir John Norton whilst on the king's service had been condemned for debt, Christopher Aske, by command of the sheriff, with '40 riotous and evil disposed persons' broke into the house of Sir John's tenants at Rylstone and, forcibly taking 20 head of cattle, drove them to Skipton at such a pace that many of them were lost and died. When the men petitioned that the cattle were theirs and not Sir John's the sheriff, with an 'angry and fierce countenance,' demanded £20, and as they 'knew they had no cow to milk and no horse to ride' they were forced to comply.

The ruined tower on the fell was built by Richard Norton, a leader in the Pilgrimage of Grace, a rebellion that shattered the family. Afterwards Richard, with some members of his family, fled abroad, and he forfeited his estates that were given eventually to the Cliffords.

Wordsworth's poem, *The White Doe of Rylstone*, perpetuates the legend that a son, Francis Norton, not implicated in the rebellion, was murdered near Bolton, and that his sister Emily, taking with her a pet white doe, visited his grave at the priory each Sunday, a custom continued by the doe after Emily's death.

As a rule, to reach Malhamdale from Skipton the traveller takes the main road north and turns off either at Gargrave or Bell Busk. The large village of Gargrave lies between the Aire and the Leeds and Liverpool Canal. It is easier to linger by the church across the river or alongside the canal than in the busy main street, where we saw the Swan Hotel that temptingly advertised Scotch salmon, chicken, or roast beef for lunch.

Gargrave was the old central parish of Craven, and once a market town. Here in medieval days was a fertile countryside devastated by the Scots raid of 1318, and here Sawley Abbey grew wheat, barley, beans, and oats. In 1674 it was discovered that the parishioners had failed to pull down the rood-loft, 'a large structure of good and valuable sapplin timber . . . neatly carved and curiously beautified and adorned.' Evidence was given that the church had several times been full and 'throng' and that the people had sat upon the loft.

The daughter of a Gargrave vicar wrote in 1730 that one of the pleasures of her childhood had been listening to the bells of the leaders of the pack-horses in the lane, and she described the arable fields as being still unenclosed and divided into strips, called lands, though these were being exchanged in order that the farmers might have them adjoining. Another diarist, William Paley of Settle, notes that a Mr Mason's power looms were attacked and destroyed by an armed mob on 27th April 1826. To-day Johnson & Johnson, the makers of toilet powder and surgical dressing, have a modern factory on the outskirts of the village, and use the old mill for storage. Leaving Gargrave we cross the canal at a wharf, where the pigs of lead from the mines in Upper Wharfedale were stored for shipment.

In this region between Skipton and Malham lies a pastoral country of heath, park land, and large houses; and lanes meander from one to another of the small villages of Hetton, Flasby, Winterburn, Eshton, and Calton, of which the largest is Calton with a population of 109. As their names imply all of them are of Anglian foundation except Flasby that is Danish, and all figure in Domesday Book. These outskirts of fell land were and still are pleasant places in which to live and prosper, as witness the lovely seventeenth-century farmhouses and barns at Hetton.

Everywhere we see marks of rigg and furr on the undulating land, for the better part of the country was ploughed until the latter half of the eighteenth century, when Craven farmers turned to stock-rearing. In the park of Eshton Hall wych-elms and beech-trees give shade for a fine herd of Ayrshire cattle. The hall, built about 1826 by the architect George Webster of Kendal for Sir Matthew Wilson, is now used as a school, and the Wilsons live at Eshton House, a good Georgian house at a junction of roads a little farther on.

The few farmhouses of Winterburn, whose name means 'the stream dry except in winter,' are spaced along the beck, and beyond them we turn a corner and come with a shock of delighted surprise face to face with the house called Friars Head, that has perhaps the best front of all the seventeenth-century houses in the dales. It stands on the site of a grange of Furness Abbey, was built by the Procters, and is now a farmhouse. Sir Stephen

Friars Head, Winterburn

Procter, builder of Fountains Hall near Ripon, was born here. A colourful small garden shows up to perfection the elaborate front of the house, that still seems to wait to welcome home its Cavalier owners.

By contrast, at the east end of Winterburn stands the old Independent church with its attractive latticed windows. One of the earliest centres of Nonconformity in the dales, Winterburn had a house certified as a meeting-house for Protestant Dissenters in 1694; and in 1704, partially owing to the generosity of Barbara, wife of John Lambert of Calton Hall, a Congregational church was erected there. It was closed in 1880, but two years later it was reopened as a chapel of ease to Gargrave church, as it still remains.

Born in 1639, 'Mistress Barbara,' one of the Listers of Gisburne, was what we should call a character and a strong Puritan. First married clandestinely in the garden of her home to William Nowell, who unfortunately was drowned almost immediately afterwards, she successfully claimed dower from her husband's estate, and later married again, this time John Lambert, son of the Roundhead Major-General John Lambert, of Calton Hall. Mistress Barbara has been compared to Philip Lord Wharton, because as he did in Swaledale, so she enthusiastically furthered the advancement of the Independent Church in Craven. In spite of her husband's lack of interest in the cause, during her life-time Calton Hall was frequented by well-known preachers such as Oliver Heywood; and for a few months in 1683 it was used by Richard Frankland as his academy for training men for the ministry.

The hilltop village of Calton was the birth-place of Major-General Lambert, who, holding several important posts under Cromwell, and being responsible amongst other deeds for the capture of Bradford, eventually died while still a prisoner in Guernsey.

The family's connection with Calton dates from 1516, when John Lambert the elder leased the manor and the hall from John Malham. The house resembled Nappa Hall in Wensleydale and was in bad repair; 'an indifferent carpenter' and four sworn men acted as arbitrators to assess the cost of the necessary repairs, to be paid for by the Malhams. This John Lambert, a lawyer, and his son held many offices under the Crown and benefited from the Dissolution of the Monasteries. At the height of their prosperity the family owned most of Malhamdale.

The hall, the major-general's home, was burnt down soon after the Restoration, and the present building on the site has nothing remarkable about it. In a small garden in front of the house an inscription on a stone pillar reads: 'IL 1688 WF 1688.' Confiscated at the time of the Restoration, the general's estates were returned to his son John, who rebuilt the hall. With the death of John's and Barbara's sons, their daughter Frances, married to Sir John Middleton, succeeded to the estates and the direct line of the family came to an end.

From Calton it is half a mile across the bridge over the river to Airton, beyond which opens out the glorious limestone scenery of Malhamdale.

2. MALHAMDALE

THE PARISH of Kirkby Malham, eleven miles in length from the boundaries of Malham Moor in the north to Bell Busk in the south, includes all the country that we speak of as Malhamdale, and it contains the townships of Calton, Otterburn, Airton, Scosthrop, Kirkby Malham, Hanlith, and Malham, all wedged into the tiny valley, only five miles long. The rest of the parish, more than half of it, is Malham Moor.

Far and away the most striking of the Yorkshire dales, considering its size, Malhamdale is renowned for its limestone landscapes, which lend a dramatic background to the head waters of its river, the Aire, whose first small streams and feeders seep and flow through fissured rock to burst out in springs and becks amongst the wonders of the cove and Gordale Scar.

The village of Malham, the focal point of the valley so far as the visitor is concerned, lies six miles from Settle and eleven from Skipton. In the eighteenth century the tourist approached from the two market towns 'by tolerably good horse paths' or by the chaise road from Hellifield; in the era of the day tripper he journeyed by train to Skipton or Bell Busk and proceeded thence on foot or by wagonette; nowadays a variety of roads, most of them narrow but none the less tarred, brings the traveller into this the most frequented of the Yorkshire dales.

Although much visited on Sundays and in the holiday months, and although hilly roads lead through it to Ribblesdale, Malham is in effect a terminus, not a place passed *en route* to somewhere else but one to be sought out and visited specially in order to see it at all. Nationally famous, its scenery has to measure up to a preconceived high standard; and in fact it does so.

Here is the quintessence of limestone country, a landscape small in compass with, in contrast, large grand details set in it like pearls on green velvet. Nearing Malham we view an extraordinarily intimate scene: the village as it were in its lair in the mountains, grizzled hills girdling the dale head, with on the one hand the bare rock of Malham Cove and on the other the folds of hills masking

Approach to Malham

Gordale; across the intervening hillside white walls enclosing fields of fantastically crooked shape; below them trees between which peep a few houses of the village hugging the foot of Cawden, a small intruding hill that divides our view in half, and on both sides plainly to be seen the terracing on the meadows of the ancient open arable fields of Malham.   What a medley it is of the natural and the man-made!

As we look we can distinguish walled roads climbing like thin silver chains out of the green bowl of the valley: one to Gordale ends there but continues as a green lane to join Mastiles Lane for Kilnsey in Wharfedale; one disappears over the hilltops to reach Malham Tarn by the east bank; and a third to the west of the cove and tarn swings a narrow serpentine way to the heights of Malham Moor and along the foot of Fountains Fell towards Ribblesdale.

As we have seen, men and women of the Mesolithic, the Bronze, and the Iron Ages came to the dale.   Airton, Hanlith, Calton, and Malham are villages founded by the Angles, whilst Kirkby Malham is of Danish origin, and all appear in Domesday Book. The scattered farms on Malham Moor have been there since the Norsemen first established them about A.D. 900.

In the eleventh and twelfth centuries the Percys of Northumberland, who after the Conquest had been given most of the dale, and their tenants, chiefly the Malhams and Otterburns, made generous grants of land to Fountains Abbey; and the Mauleverers and other benefactors similarly endowed Bolton Priory. Here, too, the Abbey of Dereham in Norfolk was given the advowson of Kirkby Malham Church and property in Calton and Scosthrop. Between them the monasteries owned more than two-thirds of the dale. At the Dissolution Fountains' lands came to the Greshams, and the Bolton estates to the Lamberts, who, as we have noted, by purchase eventually possessed almost all the dale.

In course of time many farms were sold off; and the yeomen of the seventeenth century built their houses, of which the best examples are the manor-house at Scosthrop, the post office, and William Ellis's house at Airton, the vicarage at Kirkby, Hill Top and Town Head Farms at Malham, and Water Houses near the tarn, all worth seeing as examples of the building of their period.

In past times a few linen weavers lived at Airton and Calton. In the latter half of the eighteenth century the manufacture of cotton was introduced; and new mills were built by the becks, often on the site of the manorial corn mills, as at Malham, Airton, and Kirkby Malham. At times, especially in the early nineteenth century, coal, lead, copper, and zinc were mined. But above all else Malhamdale was and still is a great sheep-rearing dale, even though the big fairs once held on its hills have gone since the railway came to Bell Busk and the auction marts were developed at Skipton and Hellifield. Cattle and sheep formed the wealth of the monks and of most people in the dale from time immemorial to the present day.

In 1785 Thomas Lister, later Lord Ribblesdale, of Gisburn Park, acquired the northern half of the valley, that in 1852 was bought by James Morrison, whose son, Walter Morrison, millionaire and bachelor, owning the estate for sixty-four years and living at Malham Tarn House for much of the time, was an outstanding figure in the dale during the last century. Lastly, after one or two changes of ownership, the tarn estate was presented to the National Trust by Mrs Hutton-Croft in 1946, and is now leased as a field centre by the Council for the Promotion of Field Studies.

Into each village in the dale can be read something of this background. Spaced about the green at Airton are old houses: in particular the Friends' Meeting House, with a small secluded graveyard behind it, and the house opposite, both with dated door-heads and the initials 'WAE' standing for William and Alice Ellis, who built the house in 1696 and the meeting-house in 1700. William, a linen weaver, and an early convert to the Quaker faith, went on preaching missions to America, and both he and Alice left several charities.

At Airton the only cotton mill in the dale still in use is occupied by Reckitt & Colman for the manufacture of the antiseptic, Dettol. Built in the late eighteenth century, it was rebuilt by Dewhursts in about 1838. A friend of ours as a child stayed at William Ellis's house some forty-five years ago, and as she lay in bed in the early morning she remembers hearing the clatter of the clogs of the mill workers going to work.

Should you go to Airton in mid afternoon of the last Saturday in August you will find in full swing the major annual event in the dale, the Malhamdale Agricultural and Horticultural Show, a show neither too small to be of only local interest nor too large to be impersonal. Undulating park land with Malham Cove in sight makes the show ground. Two men discuss the judging: 'How's t'cows gitten on? Who's winning?' to which is replied: 'Seems to be about ivverybody.'

But the pens of sheep are all-important, pens of Dalesbred, Swaledale, and half-bred sheep, and of fat lambs here, where produce for the towns is paramount. We inquired of a group of farmers how and why the fleeces of the sheep of some exhibitors were darker than natural, and were told that a weak solution of creosote or peat water was used to dye them. 'It makes 'em look more like moor sheep,' they said. Here they have sheep-dog trials, a dog show, a pony gymkhana, a fell race, motor-cycle races, and a dance at night. In the produce tent chocolate cakes, sponge cakes, biscuits, shortbread, apple pies, and other delicacies made us wish that critics of English cooking might sample this kind of fare in which the dales housewife excels.

At Airton there is a great feeling of freedom, but at Kirkby Malham, two miles up the dale, the traveller drops down into a sheltered bosky hollow. This, the parish town, is one of the smaller villages of the dale, with only 55 inhabitants and 21 houses. Quite the best approach to it is to cross the hills from Settle, and from above to come suddenly on to the church, a fine large building with many good features in the spacious well-lit interior. Two of the entries in the parish registers for 1655 are signed by Oliver Cromwell..

Recently one hot Sunday morning when the doors had been left open during morning service, the congregation was startled by a bull that walked in at the tower end; a farmer quietly left his pew and drove it out.

During the last war John Dower lived at Kirkby Malham. He was commissioned by the Minister of Town and Country Planning to write a report on national parks in England and Wales; published in 1945, this was a preliminary to the designation of the different parks.

It is extraordinary to recollect nowadays that the village was once a seat of industry: Scargill Mill, on the site of the manorial corn mill, and the vicarage building were both used for cotton spinning; and a bobbin mill stood by the beck. Scargill Mill is still to be seen between Kirkby and Hanlith up a lane alongside the Aire.

The name Hanlith derives from a personal name and means 'the hill-slope of Hagena.' A tiny village, it is dominated by the hall, part way up the hill and for long the home of the Serjeantsons, an ancient Malhamdale family. The present house has been re-modelled three times: in 1668 when Robert Serjeantson built a new house; in 1829 when a pleasant Georgian front was grafted on to the old house; and in 1912 when the front we see to-day was built by the present owners, the Illingworths. Through these changes the original doorway, inscribed 'RS 1668,' has survived, but a large stone figure in relief of a serjeant holding a halberd has been removed from above the front door to a gable.

The doorway at Hanlith Hall is one of a group of seventeenth-century doorways that incorporate a rare feature, a halberd carved on each side. We shall find others at Ingman Lodge in Ribblesdale and (though only the door-head survives) at New Hall near Settle. Here the halberds represent the holder of a medieval manor who held his land by giving a personal service to his lord.

In Tudor times the Metcalfes of Bear Park in Wensleydale held the Manor of Hanlith of the Earls of Northumberland, a connection with one of the leaders of the Rising of the North that involved Leonard Metcalfe in that rebellion. Leonard himself was eventually pardoned, but one of his tenants, William Serjeantson, and a few Craven men were hanged 'in some place nyghe the townes where they dwelt' by another rebel, William Lawson of Hanlith, who was cruelly appointed hangman.

The last of these villages and the bourn of most travellers in the dale is Malham—not by any means the few stark upland farmsteads of a dale head, but a small village of some 170 inhabitants, a genial place well sheltered and shaded by trees and at only 650 feet above sea level.   It lies on either side of the water that flows from the cove, now very close.   Crossing over Monks Bridge, near the whitewashed post office, we enter the hilly green.

Perhaps it is early spring and a cold March day; even so, a party of schoolchildren from Canterbury making a regional survey, with note-books and pencils in hand, tours the village.   Or it may be a hot August day when members of an art class from Malham Tarn Field Centre have settled on the village, and artists of all ages, even family parties, sit behind easels at every vantage point.   Or a walker bound for the youth hostel strides down from the hills, and on the way perhaps consults a Malhamdale figure, Gilbert Brown, who sits out of doors in a wheeled chair and acts as universal guide to visitors.   And all through the summer months youths and girls and their elders dismount from buses to set off to see the cove and Gordale.

But visitors or no visitors the normal life of the dale goes on. Seldom is the air of Malhamdale or of Malham itself free from the bleating of sheep.   Ewes and lambs, yellow-coated after dipping and gathered together in a small garth, call to each other, their mournful voices rising and falling in a gradually decreasing diminuendo.   Or, mingled with the whistle of a shepherd to his dog, the bleating of sheep echoes from a distant fellside, where a flock in constant movement like a moorland beck pours down the pastures.

Malham Fair may have gone, but not all trade has been transferred to the marts.   In the back-end sheep and cattle sales, perhaps five in all, are conducted by a Skipton auctioneer in the village.   The sheep sales, at which 5,000 to 6,000 sheep are sold each year, take place in the old Deer Park where the fairs used to be held.   At these events pens of 'draft ewes, horned and half-bred gimmer and wedder lambs' line the sloping field with, in the centre, a small straw-covered ring, at one side of which stands the auctioneer. Everyone knows everyone by his Christian name, the lean men from the hills, wearing caps at all angles, and the stouter men, the dealers from the towns, in flat trilbies. One lot of sheep, driven round by their owner in the ring, quickly follows another. The auctioneer keeps up his rapid patter: 'Nine pounds bid, nine bid, take nine guineas, nine guineas bid,' and in between he or the farmers comment on the stock:

'Right off t'top.'

'A grand packet o' lambs from Harry from Malham Tarn.'

'Some rare fat wedders. They'll do well.'

'Yes, they're good 'uns but a bit short.'

'How many?'

'Thirty seven. Two for luck.'

One farmer, dissatisfied with the price, slapped a sheep with his stick and remonstrated: 'They're *fat lambs*.' 'A deserving case this,' says the auctioneer of a big jolly man in a ragged coat. He raises a general spontaneous laugh that bursts out again when a youth new to the job is asked whether his father has given him any luck money for the buyer, to which he replies: 'Nut sae mich.' The sale proceeds: 'Four pounds bid. Four pounds bid . . . '

The interests of Malham divide into the natural and the man-made. Amongst the latter there are for the explorer of prehistoric sites the Bronze Age stone circle at Bordley on the east of Malham Moor and a Bronze Age barrow at Seaty Hill (where was found the musical instrument, the bone recorder), and in many places the ruinous huts and field walls of Iron Age settlements.

But of the monks' centuries-long ownership next to nothing is left except the bases of their boundary crosses, Ulfgil, Weets, and Nappa, the terraces of the arable fields, the routes they took over the hills to their monasteries, and the names of fields or buildings. They each had half the township, the beck flowing from the cove forming the dividing line, so that on the east side lay the property of Bolton, and on the west that of Fountains; and the farmhouse, Priors Hall, stands on the site of the chief house of Bolton, whilst the reading-room occupies the site of Malham Hall, the chief house of Fountains. Beck Hall, in style a kind of rustic Tudor, is also on the site of a property of Fountains, and is said to have been the dower house for Malham Tarn House; and farther up the beck is the clapper bridge, Moon Bridge, so named after Prior Moon of Bolton.

Town Head, Malham

At Town Head a seventeenth-century building with blocked-up windows is Calamine House, a storehouse for that mineral when it was being mined.   In the eighteenth century the Lister Arms on the green was called Greenhead Inn; and up the Gordale road is the ruinous old school-house, with its three round-headed window openings, founded by Rowland Brayshaw in 1717.   It and the grammar-school at Kirkby, founded by Benjamin Lambert in 1606, were united, and the new school built on the roadside between Kirkby and Malham in the last century.

Some of the people of the village now work at factories such as Johnsons at Gargrave; but in the years at the turn of the century we have to picture Malham as partially industrialized.   Not only were there the cotton mill and also tan pits, but the calamine- and copper-mines on Pikedaw, the coal-pits on Fountains Fell, and the lead-mines, still commemorated by the round smelt mill chimney on the moor, were all in production.   The mines were managed for Lord Ribblesdale by his eccentric chaplain the Rev. Dr Collins, who in 1806 sent stalactites and stalagmites from the caverns where the calamine was found to be sold as natural curiosities in Bond Street in London.   At times miners from Swaledale worked at Malham; and the minerals were taken to Gargrave for shipment on the canal.

As for the natural scene, it never palls. The sight of the cove always surprises and the sight of Gordale always astounds. Here came the eighteenth-century tourists on a tour of the North or on their way to the Lakes. Thomas Gray, the poet, found the vale dreary; Lord Torrington enjoyed himself here; William and Dorothy Wordsworth in 1807 'rested under the huge rock [of Gordale] for several hours, and drank of its cold waters.'

In an effort to describe the 'accumulation of phenomena' topographers poured out a torrent of verbiage with unrestrained zest. Even Whitaker described the cove thus: 'The imagination can scarcely figure any form or scale of rock within the bounds of probability that shall go beyond it.'

Rather than the writers it is the artists, from James Ward in the eighteenth century to John Piper of the twentieth, who succeeded best in conveying their impressions of the grandeur of the scenes, especially of Gordale. Anthony Devis, a water-colourist and a member of a family of artists at Preston in Lancashire, painted under the patronage of Lord Ribblesdale a series of pen-and-ink and wash drawings of the district. Many of them are distant views showing the pale, rain-washed atmosphere of Malham.

At the present day the artists Constance Pearson, John Parker, and William Wild, living in the dale, all produce valuable work. William Wild, artist, wood-carver, joiner, and smith, the scene of his work the blacksmith's shop at Malham, is boldly creative, and fills a niche in the life of the dale.

Malham Cove is reached along a field path from Town Head, past the site of the cotton mill by the beck and the ruins of Iron Age huts and fields, to the foot of the towering cliff 240 feet high. Here aeons ago water swept over the top in a grand waterfall, and it is recorded, although not in this century, that flood waters from the tarn have on occasion flowed over it to drop down and break into a wild confusion of spray. Many old writers speak of the screaming of the hawks nesting on the ledges of rock. When William Howson came to the cove in the 1850's he spoke of the tedious uniformity of the new fences of the recent enclosures, and of walls in general as 'a drawback to the scenery.'

It is said that the white limestone streaked with black moss and lichen gave Charles Kingsley the germ of his idea of the chimney-sweep in *The Water Babies*. This may well be so; but Kingsley first planned to use the scenery of Craven in a novel that was never written on the Pilgrimage of Grace, and again in a second abortive novel, *Alcibiades*, and from these two the scenes were carried on to *The Water Babies*.

Whereas the cove is a dry waterfall, if such a phrase may be coined, Gordale Scar is a cave that collapsed long, long ago. The upper fall splashes through a ring of rock, a new course through which the water broke in about 1730. The footpath from the road to the scar can be very wet, and the two streams, their stones covered with bright green and black mosses and the water reflecting the sky, very beautiful. Gordale Scar is seen to advantage on a sunny day in mid October, when the sunshine lights up the white torrent against the shadowed cliffs. Usually a cold wind blows down the funnel of the gorge, and always drops of water, as if hurled by a mischievous spirit of the rocks, fall from the beetling crags.

In 1780 the Rev. John Hutton, in *A Tour of the Caves*, wrote of Gordale: 'Some goats frisked about with seemingly wanton carelessness, on the brink of this dreadful precipice, where none of us would have stood for all the pleasant vales washed by the River Aire.'

Of the artists James Ward shows Gordale best in his enormous canvas, finished in 1815, at the Tate Gallery. At the foot of the scar he painted a herd of cattle, two stags fighting, and a perfectly executed white bull, so that in proportion the massive black-shadowed bastions of rock towering above look colossal. The cattle were the Chillingham breed kept at Gisburn Park, and they were transferred here to please the first Lord Ribblesdale, for whom the picture was painted.

Of all the other wonders of Malham there are for the seeking Janet's Foss, and the Dry Valley, scars, and clints on the summit of the hills behind the cove and Gordale. The tarn is away on Malham Moor.

Malham Moor is criss-crossed by tracks, some narrow motor roads over open country such as the one that runs past the tarn and past Darnbrook to Arncliffe, others that remain as bridle tracks such as those to Littondale, and Mastiles Lane, once an important highway that we shall find again continuing across Ribblesdale and alongside Ingleborough. These roads came into being as routes between the abbeys and their outlying possessions.

We have never crossed the moor other than on bright spring days when the wind blew cold and the sheep browsed ceaselessly, or in high summer when sheep and cattle, 'the cattle on a thousand hills,' stood in groups on knolls to catch the breeze where trees and shade are scarce. When the snow is 'stowering' [1] and the temperature below zero it must be a stark, grim place.

Scattered about this vast tableland that rises up to Fountains Fell and Darnbrook Fell at over 2,000 feet, the ten or so farms, occupied in turn by the Norsemen, the herdsmen of the monks, and twentieth-century dalesmen, are sited for shelter under the lee of hills and scars. All except Thoragill and Stangill appear in the bursars' accounts of Fountains Abbey: 'Mallwater hous, Tranhous, Mydlowhous, Caupanhow, Darnbrukhous,' some of them were spelt. Each consisted of one or two houses, outbuildings, and folds, run by a sheep-master and servants. Such was the remoteness and wildness of the moor that even as late as the sixteenth century the herdsmen of the abbey milked their stock with their swords and bucklers laid beside them.

At Water Houses in the Middle Ages lived the forester of the Forest of Gnoup (part of the moor) and the keeper of the Fishery of the Tarn; Low Trenhouse was at one time the storehouse and headquarters for the mining; the name Capon Hall (Caupanhow) means the traders' hill. Middle House, situated on the monks' route to Littondale, is one of the highest inhabited farmhouses in Yorkshire, with behind it the original seventeenth-century house, now disused, and near at hand many ancient sheepfolds.

In Great Close, part of the pasture ground of Middle House Farm, took place many fairs for the sale of Scotch cattle, sheep, and horses brought here by Mr Birtwhistle, the famous grazier of Craven, in the eighteenth century. As described by Thomas Hurtley in his *History of Malhamdale*: 'Mr Birtwhistle has had Twenty Thousand head of Cattle on this field in one summer, every Herd enticed from their native soil and ushered into this fragrant Pasture, by the Pipe of an Highland Orpheus.'

It is possible to make a circuit of Malham Tarn on foot but not by car. Although the roads are good enough, the field centre forbids motor-cars and preserves the area as a nature reserve.

[1] Driven fiercely by the wind.

Seen from afar, perhaps from Capon Hall, with Tarn House, the woods, and Great Close Scar as a low horizon in the distance, the stretch of water achieves a melancholy beauty.   It covers 153 acres and is nowhere more than 14 feet deep.   About 1780 it was dammed and the level raised by Lord Ribblesdale, who at the same time planted many trees and built a boat-house that cost £10 10s.   Trout and perch still abound.   Fountains Abbey and afterwards the Cliffords valued the fishery; and Lord Torrington said that here 'trout fishing is certainly to be enjoyed to greater perfection than at any other place in Great Britain.'

In the region of the tarn curlews collect whilst moulting after the nesting season, and as many as 3,000 gather together in flocks. Some of the rarer birds seen in passage are the goosander, the ringed plover, and the great crested grebe.

On its commanding position amongst trees on the north side of the tarn, Tarn House overlooks the water, a scene somewhat lacking the background of surrounding hills.   It was built on to an old house by Lord Ribblesdale as a shooting-lodge, and was altered and enlarged again by James Morrison.   Here were entertained many famous guests: Kingsley, Ruskin, John Stuart Mill, to mention a few.   A field centre since 1948, it has a resident staff, and can accommodate 50 students at once for courses on natural history, archaeology, local history, geology, geography, and so on.

From Tarn House we may reach Ribblesdale directly by foot-paths or roads past Capon Hall.   One of our favourite roads from Malhamdale to Ribblesdale is that from Kirkby Malham; from it are to be seen the spectacular Attermire Scars and the terrain of the Victoria Cave, and the site of a Roman marching camp where a by-road from Stockdale Farm meets the Kirkby road as it plunges steeply down to Settle.

V

NORTH
RIBBLESDALE

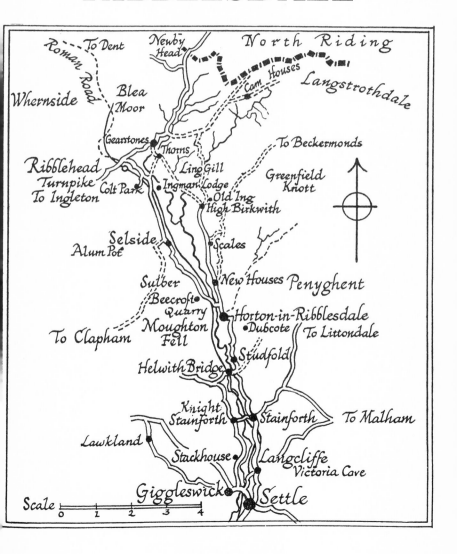

To Dent · Newby Head · North Riding

Roman Road · To Dent

Whernside · Blea Moor · Cam Houses · Langstrothdale

Gearstones · Thorns

Ribblehead · Ling Gill · To Beckermonds

Turnpike · Colt Park · Ingman Lodge · Greenfield Knott
To Ingleton · Old Ing · High Birkwith

Selside · Scales
Alum Pot

Sulber · New Houses · Penyghent
Beecroft
Quarry · Horton-in-Ribblesdale
Moughton · Dubcote · To Littondale
To Clapham · Fell

Studfold

Helwith Bridge

Knight · Stainforth · To Malham
Stainforth

Lawkland · Stackhouse · Langcliffe
Victoria Cave

Giggleswick · Settle

Scale
0   1   2   3   4

1. SETTLE

SETTLE seems to us one of the most satisfying of market towns. It lies at 500 feet above sea level on the fringe of the hills of Craven at the foot of the limestone crag of Castlebergh, where the high road running north-west to Kendal and the Lake District crosses the Ribble.

Fortunately the market-place at Settle is only brushed by the traffic of the high road, and fortunately too for the artist this open space with the shambles in the centre still presents a paintable scene. On Tuesdays, market-days, an assemblage of stalls, vans, and cars fills the square, and people from the hill farms of Ribblesdale and Malhamdale and from the low-lying farms on the flat country to the south throng the town. Here you may buy produce of all kinds, including riddle bread (thin oatcake) at a confectioner's stall and Lancashire cheese at a grocer's shop. 'I love Settle,' said a woman to us; 'I live here.'

Above the market-place, up narrow ginnels and steep lanes, crowd the houses of Upper Settle, or Over Settle as it was once called. It was here that the highway entered, before it was diverted to its present route, in the turnpike days. Here and in housing estates on the edge of the town lives an urban population; for Settle has not broken with a long tradition of industrial life that continues with cotton mills, a paper mill, and lime works in the vicinity. At the same time it has lost its importance as a mart for stock—a position usurped by Hellifield—and its population is diminishing rather than increasing.

A mile away across the Ribble in its separate township is Giggleswick, in no way rivalling but complementary to Settle. The latter is the mercantile and administrative centre with council offices, shops, banks, and most of the hotels; the former upholds the spiritual and cultural tradition with the parish church and public school. Settle clings to the hills, but Giggleswick lies snugly on a valley site: until it was drained of water in about 1830 and cultivated in 1863, Giggleswick Tarn was a natural feature. Many of the houses date from the seventeenth century, and some are charmingly swathed in early summer with *Clematis montana*.

The market-place at Settle

Settle, an Anglian settlement, and Giggleswick, a Scandinavian, in turn became part of the great properties of the Percys of Northumberland, some of whom occasionally stayed at their manor-house at Cleatop, a mile south.   In the thirteenth century their local rival, Elias of Giggleswick, a generous benefactor to Fountains and Sawley Abbeys, so impoverished himself that about 1255, in return for a pension, he resigned his Manor of Giggleswick to the Percys.   Henry Percy had been granted a market charter for Settle in 1249, a charter that was increased by additional fairs in 1708; and the market square remained the property of the lords of the manor, the Percys, the Cliffords, and the Earls of Burlington, until it and the cross were given to the parish council by Deed of Gift from the Duke of Devonshire.

In the early twelfth century a church was built at Giggleswick, dedicated like Middleham church in Wensleydale to St Alkelda; it was rebuilt and added to through the centuries, and until 1838, when a new church was built in Settle, was the parish church for that town.   In the late fifteenth century a school was founded at Giggleswick, and in 1652 William Dewsbury preached at the market cross and so introduced the Quaker faith to Settle.   In 1675 Thomas Preston built Tanner House, now known as The Folly, off the market-place.   In 1753 the neighbourhood grew more easily accessible as the Keighley to Kendal turnpike road was made, and the old route from Long Preston over Hunter Bark and through Upper Settle fell into disuse.   In 1791 the Craven Bank was instituted; later large houses were built in the town and on the outskirts; and as a result of the arrival of the railway industries were developed.

The school at Giggleswick, now one of the leading boys' schools in the North, was founded as a chantry school by James Carr.   It survived the suppression of the chantries, and was given a royal charter endowing it with lands in the East Riding in 1553.   Taking advantage of scholarships, local boys have passed on from it to Cambridge over the centuries; many have taken up legal or clerical careers and several have become famous.[1]   Following a

---

[1] Nathaniel and Josiah Shute, divines who appear in Fuller's *Worthies*; Richard Frankland, founder of the Nonconformist Academy; William Paley, archdeacon of Carlisle; Thomas Procter, the sculptor; John S. Howson, dean of Chester; John Overend, the banker; John Windsor, botanist; George Birkbeck, the founder of the mechanics institutes; and Benjamin Waugh, founder of the National Society for the Prevention of Cruelty to Children. All except the last four went to Giggleswick School.

new constitution drawn up in the 1860's many new buildings were erected; and as a jubilee memorial Walter Morrison built the school chapel that with its copper dome makes a well-known landmark.

A few people, some of them strangers passing through, give us first-hand glimpses of Settle in past times. In 1708, when the townspeople were petitioning for new fairs, George Myers, the Earl of Burlington's agent, wrote of them to the Countess Georgiana: 'Such a rabble they are as I was never concerned with . . . that would be lords themselves and domineer over everyone . . . as in the case of the market crosse, a heap of ugly stones thrown up in the middle of the town in great disorder, which I propose to remove and sett up a handsome crosse and cover it.'

In 1750 Dr Pococke remarked: 'Settle is a pretty great thorough-fare and has a small manufacture of knit stockings.' Nineteen years later the poet Gray, staying two nights in Settle, wrote: 'There are not in it above a dozen good-looking houses, the rest are old and low with little porticos in front.' John Housman, the topographer, noted in 1800 that Settle was a considerable market town containing about 900 inhabitants, that the leather and hide trade was in decline, that there was a sale once a fortnight for these and fat cattle, and that the inhabitants had lately cut an easy, winding path to the top of Castlebergh.

William Lodge Paley (1785–1847), who was the master of Giggleswick National School and who sold books to the local gentry and to parsons and schoolmasters in the dales, kept a diary. On 16th May 1842 he ordered Whitaker's *Craven* for himself and hoped 'it is as good as reported.' He gives a picture of the rowdiness and general drunkenness that prevailed on all public occasions such as the fairs.

On 18th April 1821 he wrote: 'Was shocked to hear that Charles Duckett late of Folly has cut his throat, having betrayed Mr Kayley's daughter and can't bear the reproach,' and on Easter Sunday 1826: 'Parents let their children go to Ebbs and Flows to suck Spanish juice and water. Others more vitiated take liquor, and these children will doubtless do so when they get older, so these ridiculous and sinful customs get perpetuated.' Ebbs and Flows was of course the well that has been ebbing and flowing since time immemorial at the foot of Buckhaw Brow.

He writes of the market as being sometimes full of apple or potato carts, and of the visits of travelling companies: for instance, four large caravans with the skeleton of a whale 85 feet long, and Wombwell's menagerie 'drawn by 45 stout horses in 14 caravans, the largest collection in Settle since I came.'

At the present day such arrivals as these would present traffic problems; and as the summer days pass, with motor-coaches and cars threading their way through the narrow main street, we may well echo: 'Settle is a pretty great thoroughfare.'

This brief survey treats of little more than a thousand years; but far more ancient times are to be glimpsed at Settle from the finds in the famous Victoria Cave in Langcliffe Scar near by.

In May 1838 a local man, Michael Horner, was walking with companions near the scar when a dog they had with them disappeared into a foxhole that was found to be a cave, its entrance almost blocked by scree. Horner reported the discovery to his master, Joseph Jackson of Settle. Examining the place, Jackson began to pick up in it relics left by Iron Age man, and in course of time, first under Professor W. Boyd Dawkins and later under R. H. Tiddeman of the Geological Survey, he took charge of an organized excavation of the Victoria Cave, so called because it was found in the coronation year.

Apart from small collections of bones and flints at the British Museum and the Manchester Museum the best of the cave finds are preserved at Settle itself, so that after scrambling out to the scars to look at Victoria Cave and Jubilee near it, or at Attermire, Sewell's, Kelco, and Kinsey Caves in other scars, all once inhabited or used by early peoples, seek out the private museum of a local man, Mr Tot Lord, through whose enterprise a comprehensive collection has been preserved and splendidly displayed. It was begun about 1928 in connection with Settle Pig Yard Club, and enlarged by objects from Giggleswick School Museum.

Here you will find evidence that over the hills of Craven straight-tusked elephant, slender-nosed rhinoceros, woolly hippopotamus, and ox (*Bos primigenius*) once roamed, and ended their days in the Victoria Cave, a hyena's den, probably during the tropical climate of the Great Inter-Glacial period.

Above the bones of these a layer of clay was deposited after the retreat of glaciers at the end of the Ice Age. Next came the fauna of a cold time—reindeer, arctic fox, badger, horse, dog, and sheep.

Eventually man arrived—Mesolithic hunters who left in the cave a harpoon, and lastly Iron Age man who appears to have used the caves in Langcliffe Scar as a refuge in Roman times, and who left behind superb examples of Celtic art in the silver and bronze brooches, and armlets, rings, Roman coins, spearheads, spindle whorls, daggers, and much else.

To complete this picture of early man, we must add that when Giggleswick Tarn was drained a canoe of the Early Bronze Age (1600–1400 B.C.) was found. This canoe was sent to the Leeds Museum, where in an air-raid in 1941 it was shattered to pieces.

The cave relics form the major part of the museum collection, but for the local historian there are documents, for example: inventories of yeomen, the Settle township book for 1677, an advertisement for a concert given by Signor Malgarini on 31st December 1841 at Hartley's Golden Lion Hotel, a famous posting house in the coaching days, a theatre bill of 1838 announcing the play 'Heart of Midlothian or the Lilly of St Leonards to conclude with the very Laughable Farce the Village Draper or the Lawyer Bit,' bank-notes of the Craven Bank, and an enormous parchment book, the Craven Legion Muster Roll, that gives lists of names of the volunteers, the local Home Guard of the Napoleonic wars, and the counterpart of the Loyal Dales Volunteers of the dales of the North Riding.

Before leaving for North Ribblesdale we might look briefly at some of the villages and farmhouses on both sides of the river immediately south of Settle. No doubt a good parish history could be written on Long Preston with its Roman fort, open fields, and early church. Most people know Hellifield as a railway junction, and to its large and important cattle mart come buyers from far and wide.

In the park near by stood Hellifield Peel until it was dismantled and partially demolished in 1954. This property came by marriage from the Knolle family to the Hammertons, who, in 1441, obtaining a licence to enclose, crenellate, and furnish with towers and battlements their Manor of Hellifield, built the Peel with a tower at each corner of a central square. Later it was altered and the structure weakened by the insertion of large sash-windows. It was occupied as a private house until 1944, after which it served for a time as a hostel for displaced persons.

On the other side of the Ribble three farmhouses display the richness of the seventeenth-century domestic architecture of Craven: Swinden Hall is three-storeyed and cream-washed, Arnford and Wigglesworth Halls were granges of Fountains Abbey; and the tithe barn at Wigglesworth, hanging with cobwebs and dimly lit and quiet as the interior of a cathedral, is so large that eighty cows may be tied up in it. Returning towards Settle we pass the house that was the Rathmell Academy, the first Nonconformist college, founded by the Rev. Richard Frankland, and in effect the forerunner of Manchester College, Oxford. Lastly Newhall has built into a barn an elaborate if weathered seventeenth-century door-head with the initials JM, which commemorates James Moore's victory after a long legal struggle for possession of the farm that his father had bought.

Doorway, The Folly

2. SETTLE TO HORTON

F ROM Settle Bridge the view northwards looks over the swift-flowing Ribble beyond green ings and two black mill chimneys to foot-hills of limestone, and away in the distance to Penyghent, peeping above moorland in North Ribblesdale.

In 1724 Daniel Defoe saw this same view and wrote: 'Looking forward to the north-west of us we saw nothing but high mountains, which had a terrible aspect and more frightful than any in Monmouthshire or Derbyshire, especially Penigent Hill. So that having no manner of inclination to encounter them, merely for the sake of seeing a few villages and a parcel of wild people, we turned short north-east.'

To-day the view has the opposite effect. Penyghent beckons us to explore it and the far reaches of the dale. A road on either side of the bridge leads off to rejoin four miles away at Helwith Bridge, and to continue as one a further eight miles to Ribblehead.

When the Settle–Carlisle railway line was built in 1869–76, the horse age was superseded here by the railway era, and although the roads of Ribblesdale are being widened in places, partially on account of the traffic from the lime works, they have not caught up with the motor age, and they twist and turn up and down banks between walls that bulge out in an alarming fashion and endanger the safety of traffic. A private bus service to Horton-in-Ribblesdale caters for workmen to the quarries, schoolchildren, and the dalespeople.

North Ribblesdale was neither a royal forest nor a private chase, as might be expected of this territory of moor and exposed peaks, but it was and still is a vast sheep walk. Once it was a country of huge estates, as now it is a land of large farms: after the Conquest, Roger the Poictevin was said to possess all the land from Ribble to Mersey; and following him the Percys' wide-flung domains extended from Sawley Abbey to Penyghent.

After the earliest medieval days until the Dissolution scarcely any property in the dale remained outside the hands of the abbeys. Furness owned all the southern slopes of Ingleborough, including

Selside, and much of the head of the valley east of the Ribble to the watershed; Jervaulx, soon after its foundation, had been given the rectory and the Manor of Horton-in-Ribblesdale by William Morville; the property of Fountains lay along the eastern boundary; and part of the lower dale belonged to Sawley. It was a partition fraught with difficulty and fruitful dispute. Most of the villages and hamlets—Stackhouse, Stainforth-under-Bargh, Langcliffe, Studfold, Helwith Bridge, Horton, Selside, and Gearstones—belonged at least in part to the abbeys; and many of the farmhouses, such as Colt Park, Nether Lodge, Ingman Lodge, and Cam Houses, stand on the sites of monastic granges.

Langcliffe formed part of the property that Elias of Giggleswick gave to Sawley Abbey. Traditionally the village was rebuilt half a mile to the south after the devastating Scotch raid of 1318. At the present day it is peopled by millworkers and is refreshingly independent of the tourist trade; its church, the school, the Wesleyan chapel, and a row of cottages surround a green where in summer boys play cricket; near by a fountain plays, and railings and a seat for the elderly ring a sycamore.

Whilst Settle has a Naked Man Café, so called from a seventeenth-century carved stone figure, for a similar reason Langcliffe had a Naked Woman Inn, though the inn has gone, and only the stone with a figure and the date and initials, '1660 ISMS,' remains high on a house side. (Actually neither of these figures is naked.) There are other carved door-heads to be seen; but they and any others in Craven pale into insignificance before the magnificent doorway of Langcliffe Hall. It bears the inscription 'ISH 1602.' The hall was probably built by Henry Somerscales, but it has long been owned by the Dawson family, and was the home of Geoffrey Dawson, editor of *The Times* from 1912 to 1919 and from 1922 to 1941.

In 1855 'grass grew in the streets of Langcliffe.' In that year the cotton mill, originally the old corn mill converted some seventy years before to cotton, failed, and in consequence many people left the district. Six years later Hector Christie took over and brought in 'foreigners' from Devonshire and the eastern counties. After the last war real foreigners, some twenty-six Italian girls, who lived in a hostel specially provided for them, for a time augmented the labour force. At the present day Langcliffe Place Mills is worked by a combine.

Opposite to Langcliffe across the Ribble, and until 1953, when it was washed away in a flood, joined to it by a footbridge, is Stackhouse. Several large houses, including the seventeenth-century Old Hall, with their gardens, and a few cottages make up the sheltered bosky hamlet where lilac and laburnum blossom in May.

The initials and date, 'TCE 1695,' and a coat of arms with three cocks identify the Old Hall as the home of the Carrs, the principal tenants of Furness Abbey. As founder of the Chantry of the Rood and the Chantry School in Giggleswick Church, John Carr was virtually founder of Giggleswick School, and his nephew, Richard, was the first chantry priest and probably the first master of the grammar-school. This branch of the family died out in 1875.

Road, railway, and river hug each other closely in this stretch of the dale. Where Winskill Scar thrusts into the valley were the workings of the Craven Lime Co., now abandoned. Stainforth and Little Stainforth, once a single village at 'the stony ford,' lie within half a mile of each other on either side of the Ribble, and they should be given their full names of Stainforth-under-Bargh and Knight Stainforth. The first, also called Friar Stainforth because owned by Sawley Abbey, and the second, in the lay ownership of the Tempest family, grew unequally. The monks developed their property so that when they left there were two windmills and two water-mills at Stainforth-under-Bargh. To-day the village possesses a new church and houses overlooking a rough green; but Knight Stainforth has dwindled to a few farmhouses.

To approach one village from the other on foot you first cross the railway bridge and then the river over the lovely pack-horse bridge that here graces an equally beautiful reach of the Ribble. On hot summer days the deep pool below the waterfall, making an ideal swimming-bath, is a popular resort.

In 1547 the Watson family bought Knight Stainforth, and in the 1670's Samuel Watson built both the bridge and the hall there. Some of the tradesmen of Stainforth-under-Bargh, in return for 'full egress,' paid him a little towards the cost of the bridge, that was useful locally and for 'ye rest of ye country,' it being on the pack-horse route from York to Lancaster. In 1931 the present owners of Stainforth Hall, the Maudsleys, gave the bridge to the National Trust.

We look towards the dome of Penyghent

The three-storeyed Stainforth Hall is comparable with other Ribblesdale yeomen's houses that are now farmhouses, and it enjoys a pleasant uninterrupted view down the valley towards Settle. It retains many of the original oak doors, a wide, handsome oak staircase, a powder closet, and in the cellar a fifteenth-century stone doorway from an earlier house on the site. Part of the building makes a house for a farm-worker, and part was burnt out in about 1773. Mrs Maudsley, who showed us round her home, pointed out a well from which in days gone by a maid fetched water for the family's luncheon.

Samuel Watson, who was a Quaker, obtained a licence for a meeting-house at Stainforth Hall. From him the Weatherheads of Ingman Lodge (to be mentioned shortly) bought the house; and when in 1774 Christopher Weatherhead, a merchant of Liverpool, became bankrupt, his assets included Stainforth Hall, and plantations, mules, stock, and numerous slaves in the islands of Dominica and Tobago in the West Indies.

Following the moorland road from Knight Stainforth to Helwith Bridge, we look towards the dome of Penyghent and the beginnings of the thousands of acres of billowing meadow, pasture, and moorland of the dale head, and immediately before us and on the eastern flank of the hill called Moughton (pronounced Mooton) a territory given over to quarrying. Accustomed as we are since the Industrial Revolution to the segregation of industry, these quarries and similar ones elsewhere in the dales always come as a surprise. Yet the tall smoking kilns, the artificially bared rock faces, and the raw tippings disfigure only a small area of the vast landscape that lends to them a dramatic setting.

Two types of stone, limestone and slate, are quarried near Helwith Bridge, where in consequence of the Craven Fault the Silurian rocks under the limestone have been exposed. Geologically Coombs Quarry at Foredale on the side of Moughton is famous. The horizontal strata of the limestone rest on the pressed and upthrust Silurian mud-stone, and even from a distance the zigzag contortion of the Silurian draws the attention of the passer-by.

In former days thick flags of slate were quarried and cut here to serve a multitude of purposes—to pave cottage floors, and to make doorsteps, cisterns, tombstones, porches, gate-posts, and partitions in cow-sheds, most of which are still a feature of Ribblesdale and of neighbouring villages. Great smooth slabs of blue-green slate pave the paths of Giggleswick churchyard, and two long thin slates meeting in a point and built into a house wall over a front door make characteristic porches in many neighbouring villages. The slate, erroneously called granite, is still quarried, but it is crushed into chippings chiefly used for road metal.

A few quarrymen live at Studfold, the next hamlet beyond Helwith Bridge. The latter name derives from the Old Norse, and means the ford paved with flat stones, whilst Studfold is Old English and implies that the Angles used enclosures there as folds for horses. It belonged to Furness Abbey, and was bought from Sir Arthur Darcy by Thomas Procter after the Dissolution.

Here the Ribble, winding along the bed of a post-glacial lake, finds its course less constricted than in the rocky lower reaches. As we approach Horton-in-Ribblesdale long slopes of pasture land rise to Penyghent. Newland House, one of the isolated farms backed by a lofty hill so characteristic of the dale, and a little farther on Dubcote, once a place of several dwellings, appear. Judging by the ranes behind the present solitary farmhouse at Dubcote, it is a settlement of great age. Lying in the Manor of Horton, it belonged to Jervaulx, and in the eighteenth century it formed part of the grammar-school endowment, as in fact it still does.

We reach Horton-in-Ribblesdale, where the road crosses Douk Gill Beck, turns a corner round the church and churchyard, and passes the Golden Lion Hotel. The village straggles on for half a mile to a second cluster of houses and an inn near two bridges, one over Brants Gill Beck and one over the Ribble, and turning left continues with houses placed haphazardly along it towards Horton station on the hillside, and after a sharp right turn at length ends at Blind Beck Farm.

Most views of Horton lead the eye on to Penyghent, a grand background to farmhouses, bridges, and ancient church whose squat grey tower so perfectly fits the scene. Yet, in contrast, on the opposite side of the valley behind the village a limestone quarry and lime works continually eat into the flank of Moughton. The houses of Horton reflect the development of the dale—fine old farmhouses built by the yeoman, such as Blind Beck and Raw Farm near it, Victorian terraces of early railway times, and modern villas of the quarry era. With two hotels, a guest-house, and private houses catering for visitors, Horton is a centre for geologists and for walkers. Footpaths and green roads that are some of the joys of Ribblesdale lead off in many directions.

When Domesday Book was compiled Horton was a small village. We may picture the manor growing up with its church, built in about 1100, its corn mill, and open fields of arable land lying round it—many ranes can be seen south-east of the village. Its name means the settlement on muddy land; and no doubt this flat site near river and becks was muddy enough.

Armitsteads, Wilsons, Weatherheads, Howsons, Burtons, Lodges, Batemans, Hesledens, Clarks, Sidgwicks, and Benthams—these were some of the yeomen of Horton in the seventeenth and early eighteenth centuries. John Armitstead founded a grammar-school at Horton in 1725 by assigning houses and land for the maintenance of a master in orders. The school buildings, now occupied as a house, abut on to the churchyard, and opposite the south porch of the church a table-tomb with an almost illegible Latin inscription on a brass tablet commemorates the school's founder.

The Howsons and later the Wilsons, families with distinguished clerical associations, lived at Beecroft Hall on the opposite side of the river and railway from Horton, and near the lime works. Though with only an undated door-head as visible proof of its age, Beecroft was in fact the chief seat of a manor that in Elizabethan times consisted of some twenty houses. So near to industry, yet secluded in green meadows and sheltered by a copse of fine sycamores, it keeps an air of quiet self-sufficiency.

The present owner, Mr R. C. Ford of Bentham, has told us that when invasion was expected in the Napoleonic wars his great-grandfather, who lived at Yealand, near Carnforth, stored food at Beecroft. The French were pictured sailing into Morecambe Bay; and all was made ready to flee into the then remote Ribblesdale.

Beecroft gives its name to the quarry worked by Settle Limes Ltd near by. As an industry lime-burning is not new in the dales; the ruined semi-circular kilns remain on many hillsides near convenient outcrops of rock. In the mid seventeenth century the Rev. John Hutton speaks of a company of lime-burners at Castlebergh at Settle, and there were others at Buckhaw Brow. But it was not until the late nineteenth and twentieth centuries that the industry exploited fully the great limestone escarpments of Craven.

The quarrying of limestone in Ribblesdale began at the Craven Quarry, disused since 1940, which we passed between Langcliffe and Stainforth. Here Winskill Scar visibly receded as the quarry excavation developed over the years. The first venture at working in this vicinity by a Mr Murgatroyd failed. Next three Settle men, Messrs Clarke, Wilson, and Shepherd, after starting quarrying at Feizor, near Austwick, and at Giggleswick, moved to the Craven Quarry in 1870, and built the Craven Kiln there. The kiln chimney with the date of its completion, 1873, picked out in white bricks made a familiar landmark for almost eighty years until it was demolished in January 1951. In those days coal was carted from Fountains Fell; and development went hand in hand with the building of the Settle–Carlisle railway, then nearing completion.

At Horton John Delaney, a Norfolk man who first came to work at Langcliffe Place Mills, started lime works at Beecroft Quarry in 1887, and he brought skilled quarrymen from Derbyshire. Quarrying with various changes in ownership continued in the dale until, in 1939, Settle Limes Ltd was reconstructed to include the three local firms then in existence—the Craven Lime Co., John Delaney Ltd, and the Ribblesdale Lime Co. At the present date there are five quarries in North Ribblesdale run by three firms.

Since Settle Limes Ltd introduced large-scale mechanization, gas-fired kilns, and other processing plant at Horton, the works rank as some of the most modern of their kind. For instance, the enormous crusher reduces blocks of limestone weighing $2\frac{1}{2}$ tons to pieces measuring less than 10 cubic inches; and the quarry face extending for over a quarter of a mile varies from 80 to 150 feet in height, and is blasted away not by means of charges in short hand-drilled holes as in former days, but by high-explosives in holes sunk from top to bottom of the face by a well-hole drill. It says much for the open spaces of Ribblesdale that they dwarf almost into insignificance this huge concern.

The quarries in North Ribblesdale employ some 200 to 250 men, who either live in the valley or journey to work by special buses from Austwick, Ingleton, Bentham, and Hawes. A few also travel from Gargrave and Skipton. The works are by now of such long standing that men who have spent all their working lives in them live in retirement at Horton.

Lime is sent from the quarries throughout the North of England and to Scotland. 'Scotch lorries,' as they are called locally, constantly pass through the villages near Ingleborough; and Horton station, with $4\frac{1}{2}$ miles of sidings, deals with about a quarter of a million tons of goods a year, probably more tonnage than that handled by any station of its size in England. The uses for lime and limestone are manifold: blast-furnaces, agriculture, paper mills, gas-works, and the building, dry-salting, tanning, and chemical industries; and besides its ancient but now insignificant use as whitewash, lime softens and purifies water, and is used as a filler in many commodities ranging from paint to cattle food.

The railway, like the quarries, is bound up with the life of the dale. Part of a great main trunk-line that links north and south, it provides work and transport for the people who live on its route. At Horton alone the station-master has under him two clerks, three porters, ten signalmen, and thirteen platelayers. From the station we see below us some of the railway cottages, and look beyond them to Penyghent. These blocks of cottages dotted here and there along the line never achieve beauty. Victorian, sash-windowed, heavily built, black, and stony, the product of industrial towns rather than a countryside such as this, they yet form part of a grand design; and what is more important they provide comfortable homes.

The Settle–Carlisle line came into being through the resolution of the directors of the Midland Co., the inspiration of the engineers, and the dogged spirit of contractors and navvies. This route over the moor, bog, and mountain of the Pennine watershed, swept by storms of snow, wind, and rain, came to be considered only because it was the last route left for a new line to Scotland. It cost £3,467,000; some million tons of stone went into the construction of viaducts, tunnels, bridges, and culverts, and thousands of navvies, many boarded in houses, others living in shanty towns, invaded Ribblesdale for seven years from 1869 to 1st May 1876, when the line was opened for passenger traffic. Numbers lost their lives, in brawls, in a smallpox epidemic, or in accidents incurred on the difficult and dangerous work.

Even nowadays few people fail to marvel at the long-distance trains as they speed their way amongst the hills. One of our recollections of a recent climb up Ingleborough is of seeing from the top the Thames–Clyde express emerge from Blea Moor tunnel, and swoop as if by a miracle over Batty Moss Viaduct at Ribblehead.

We witness at Horton a later aspect of railway history. Mr J. M. Taylor, coming there as station-master in 1947, the following year won the fourth prize for the best-kept station out of the seventy-two in his particular district, and each year since then the station has been awarded the special prize and shield, even when in 1953 the prize was divided into two. Horton station is a revelation—the waiting-room shining with green and cream paint, new chairs, and clean, up-to-date magazines neatly arranged on a table; and on the platforms freshly painted signs showing the altitude, points of interest, and basic industries of the district. In summer the staff runs an art show. When we were there wallflowers and tulips filled many flower-beds, and rare plants grew in specially designed rockeries. The station makes a point of interest in the dale, and is visited by many people.

3. HORTON TO RIBBLEHEAD

TURNING our backs on the works of man we press on to the head of the dale, to far-flung ancient roads, caves and pot-holes, gills and limestone scenery, and to the dale's own hill—Penyghent, 'the hill of the open country.'

At the end of March the botanists, amateur or professional, climb Penyghent; for at this time of year, before winter has left, when hailstorms and even snowstorms may rake the hills, purple saxifrage, *Saxifraga oppositifolia*, blooms on the limestone out-crops south-west of the top. To see the small cushions and hanging clusters of this rare and colourful flower, deep pink rather than purple, fills heart and mind with pleasure long remembered. In early June cloudberries, amongst other rare flowers, star the bogs of the summit.

Penyghent, like Saddleback in the Lake District, rises up close to habitation, so close that the noise from the lime works, two and a half miles away across the valley, can be heard at the top. A turquoise-blue lake near Beecroft attracts the eye. It is a dis-used quarry filled with water, and the coloration is caused by suspended particles of waste lime.

Rather than spectacular distant views that are better seen from Ingleborough, Penyghent offers a panorama of the dale: sparsely inhabited, scored with walls as far as the eye can see, and north-wards filled with acres and acres of hump-backed pastures shaped thus by drumlins, the mounds of debris left by glaciers after the Ice Age. Friendly enough on a calm day, the hill has many moods and at times attracts above it the most fantastically shaped clouds. Long ago it was the haunt of the red deer, and over it the Penyghent Beagles hunted in the last century. Sometimes from the crags of the summit ravens croak their menacing cry as you approach; and sheep pasture on its slopes as they have done since time immemorial.

To look at an early map of the district, for example the 'Environs of Sedbergh, Dent, Hawes, Askrigg, and Settle' in Jefferys' *Yorkshire Atlas* published in 1771, is to visualize a different

Ribblesdale. Without the railway, the effect enhanced by the cartographer's crude but realistic engraving of mountains, it looks a wilderness through which only one road penetrates north, that from Horton through Newhouses, Birkwith, Old Ing, and across Ling Gill, to join what was then the Richmond to Lancaster turnpike coming over Cam Fell from Bainbridge in Wensleydale. This is now a by-road tarred only as far as High Birkwith Farm. The present main road from Horton through Selside to Ribblehead is not marked, and it is in fact comparatively modern. The map best shows these old and new roads.

A Roman road, known far back in the past as the Craven Way, started out from the fort at Long Preston up the dale to Horton, possibly then taking the route through Birkwith, past Thorns and Gearstones, and over Whernside to Dent. It has been plotted by F. Villy, and it shows well-marked pavements over Whernside— a road worth exploration. Near Gearstones this track crossed the Roman road from Bainbridge Fort to Lancaster; the latter was adopted by the turnpike.

These by-roads of Ribblesdale—Roman, monastic, and eighteenth-century turnpike—are mostly green tracks that make the dale a paradise for the walker. There are the pack-horse roads: that which comes from Beckermonds and Greenfield in Wharfedale to join the Horton–Ling Gill Road at Scale Farm and to cross to Selside and continue over Sulber Nick to Clapham; and that which comes from Littondale past Hull and Hunt Pots to Horton.

Three miles beyond Horton the road twists rather than winds— that would imply too large a place—through Selside. The houses draw close with the Red Lion Inn, now a house, on the right, and Shaws, a farmhouse with a superb doorway and the date 1738, on the left. The road opens out on a tiny green with a row of cottages, of which only one is occupied, on one side, a farm and a school on the other. A small gill, by which you scramble up to North Cote Farm, runs through this grey hamlet occupied almost entirely by a farming community.

Selside, like other place-names ending in 'side' or 'sett,' derives from the Old Norse, and means 'sallow shieling' (the croft by the willows). At the time of the Domesday survey it was a small Norse settlement rated at a hundred acres, and the farthest one up Ribblesdale to be recorded. It belonged to Furness Abbey at the Dissolution. Within living memory a fair, called Selside Pot Fair or Cheese Fair, was held each year on 24th June; but about 1890, when the topographer, Harry Speight, passed through, the place was half derelict. It now consists of seven farms and eleven cottages in the hamlet and round about. Thirteen to fifteen children attend the tiny school, which was built in 1877 when £30 a year became available from the endowments of Horton Grammar School. Selside not only boasts a school but a town hall, which now looks like a derelict barn, but was once a forgathering place for the men.

The railway runs very close. During the Second World War Selside signal-box was operated on all three turns of duty by women, and up to the summer of 1955 one signalwoman still took regular turns. It is remembered that many navvies working on the building of the line lodged in the hamlet, and that an old woman who lived in the top cottage of the row, after preparing dumplings for her lodgers, always went off with a jug to the Red Lion for refreshment for herself.

As we approach the head waters of the Ribble the country's land surface appears deceptively featureless. Scarry outcrops of lime-stone mingle with close-cropped grass on the lower slopes of Simon Fell; acres and acres of swelling hillocks of brown pasture land formed by the drumlins fill the valley, and afar off, tucked in the dented hillsides between Penyghent and Cam Fell, lie isolated sheep farms ringed by meadow land. Old Ing is the highest at 1,200 feet above sea level. Down in the valley, Gayle and Cam Becks join below Selside to form the Ribble, that here flows at 800 to 850 feet above sea level. In this wide, bare, shallow valley a copse standing sentinel on a hillside or a glimpse of the tops of a few trees no more than hints at those other features of the dale—the caves and gills.

The caves cluster in groups—five west and two east of Selside, sixteen along the eastern slopes of the valley between Hull Pot and Brow Gill Cave, and eight at Ribblehead. Of all these Alum Pot is the most fascinating.

Alum Pot (or Helln Pot) may be approached by first taking the lane, the Clapham road already mentioned, leading west at the north end of Selside, and after a hundred yards turning off right through a gate to the plantation of wind-swept larches and pines that marks the pot, which is surrounded by a well-built wall.

You look over into the steep-sided mossy rift to the black chill depths down which a waterfall pours. Perhaps a shaft of sunlight slants into the chasm; the rocks steam with heat and damp. A ring-ouzel flies to its nest in a crevice in the vertical side; a willow-warbler sings, and *Primula farinosa* blooms on the boggy ground beside a small stream that trickles down limestone steps. Where the entrances to many pots repel, this, like the scene at Weathercote Cave, delights the eye.

The underground stream at Alum Pot drains the system of caves on this hillside, and it has the curious distinction of eventually flowing under the Ribble, and appearing again at Tarn Dub, a pot-hole near Horton Tarn.   Long Churn Cave near by provides a side entrance to Alum Pot, and down it the Rev. John Hutton penetrated in about 1781.   In 1847 ten people led by John Birkbeck of Anley House, Settle, and William Metcalfe of Weathercote, Chapel-le-Dale, made the first descent of Alum Pot, as is recorded by Professor W. Boyd Dawkins, who himself explored it in 1870.   A stone dropped irresponsibly killed a woman pot-holer resting at the bottom on 5th July 1936, and in the summer of 1955 a member of a pot-holing expedition fell from a rope-ladder and was killed.   On fine Sundays Alum Pot attracts many people, both to watch pot-holing operations that may be afoot and to look out to the fine panorama of the dale.

Instead of subterranean wonders, the moorland gills of Ribblesdale give a surface view of the contorted shapes of water-worn limestone; the deep channels with brown water flowing over white rock set amidst acres of moorland make pleasant places for exploration on a summer afternoon.   We have left behind Douk Gill and Brants Gill near Horton; but from Alum Pot we can see Brow Gill and Ling Gill on Cam Beck, the little gill above High Birkwith, and Thorns Gill on Gayle Beck near Gearstones.

Ling Gill, two miles north-east of Selside, can be reached by Nether Lodge, a farm in the valley bottom, or from Horton, by taking the old route to High Birkwith and past Old Ing to the pack-horse bridge at the head of the gill.   Ling Gill Bridge, with an inscription carved in relief on a small block of millstone grit let into the parapet, bears visible witness to the one-time importance of the route.   The lettering records that it was repaired in 1765 'at the charge of the whole West Riding.'   The ruins of two farmhouses, almost razed to the ground and grassed over, remain not

Pack-horse bridge in Thorns Gill

far from the bridge, and below it the open mountain stream disappears down amongst the tumbled rocks of the deep ravine, a bower of bird cherry blossom in May. The gill has its own beauty, but for us the charm lies in the bridge, the ruins, and the imagined happenings in this wild bleak place.

Thorns Gill, smaller, shallower, and more approachable in every way than Ling Gill, is reached from the main road a little west of Gearstones by a lane that leads to a wooden footbridge. Continuing down-stream and passing the openings to Cat-Not and Thorns Gill Caves, we come to a tiny pack-horse bridge, the Roman bridge as it is called locally, its narrow arch springing above the beck from the cliffs at either side of a rocky gorge. Rowan-trees surround it; there is the continuous roar of a torrent as the water swirls past circular and horse-shoe-shaped cavities in the extremely white limestone, and not far from it thyme, milkwort, and butterfly orchis bloom. If you find a way through the meadows across the beck you reach a barn amidst trees, and near it the ruined farmhouse of Thorns, once a grange of Furness Abbey.

Between Selside and Ribblehead a solitary house by the roadside marks a site of one of the shanty towns of the railway-building era. It was, and is, called Stone Cottage to distinguish it from the wooden huts—with albeit their Dent marble fire-places—now pulled down. Farther along on a scar at the end of the only belt of trees of any size for some miles is Colt Park, a Furness Abbey grange and perhaps the farm for the monks' horse park at Ribblehead. On Saturday, 29th September 1844, Mr Henry Procter of Colt Park, returning from a fair at Gearstones, was brutally attacked and almost strangled by five men bent on robbery.

A track past a green-painted gate with Lodge Hall and Nether Lodge printed on it leads to the site of another one-time grange of Furness, now one of the finest yeoman's houses that we know of so near to a desolate dale head. Lodge Hall, or Ingman Lodge to give it its old name, was rebuilt or considerably altered by Christopher Weatherhead in 1687, as the initials and date over the elaborate doorway testify.

Mrs Mason, the farmer's wife, showed us over her three-storeyed old house: the large pleasant rooms with two wide arched fire-places, and a third of a more delicate design left behind the modern kitchen range in what must originally have been the parlour; the large bedrooms, and a powder closet with a lozenge-shaped

Doorway at Ingman Lodge

window on the second floor; and up the wide stone staircase the big attics, once occupied no doubt by menservants and maid-servants. In 1954 Mrs Mason's black-haired maid came from near Naples, and had a sister working at Horton. The unusual design of the main doorway incorporates a halberd at either side of the door, a feature as we have seen of the door-heads at New Hall, near Settle, and at Hanlith Hall, near Malham.

Across the lane from Ingman Lodge is a Quaker burial-ground, a small enclosure marked by large trees. John Moore of Ingman Lodge was prosecuted for the non-payment of tithes in 1696, and imprisoned in York Castle. At that time there were perhaps two houses here.

The rough road leads on half a mile across the valley, where curlew, plover, titlark, and redshank fill the air with their cries in spring, to Nether Lodge Farm, a new building, with near it two long, low, ruinous houses with barns attached to them that are the original buildings of the yeomen who followed the monks at this, yet another grange of Furness Abbey.

At Ribblehead we join at right angles the Hawes to Ingleton

road, once the Roman road, and more recently the Richmond to Lancaster turnpike. The whale-back of Whernside looms beyond the arches of the Batty Moss Viaduct; the main massif of Ingleborough, hidden until now by Simon and Park Fells, shows up in Chapel-le-Dale, and over to the east the cairn on Greenfield Knott stands out against the sky. Sheep browse beside the open road, heifers graze in the pastures. There is a group of farms and a shooting-lodge at Gearstones, and the Station Inn and a lime works near Ribblehead station. The few works of man are dispersed over a huge landscape, as often as not blotted out by mist and rain; and Ingleborough and Penyghent rear dark blue heads in a vast grey sky.

Weather is here the chief factor of existence; everything seems reefed against storms. At Ribblehead since 1938, successive station-masters, in addition to their normal job, have operated a weather-reporting station for the Air Ministry. At ten minutes to the hour throughout the day messages are sent in code to Dishforth aerodrome in the Plain of York; and, passed on from there, they eventually swell the information necessary for many weather reports, some of which we hear on the radio and television. The rain gauge at Ribblehead recorded $109\frac{1}{2}$ inches of rain in 1954 (about 70 inches is average), and on 2nd December 1954, 5·2 inches fell, perhaps a record for normal rain. In contrast the rainfall for 1955 was only 59 inches.

The wind can and does stop trains. This is not a frequent occurrence, but it is by no means uncommon. On 15th January 1954 a wind blowing at eighty-five miles an hour (the highest on record) stopped three. We inquired whether there was a speed limit over the viaduct. There is—but it is eighty miles an hour! A hundred trains pass over it in one direction or the other each day. On 18th April 1952 two engines fouled the points on Blea Moor and were derailed. Wreckage and overturned engines strewed the line, but by a miracle no one was killed.

As we have said, the railway is part of the life of the dale. Here in the booking-hall the vicar of Ingleton holds an evening service once a month, and children assemble each week for Sunday-school. As the station-master told us proudly, after the last harvest festival service the sale of produce raised £23.

One of the largest of the navvies' shanty towns, Batty Green, which housed some two thousand people, was located at Ribblehead. Other smaller camps were Jericho, Garlic Huts, Battle-barrow Bank, Sebastopol, and Salt Lake City, the last two still perpetuated in the names of some of the railway cottages. Batty Green boasted, besides the dwellings, a school, post office, library, mission house, run by the Manchester City Mission, and a hospital built to cope with the smallpox epidemic that broke out in May 1871. Local trade in food-stuffs, not to mention drink, flourished. Beef was the favourite diet of the navvies. Now empty and desolate, the scene and its complement of rough workmen, like a gold-rush town, is hard to visualize.

In June 1792 Lord Torrington travelled on horseback from Askrigg to Gearstones, and found one of the two annual fairs for Scotch cattle in progress there. He writes that he reached 'a public house—call'd Grierstones, the seat of misery, in a desert; and tho' (unluckily for us) fill'd with company, yet the Scotch fair held upon the heath (there I go to meet Macbeth) added to the horror of the curious scenery: the ground in front crowded by Scotch cattle and drovers; and the house cramm'd by the buyers and sellers, most of whom were in plaids, fillibegs, etc.'

Again in this desolate place it is not easy to picture either the fairs or the customary market that, held for the sale of corn and oatmeal every Wednesday, ceased about 1870. In the early nineteenth century as many as twenty to thirty carts laden with grain trundled to market along the turnpike from Wensleydale, and gangs of pack-horses, travelling by the green roads, came from all the dales.

Standing by the roadside, Gearstones Inn, where Lord Torrington stayed, was turned into a shooting-box by the Farrers of Clapham, who once owned the estate. It ceased to be an inn in 1911. But Far Gearstones a little farther east appears the more likely site for what was again monastic property: a farmhouse remarkable for limestone rocks in the paddock in front of it, transported there by glacier action, and with sheltering sycamores seen against a background of Ingleborough. Near it a rough road leads down to a footbridge over Gayle Beck to mount Cam Fell, the Roman road and the one-time route of the turnpike, visible against the brown moor as a green track.

From Holme Hill Cave on the beck (close to the fork of ancient and modern roads) a strong force of water rushes out to swell this tributary of the Ribble. Some favour it as the source of the river; the ordnance survey marks a cave near the road three-quarters of a mile west of Gearstones as 'Ribble Head'; others choose the source of Cam Beck, the second tributary of the Ribble, rising close to the head waters of the Wharfe at Cam Houses; whilst local opinion plumps for the springs of Gayle Beck in Newby Head pasture.　It seems a matter of choice.

Gayle Beck, the larger of the two tributaries, winds alongside the open road, between heather-clad hillocks, through three miles of the wild country of the watershed, where in summer curlew call and a heron fishes from banks pink with thyme.　The Dent road turns off left.　Half a mile beyond it, at 1,400 feet above sea level, we reach Newby Head farmhouse, an inn until 1919, and in another half-mile the boundary of the West and North Ridings, whence the road drops down Widdale into Wensleydale.　Looking back we see an appropriate last view of farmhouse and mountain: Newby Head, flanked by barns, a solitary hawthorn, and the long outliers of Park Fell and Simon Fell rising to Ingleborough's flat summit.

VI

INGLEBOROUGH

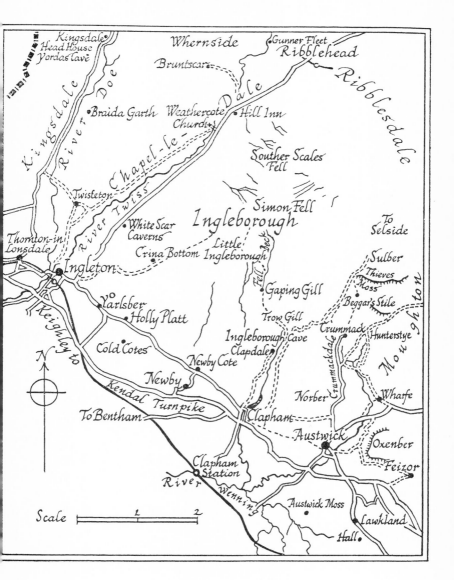

1. ROUND AUSTWICK

IN THE west of Craven the mountain mass of Ingleborough rearing its head to the clouds dominates the countryside. It is bounded on the east by Ribblesdale, on the north-east by Chapel-le-Dale, and on the south-west by the highway between Settle and Ingleton. Except for Ribblesdale, the present chapter concerns this rough triangle of land, the hill itself, and the villages and farms in the dales at its feet.

Ingleborough means not a single peak but a whole range of hills —Simon Fell, Park Fell, Souther Scales Fell, and Little Ingleborough—from which the distinctive angular summit, 2,373 feet above sea level, stands out as the highest point of a huge acreage of grassy, treeless moor. So great are the billowing folds of its foothills that the summit is invisible from many of the villages near it; but at a distance, from fell-tops and fell passes, we eagerly pick it out as the hill above all others to be recognized. Seen best at close range from Chapel-le-Dale, Ingleborough looks and is a big hill: it was long thought to be the highest in the North; in fact, it is the third highest in Yorkshire, being topped by Whernside and Mickle Fell. The mountain is of supreme fame in the county and without parallel in England for interest to many branches of science.

Geologically Ingleborough may be likened to a huge-scale natural monument of which the footing is ancient Silurian rock; the base, 500 to 600 feet thick and twenty miles in circumference, Great Scar Limestone; the central pillar, 1,000 feet high, the shales, sandstones, and limestones of the Yoredale series; and the pinnacle, a plateau of fifteen acres and a mile in circumference, millstone grit. The sweet herbage of limestone land partly covers it; but the coarse grasses that grow on the glacial drift that has buried the limestone largely clothe its slopes.

The Great Scar Limestone is all-important. On its outskirts the villages rest in a setting of the pale greens and greys of meadow and scar. Into its upper surface mountain becks disappear down cracks and fissures, and flowing through echoing corridors, splashing down sunless waterfalls, filling black lakes, eventually gush out of slits at the base. These subterranean channels, the caves and pot-holes of Ingleborough, where explored by man, have their individual characteristics and reputations.

Here too the botanists, from John Ray of the seventeenth century to Geoffrey Grigson of the twentieth, have come to seek and find the rare flowers that grow on the upper surface of the limestone, exposed in many places at flat fissured pavements called clints and grikes.

For the archaeologist there are the Bronze Age tumulus near Ribblehead, the Iron Age fort on its summit, the earthworks of similar date at Yarlsber on the south-west, the Iron Age villages in Crummackdale and on Oxenber, and the Celtic wall on Smearsett.

The people who know the mountain well call Ingleborough the Big Hill and Little Ingleborough t' Lile Hill; they speak of the names of its features with familiarity as of those of old friends. They know the shades of the hill's expression in all weathers, and note the changes of the seasons from the tones of the herbage or the first sprinkling of snow. On the plateau top in past times the people of the neighbourhood lit beacons, ran horse-races, and built a tower as a shelter for shepherds; once an electric tramway was planned to run up there; and to-day they build bonfires on the summit to celebrate national events.

The commons of Ingleborough are divided amongst the four townships of Austwick, Clapham, and Horton that meet on Simon Fell, and Ingleton and Clapham that divide the summit; and the sheep of many farms, sheep that know their own heaths where they were suckled by the ewes, graze it on their customary grounds. Much of it is unstinted common that has been overstocked for many years.

No hill in Yorkshire is more climbed—from Ribblehead, from Selside, from Crummackdale, from Newby Cote, from Clapham up Trow Gill, from Ingleton past Crina Bottom House, from the Hill Inn in Chapel-le-Dale. A hundred years ago it was considered a feat to reach the summit. Now the three-, the five-, the twelve-peak walkers rush over it. Elderly men in their eighties make a practice of climbing it. Some enthusiasts have camped on its summit many times to see the sun rise; others have played an annual hockey match there on New Year's Day. The most unlikely people, who would never trouble to climb any other hill, have been up it. Groups of schoolchildren, youth hostellers, members of societies, cross the top from all sides. Yet gales sweeping it, mist capping it, snow shrouding it, often make it formidable and unapproachable; none the less Ingleborough is more than a mountain: it is an institution.

Between Settle and Ingleton on the south side of Ingleborough, Angles, Danes, and Norsemen chose dry, sheltered positions for their settlements; and the present-day rural villages and hamlets that they founded—Austwick, Feizor, Wharfe, Clapham, Newby —lie peacefully ensconced with their backs against the hill and away from main road and railway line. They face open country drained by the head waters of the River Wenning, and look afar off to the fells of Bowland and Lancashire. They are in truth on the fringe of the dales.

The busy high road linking the villages follows the line of the Keighley to Kendal turnpike road, part of which from early times followed the main route from York to Lancaster. Originally the road left Settle by Giggleswick over High Rigg to Lawkland and so to Clapham, whence it continued by Newby Cote to Ingleton. But in 1753, after the turnpike Act was passed, the first move was to abandon the route through Lawkland and to bring into use the now familiar one up Buckhaw Brow; and in 1823 the route through Newby Cote was changed and a new road made from Clapham over Clapham Common to Ingleton.

Because of the building of a bridge over the River Greta at Ingleton this latter section cost £11,000. In the turnpike heyday the many toll-gates let for a total of £1,000 a year; and in 1856 a carriage and pair paid 9s. 4d. in tolls from Keighley to Kendal.

A sidelight on the traffic on the road is given in the *Wensleydale Advertiser* of 30th September 1845: 'We hear, from high authority, that the Postmaster General is seriously displeased with the wags, who cut off the tail from the red coat worn by the Austwick and Settle Mail Guard. We advise them to look to themselves.'

Austwick, Lawkland, Feizor, and Wharfe form a group of places of Norse origin. Austwick's name means 'the eastern settlement,' Lawkland's 'the land where leeks are grown,' Feizor's (pronounced Fazer) 'Fech's (or Feg's) shieling,' and Wharfe's 'a group of homesteads.'

In a nook of the bleached and rocky sides of Ingleborough, Austwick is sheltered from cutting winds and warmed 'by the reflection of the sunbeams,' as Whitaker noted. Speight, commenting on a first visit, says that it is a case of 'love at first sight.' The village, with its grey stone houses straggling down lanes or round little greens, seems to welcome the stranger. The Gamecock Hotel is renowned for its catering, and the blacksmith's shop, with hayrakes, pails, and farming requisites spread out for sale by it, makes a focal point.

At the time of Domesday Book Austwick was the head of an honour of twelve manors; and an ancient base of a cross surmounted by a new shaft on one of the grassy plats points to an early market. But the village soon lost its importance to Clapham.

Here the families connected with the district are the Darcys, Yorkes, Shuttleworths, Ingilbys, Claphams, and Farrers. The Ingilbys bought Lawkland Hall and Austwick Hall, the latter a small fortified manor-house, in 1573, and it is this family of whom we are most conscious in the neighbourhood. Different members have lived at one time and another in most of the large houses, and their initials are to be found on many of the dated door-heads, of which several are particularly elaborate. The last member of this branch of the family still keeps a connection with Austwick.

In medieval times the men of Austwick grew oats in their townfields, the terracing of which can be seen west and south of the village. A division of the commons and wastes of the whole countryside took place in 1622, and the commons of Austwick were enclosed in 1814.

The hall has been much altered; but part of the massive wall of a peel tower that stood on the site has been kept. Near it is a farm with a field on it called Dearbought, of which the story goes that a man wanted to buy the field and for a wager said that he would mow it. It was so rough and it took him so long to finish that he called it Dearbought.

Up to about 1850 worsted cloth was woven in the weaving-shed, a long, low, deserted building on the outskirts. Many people now work in Settle or at the quarries in Ribblesdale. A racehorse trainer keeps horses in the village; and Joe Holmes and his son, the smiths, make fine ornamental ironwork such as the gates of Ingleborough Hall at Clapham. But the real industry of Austwick at the present day is catering for holiday-makers, who have come to the neighbourhood since the geologist, Professor Phillips, made the district known. As well as the hotel, the large Georgian houses, Harden and the Traddock, provide for the visitors who forgather here for the conferences of societies.

With the latter we link a man such as Christopher Cheetham, who was secretary of the Yorkshire Naturalists' Union for twenty years until his death in 1954. Coming from the industrial West Riding to Austwick, he threw himself whole-heartedly into the study of natural history, and he typifies the townsman born with a deep-rooted nostalgia for country life.

In the footsteps of the geologists, the naturalists, and all the rest of the visitors who have come to Austwick, we may start out to explore what is the real attraction, the background of the village. We shall follow narrow walled pack-horse lanes and perhaps cross the clapper bridges, called the Pant and Flascoe, to reach the limestone hills of Moughton and Oxenber, Long Scar, and the Norber boulders, Crummackdale, Austwick Moss, the hamlets of Feizor and Wharfe, and the village of Lawkland.

To climb the almost isolated little hill called Oxenber, the hill of the oxen, makes a pleasant morning's walk. Covered with scrub, it forms part of the commons of Austwick, and in 1814 was allotted 131 sheep gaits, now reduced to 40. Every gait-owner has the right to shoot rabbits, to gather fuel, and to quarry stones on the hill; and the path up it passes through Austwick Little Wood, let to pay for the repair of the walls. In the past trouble has arisen from people from a distance who came nutting and gathering pea sticks. All over the summit is a jumble of enormous rocks of the tumbledown walls of crofts and huts of Iron Age people; and from the edge of steep crags we see fine views of the Wenning valley, and in the opposite direction the perched boulders on Norber looking like black hawthorn bushes on the white limestone.

The Norber boulders are geologically famous. They are freaks of nature, being blocks of Silurian Grit swept up the hillside from the valley floor by glacial action, so that they rest quite out of place on the top of the limestone instead of underneath it.

The boulders thickly cover the fields on the west side of the road to Crummackdale, one of the most entrancing of Yorkshire's small dales. From Austwick a good if steep and narrow road runs for two miles as far as the one habitation, Crummack Farm, with its whitewashed house and modernized buildings.

Late one afternoon in spring we walked from the farm into the

Crummackdale

lonely green dale enclosed by Norber and Moughton and on to
Austwick Beck Head, where the stream first issues from a cave,
one of those slits in the Great Scar Limestone which are a most
common sight in Craven.   Penyghent peeped above Moughton's
scarry head.   The limestone glowed pink in the sun; bracken
grew on the hillsides, and across the valley the shadowed walls of
the bridle road by Hunterstye to Horton stood out clearly.
There were black Galloway cattle in the meadows on the bottoms.
The whole wild rocky scene might have been in any century.

Later, on a summer's day, we picnicked beyond Beck Head at
Beggar's Stile, a cleft by which the footpath mounts an extensive
semicircular cliff.   Here, so it is said, inquiries about stolen goods
were made.   A great amphitheatre of clint and pasture enclosed
us.   Not a farm or habitation could be seen; Austwick Beck
wound along the valley; beyond lay Oxenber and in the distance
the fells of Bowland.   As we sat there a pair of wrens fluttered
near; and almost within reach a gooseberry bush, sheltered by an
ash-tree rooted in the scar, fruited with berries no bigger than
small peas.

Above Beggar's Stile an area of clint is circled by a second
amphitheatre with a brown bog called Thieves Moss at its foot.

Both these curious names derive from age-old recollections of people living there. The general scene of devastation, of exposed clint and little valleys choked with boulders, is natural; but amongst it can be traced the more orderly arrangement of the half-buried walls of Iron Age fields, and the ruins of round huts with the up-ended stones of their walls fallen outwards. In the Dark Ages a considerable population must have lived here.

From Thieves Moss we climbed out by Sulber Gate, from which point is to be seen the grandest expanse of clints in the dales, the fissures in the flat limestone forming radiating patterns and the scene backed by Penyghent. We could pick out black clumps of juniper growing at 1,300 feet on Moughton, but down below on Thieves Moss, where the shrub has been dying out since 1900, we had found only one old bush alive. Sulber Gate is on the Clapham road that we saw at Selside, a wild open track easy to people in imagination with the pedlars, pack-horse strings, drovers, and 'sturdy beggars' who once trod it.

Just below Crummack Farm, White Stone Lane leads to the hamlet of Wharfe at the foot of the southern side of Moughton and situated off the by-road from Austwick to Helwith Bridge in Ribblesdale. In Wharfe Gill can be seen the ruins of Wharfe corn mill, whose owner was allowed a brief for its loss by burning in 1829. We remember visiting in this secluded hamlet a retired farmer and his wife who lived in the smallest and neatest of cottages. Forty years ago they had lived at Cosh, that very lonely farm in Littondale, and for twenty years they had farmed at Crummack. Such people, who have for long lived apart from their fellows, often are the most unworldly of dalespeople.

Feizor lies on the other side of Oxenber from Wharfe. It was on the route from Kilnsey by Mastiles Lane and over Stainforth Bridge used by the monks of Fountains Abbey on journeys to their granges in the Lake District. Both Fountains and Sawley Abbeys had possessions here. The three farmhouses and a few other houses across a ford shelter under the scar called Smearsett. Feizor Hall, originally monastic property and now a farmhouse, still retains several old features, and it once had a great yew-tree in the garden. Mr Frederic Riley, who has described the history and legends of Craven in many books, lives in the hamlet.

Leaving the buttresses of Ingleborough for a moment, we will go across the main road from Austwick to Lawkland out in the

Lawkland Hall

valley, and in between the two villages turn down a muddy lane for Austwick Moss, or Red Moss as it is sometimes called. This sixty-acre swamp is now a primitive mosquito-ridden place, and is of interest to the naturalist rather than the farmer. The scrub that covers it marks it out amidst the bare wind-swept fields that surround it.

In 1757 Red Moss was allotted to people in dales (strips of land), and to-day it is shared amongst eighteen householders each with a dale twenty yards in width. Peat has been dug, bedding cut, and geese grazed there; and the story is told of an old farmer who kept a telescope directed on to it to spot when other men's stock were trespassing on his dale. Here rare specimens of beetle, moth, and fly are found, and uncommon birds such as the reed-bunting, lesser redpoll, sedge-warbler, harrier, and, though more rare than formerly, the grasshopper warbler.

The chief point of interest amongst the scattered farmhouses that go to make up Lawkland is the hall. This Elizabethan house with an even earlier south front and tower dating from the reign of Henry VII is an architectural treasure. Built of warm-coloured sandstone from the quarry at Knot Coppy near by, it is set in a formal Elizabethan garden and orchard sloping down to a beck.

In the east wing under the floor of a room, once a chapel, on the second storey is a priest's hiding-hole, a dungeon-like cavity with a stone seat.

For three centuries Lawkland Hall was the home of the Ingilbys, whose coat of arms appears on the shield over the entrance on the north front.   In 1573 John Ingleby, as the name was then spelt, of Acomb Grange, York, the second son of Sir William Ingleby of Ripley Castle, bought the Manor of Lawkland from his uncle, Peter Yorke of Middlesmoor, and at about the same time acquired Austwick Hall and the Manors of Clapham and Feizor.   After leaving the hall in 1860 the Ingilbys sold it in 1912.   Near by two fine tithe barns date from the early eighteenth century, and a small Roman Catholic chapel in the village was built by the family for public worship in 1790 after they had turned Protestant, and no longer used the chapel in the house.

From Lawkland we can make a round tour, looking in at Eldroth Hall, a farmhouse with a delightfully ancient appearance, and the Quaker burial-ground near it, and so return to Austwick.

The Pant

2. CLAPHAM AND INGLEBOROUGH

OMPARED with Austwick, Clapham, a mile and a half west of it, is more obviously a pretty village. Formerly, until the route was diverted, the whole of the traffic on the turnpike road to Kendal passed through the top of the village, that now mostly lies quietly aloof from the high road that cuts across its lower end.

Clapham Beck, dividing the houses and the two roads, runs down a wooded ravine; and trees and shrubs, including acacia and rhododendron, bordering the beck are matched by colourful little gardens in front of the houses, and evergreen and flowering shrubs planted to screen walls. Four bridges, of which the one by the church took the traffic on the turnpike, cross the beck. At the top of the ravine a waterfall flowing from the artificial lake in the grounds of Ingleborough Hall keeps up a thudding boom after rain. In summer Clapham is a bower of foliage.

The village is remarkable in that during the early years of the nineteenth century it was largely shaped by one family, the Farrers, to whom most of it still belongs. It has three claims to fame: firstly for its associations with Reginald Farrer, the botanist, secondly as the home of the magazine, the *Dalesman*, and thirdly in that the father of Michael Faraday was born in the township.

The *Dalesman* is edited by Harry J. Scott, who also publishes books and booklets on various districts and specialized subjects. The first number of what was then called the *Yorkshire Dalesman* came out in April 1939, and was described as 'a monthly magazine of dales' life and industry.' Published under its shorter title since April 1948, the magazine, increasing in size and circulation, has become a feature of the Yorkshire Dales, a vehicle for the preservation of present-day commentary on them and for historical articles such as those by Dr A. Raistrick, and a venue for advertisements of property, lodgings, books, events, and much besides.

Clapham was an Anglian settlement, the home or enclosure of a

Clapham church

person called Clapa. Not mentioned in Domesday Book, it early surpassed Austwick in importance, and was granted a market charter in 1201. The parish, originally carved out of Bentham, is itself of great antiquity, and was one of the foundation parishes with which the archdeaconry of Richmond was endowed. Except for the tower, the church was rebuilt in the last century; and the abnormally lofty aisles give it a curious look of possessing permanently shrugged shoulders.

Although the autumn fairs only ended within living memory, the market vanished long ago. The market cross is to be seen near the bridge on the main road; and here were two inns besides the present New Inn, one called the Bull and Cave. At Clapham was a school founded by George Ellis, who in 1712 left £30 a year for schools at both Clapham and Newby.

In the reign of Henry II the manor was granted to William Clapham, whose descendants subsequently owned the Manor of Beamsley. According to tradition the Claphams were buried upright in a vault at Bolton Abbey; Wordsworth pictures the 'grisly sight' in one of the less inspired verses of *The White Doe of Rylstone*. From the Claphams the Ingilbys bought the manor with Clapdale Hall and a water and fulling mill in 1573, and the elaborate door-head of the reading-room has the inscription 'WCI 1701.' After passing to the Morleys it was bought by James Farrer in 1856.

The crest of the Farrers is to be seen on the inn, the Flying Horseshoe, a mile and a quarter out of the village near Clapham station. A family of yeomen, they hailed from the neighbourhood of Halifax and from Chipping in Lancashire, and a Richard Farrer settled in Clapham in the early eighteenth century. His grandson, James, built the three-storeyed Georgian house, Yew Tree House, on the west side of the village.

Oliver Farrer, Richard's great-grandson, called Penny Bun Oliver because of his frugal habits whilst a legal junior in London, founded the family fortunes; and, buying first shooting rights on Ingleborough and then a farm here and another there, built up a large estate that eventually reached to the head of Ribblesdale. He converted a farmhouse into a shooting-lodge, called Clapham Lodge, and this, added to from time to time, became the present Ingleborough Hall.

In the first years of the last century thousands of trees—larch, spruce, pine, oak, and other varieties—were planted in Clapham Gill. Later the two brothers, James William and Oliver Farrer, nephews of Penny Bun Oliver, carried out the major alterations, including the building of the front of the hall. About 1833 they completely transformed the top end of the village. They demolished several buildings, including the vicarage and tithe barn, which stood south-east of the church, rerouted roads, and made the tunnels that still lead under the grounds to the lanes to Austwick and Selside, and to the back door of the hall. They dammed Clapham Beck to flood eight acres of land for a lake in the grounds; and built a new vicarage on the west side of the village.

The Farrers were true lovers of their native countryside, and some of them were the first to explore the caves in those exciting early years of discovery. One branch of the family was given a peerage, and another counts amongst its members Reginald Farrer, the botanist. Owing to many deaths in recent years much outlying property has been sold, and the present owner, Dr John A. Farrer, came from Australia to succeed to the estate in 1953.

Ingleborough Hall has an elegant staircase and pillars of Dent fossil marble. During the last war it was occupied by a boys' preparatory school from Broadstairs, and in 1947 it was sold to the West Riding County Council for use as a school for delicate children. The kitchen garden, the famous shrubberies, and the moraine and water gardens, made by Reginald Farrer, were eventually sold by the council; and though still visited by botanists they have fallen into neglect.

Reginald John Farrer, who died aged forty in Upper Burma in 1920, won fame by his writings on rock-gardens and by his plant-collecting travels in all parts of the world. In 1902, after leaving Balliol College, Oxford, he lived in Japan and wrote his first book, *The Garden of Asia*. But attempting novels, plays, and poems he failed as a writer, and at length found his true vocation in ambitious and often dangerous journeys, sometimes taken with fellow botanists, to Japan, China, Tibet, the Alps, and the Dolomites.

Reginald Farrer introduced over a hundred new plants into Europe, including the famous *Gentiana farreri*, and two of his books, *My Rock Garden* and the two-volume *The English Rock Garden*, published in 1907 and 1919, have lived. The former, and the fame of his moraine garden at Clapham, stimulated the fashion for the building of rockeries in the years just before the First World War. In a chapter of *My Rock Garden*, 'Our English Alpines,' he describes from intimate knowledge the rare wild flowers of Craven, and, as we still do, laments the disappearance of the lady's slipper orchis.

We remember walking alongside the lake with a friend who had helped Reginald Farrer to plant many of the shrubs in the deep gill beyond, a gill that in springtime appears so strange as it burgeons with the lush growth of Eastern shrubs close to the wastes of Ingleborough. We were told of his elaborate plans for the planting of the gill. A man of great energy, he painted delicate flower sketches, wrote prolifically, if a little exuberantly for modern taste, and filled the pages of his books with sympathetic descriptions of strange places and people and original and stimulating views on gardening.

In half an hour's walk from Clapham the lovely wooded drive through the grounds of the hall leads to Ingleborough Cave. From there the path continues up Trow Gill past Gaping Gill to the summit of Ingleborough. But first, like eighteenth-century tourists who hired a guide for every conceivable excursion, we find a house with a notice reading CAVE GUIDE, buy a fourpenny ticket for the grounds of the hall, and make arrangements with Arnold Brown, woodman and in his spare time guide, to see the cave.

There is an alternative route to the cave along the cart-track to Clapdale Farm.   With little of interest left Clapdale disappoints; a 'castle large and strong . . . on ye outskirts of the high hill Ingleborough,' Dodsworth, the historian, described it.

Each year over a thousand people, from children in arms to grandmothers over eighty, visit Ingleborough Cave.   It is dry, not at all artificial; and though tall people must duck their heads here and there, bending double is necessary in only one place.   It was made accessible in 1837 by the Farrers, with the help of Josiah Harrison and other estate workmen, who broke down a barrier of stalagmite to release an underground lake.   Professor Adam Sedgwick and Professor John Phillips were amongst the first visitors.

The guide unlocks the door covering the entrance, gives each visitor a candle in a home-made wooden holder, and leads the way with a high-powered lamp.   Stalactites and stalagmites, water-falls of them, pinnacles, columns, clusters of them, fancifully named the Pillar, the Jockey Cap, the Coffee Pot, the Elephant's Legs, the Shower Bath, the Peal of Bells, the Organ Pipes, the Sword of Damocles and so on, meet the eye.   How extraordinarily like the folds of an elephant's hide many seem!   The guide taps the brittle columns with his key.   At the end is the Pool of Reflections, and without prompting we see an inverted picture in the pool of the skyscrapers of New York.   Phillips wrote: 'If the stalactites of this Cave could be drawn by the aid of Photography, very beautiful effects would be produced.'   He was right. Stalactites show up brilliantly white in flashlight photography, but in reality they are often mud-coloured.

The hardy pot-holer penetrates farther by crawling and wading to the Giant's Hall and on to meet the underground waters of Fell Beck, from where cave-divers have not yet succeeded in reaching the main chamber of Gaping Gill, by estimation only 1,350 yards away.   The cave is in fact part of the channel of Clapham Beck, which begins as Fell Beck near the summit of Ingleborough, plunges underground near Gaping Gill, down which it also rushes in times of flood, flows through part of the cave, and emerges near the entrance at Clapham Beck Head.

Overland it is about a mile to Gaping Gill, with in between a scramble up Trow Gill, itself a tremendous collapsed cave so lofty that people appear like pygmies in the bottom. Once in the gill we shouted at a hawk perched in a tree far away at the top of the crag, and the sound echoed hollowly round the limestone walls.

Here on two consecutive Sundays in 1947 tragedy came to light. On 24th August pot-holers, casually exploring shakeholes in Trow Gill, entered a roughly walled-up cave, and in it found the skull of a dead man with a scarf round the mouth. A week later a caver, his memory stirred by this discovery, led a party down Gaping Gill to recover bones noticed previously. They were human. The grim finds became national news; rumours circulated that the dead men had been Nazi agents parachuted on the fells. But the mysteries to this day remain unsolved.

In this part of Yorkshire it is not only the hill summits but the pot-holes that are a basis of fellowship. If you have been down Gaping Gill you have earned the freedom of Craven. As its name implies it is a great gash in the open fell, and the descent can be made when the Yorkshire Ramblers or other pot-holing clubs are in camp there, usually at Whitsuntide or in early August.

Prior to 1850 (the exact date is unknown) John Birkbeck of Anley, Settle, first attempted the 340-foot drop to the floor of the main chamber of Gaping Gill. As his tackle only consisted of ropes, that frayed and dislodged stones, he failed. In 1895 a Frenchman, E. A. Martel, and his wife arrived with rope-ladders; and on 1st August, keeping constant communication by telephone with his wife on the surface, he reached the bottom in twenty-three minutes. A translation of M. Martel's thrilling account of the descent can be read in *Yorkshire Caves and Pot-holes—No. 2, Under Ingleborough* by A. Mitchell. Nowadays a winch, driven by a petrol engine, enables the visitor, sitting in a bosun's chair, to be lowered in ninety seconds.

From Gaping Gill a short but steep climb leads to the summit of Ingleborough. On a fine day the view from it is superb; and, especially on the north side, where the shales have worn back, the precipices give a sensation of great height above the valley. To the west may be seen the Cumberland and Westmorland Fells, and nearer at hand the familiar hills, farms, and corners of valleys of the Yorkshire Dales. In the centre of the plateau a direction plaque, set up by the Ingleton Fell Rescue Team to commemorate

Ingleborough irresistibly draws the eye

the coronation of Queen Elizabeth II in 1953, gives the many hills to be seen and their distance from the summit.

Lucky indeed is the walker who sees all the hills marked on the plaque. The last time we climbed Ingleborough, one hazy, warm Easter Monday, we saw the near landscape shimmering in the sun, but the Lake District mountains and Morecambe Bay melted into the soft mists of the horizon. Many people were crossing the top, and one man asked us what time there was a train to Bradford from Ingleton!

In *The Rivers, Mountains, and Sea Coast of Yorkshire* Phillips prints a plan and a description of the Iron Age fort on Ingleborough and says: 'The huts and walls exhibit principles of construction which remove them from the catalogue of barbarian works.' The massive defensive wall ringing the summit, though in ruins, is impressive; but the huts once scattered about the plateau have been plundered for building material, in particular for a beacon, and in 1839 for the tower, designed as a refuge for shepherds, but on the day of its opening destroyed by the crowd. How the Brigantes endured it up here is difficult to imagine. They must have been conditioned to gales of wind and rain.

From Clapham to Ingleton there is a choice of two routes, the turnpike by Clapham Common and the old road past Newby Cote. In between are Newby and Cold Cotes. Newby Head in Ribblesdale takes its name from the former, the Manor of Newby, owned by Furness Abbey, being originally in two parts, one here and one some ten miles away. On the south side of the road the pastures show well-defined and extensive ranes, the townfields of Clapham and Newby.

The houses of Newby spread round a large rough green with a stream running through it. At the east end the hall, the manor-house, stands on the site of a grange of Furness Abbey, and was a stopping place for the wool traffic on the route from Furness to the east coast. The present seventeenth-century house has a dated door-head and a fine barn alongside, also dated and with an unusual feature, a penthouse roof over the entrance doors.

At Newby we spoke to the shepherd of Ingleborough Fell, the name of the commons of Clapham township. He is hired from the middle of April until November to look after the two thousand Dalesbred sheep belonging to ten farmers. Going on to the fell every day in early summer, he has chiefly to drive the sheep to the tops of their heaths. Sheep tend to move downhill, especially in bad weather, which they sense approaching. The numbers of each flock depend on how many sheep the farmer can satisfactorily winter on his low ground, his 'inside land.' Five times a year gatherings take place: two for dippings and one for clipping, one for separating the ewes and lambs, called spaining, and one for sorting out the draft ewes for sale in the autumn.

Even the shepherd, who knows his ground as well as a townsman his streets, can lose direction when mists completely alter the look of the fells. For sensing 'owt amiss,' a sheep rigged, for example, his dogs are invaluable. Nowadays shepherds are difficult to find, and the farmers of Austwick, who used to employ several, do the work themselves.

On the old road we pass the farmhouse, Holly Platt, a former coaching inn. It has a raised platform from which coaches were boarded and where luggage was unloaded, and a two-storeyed porch supported on columns, whose upper storey acted as a look-out for traffic. Holly Platt's chimneys are supported on slates that for strength project at each side, a characteristic of the building style of the district. The slate ledges, you may be told, make seats where witches sit and rest in between their broom-stick rides in the sky.

3. INGLETON AND
CHAPEL-LE-DALE

ROBUST figures in fancy jerseys, in checked shirts, in shorts, sitting in small cafés; young people, weighted down by rucksacks, marching through the narrow streets; a bus-load of men and women on an outing from a West Riding or a Lancashire town gazing round the square: all these are everyday sights in the summer months at Ingleton; for Ingleton has a season—the tourist season—and it has an industry—the tourist industry—and both are obviously successful and deservedly so.

Just as Keswick has developed as a centre for those who climb the mountains of the Lake District, so Ingleton has exploited its setting as a natural centre not only for climbing the hills of Yorkshire, with the most famous of those hills, Ingleborough, at its backdoor, and for walking the fells for their geological and botanical interests, but also for penetrating into the caves and descending into the pot-holes under the hills. Not content with all this, Ingleton, situated near the meeting of the waters of the Twiss and the Doe, provides a unique series of waterfalls in the river glens that for this type of picturesque scenery are unrivalled in the county.[1]

Ingleton perches high up alongside a deep valley, with the church dominating it, a railway viaduct spanning the ravine, and down below two bridges crossing the rivers. In the narrow main street every house is either a shop or a café. Hotels, boarding-houses, and bed-and-breakfast establishments abound. The youth hostel accommodates 60 people, and in the holiday months may put up some 1,300 members and schoolchildren. Yet many parts of the place are spoilt by indiscriminate building, and on the

---

[1] Some confusion as to the nomenclature of these rivers has arisen for two reasons: a mistake on the ordnance survey map that identifies Dale Beck with the River Doe, and the existence of a variety of local names for each. We have gone by eighteenth-century guide-books, the *Geological Survey of Ingleborough* (1890), and by what they are called locally to-day. The River Twiss or the Dale Beck flows down Chapel-le-Dale, and the River Doe or the Thornton Beck down Kingsdale. They meet below Ingleton to become the Greta.

outskirts is a red-brick housing estate. It speaks well for the natural landscape that Ingleton still attracts.

Underlying the modern scene, Ingleton's past follows a similar pattern to those of other dale villages. In 1086 Ingleton was in the Manor of Whittington, now a small village seven miles west, and in Elizabethan times the owners of the manor, the Cholmondeleys, quarrelled about rents with their tenants and reduced them to destitution before the dispute was settled. Old names of the yeomen of Ingleton include Kidd, Redmayne, and Foxcroft. The Kidds are associated with Chapel-le-Dale and Blue Hall at Ingleton. John Kidd, said to have made a fortune from printer's ink, built the Ingleborough Hotel, but no members of this branch of the family remain in the district. The once moated manor-house, now a farmhouse, has a fine tithe barn alongside it.

Within recollection Ingleton has changed. An annual fair that took place on 17th November specialized in 1770 in leather and oatmeal; but it is remembered that about sixty years ago it was solely a cattle fair with stock crowded into the main street, and with the day ending in sports—quoits, brasses,[1] and races. Bell Horse Gate, the present steep road to the rivers, commemorates by its name the leader of a pack-horse train, and it once had an inn of the same name on it. The post office block was once the Bay Horse, and the stationer's, Tennants, was a bakehouse for riddle bread, as the thin oatcake of the district is called. Like Askrigg in Wensleydale, Ingleton has a bullring, that was once turned over by pugnacious persons who had had 'a sup ower much' as a signal for a fight.

In the past Ingleton has been partially industrialized. Coal was worked for centuries; and before the advent of steam power 'a good deal of wool was spun here for the Bradford market.' Near Thornton Bridge over the Doe stands a partially ruined cotton mill with the manager's house beside it. It was burnt down on 1st April 1854, but was rebuilt. After standing empty for twenty years it was restarted for hemp, but three months later, on 13th October 1904, was burnt down again. Beyond the mill across the river is Mealbank Quarry and the limekilns of the Craven and District Lime Co. that closed in 1909. A railway bridge, of which the piers only remain at the entrance to the glens, once connected the quarry with Thornton station, and a short

[1] A game similar to quoits, but played at a range of four to five yards only.

red-brick chimney on the wooded hillside is the outlet for the surface flue of the limekilns.

The most important recent attempt at industrialization was the reopening of the colliery in 1913. In its heyday two or three hundred miners were employed, and what is known as the Model Village, the red-brick housing estate, was built. When the colliery closed in 1937 Ingleton became temporarily a distressed area; but now the once unwanted houses of the village sell at high prices. A link with the cloth trade, a burling and mending shop, housed in the old elementary school, employs girls; a laundry has a depot here, and many people work at factories at Bentham, four miles away.

The story of Ingleton as a tourist centre begins in 1849, when the railway was brought from Skipton; twelve years later the viaduct was built and the line extended to Sedbergh and Low Gill. Then there were two stations, Ingleton and Thornton, on either side of the viaduct; and a favourite pastime for the boys of a past generation was to ride from station to station, for which they paid 1*d*. fare.

In the following years a Joseph Carr publicized the place by writing articles for newspapers, and in 1884 the Ingleton Improvement Society was formed. Paths were made and bridges built over the Doe. But the glens and falls of the neighbouring Twiss belonged to local farmers, so that for some years there were two groups of purveyors of the picturesque. A story goes that each group employed a man to meet excursion trains and to distribute handbills extolling the beauties of the glens, and that one man, finding that he had a drunken rival, substituted his own bills for those in the other man's pocket.

Eventually the rights on both rivers were amalgamated, and shortly after the First World War they became the property of W. S. Worthington, who levelled the paths and built steps and bridges. The glens remain his property—you may meet Mr Worthington when you pay your sixpence at the hut at the entrance—and repairs and improvements continue to be made.

The round walk up the Doe and back by the Twiss, four and a quarter miles long, takes two and a quarter hours. For perfection choose a fine day in spring after heavy rain to see the sun on fresh green leaves, clear sparkling water, towering cliffs, and river gorges. There are concrete steps to scale the once almost impassable cliffs to see Pecca Falls, Beezley Falls, Thornton Force, and, as old guide-books said of the environs of Ingleton, 'many objects worthy of the attention of the admirers of romantic scenery.' The slate quarry at Pecca Falls was worked in the eighteenth century for roofing slates, and at Thornton Force is to be seen the ancient Pre-Cambrian rock. Walkers, school parties, bus-loads and car-loads of people, the majority from Lancashire, set out on the walk. They return flushed with exertion and beaming with the pleasures of enjoyment and achievement.

If the crowds fill Ingleton, they soon disperse on the fells. The summit of Ingleborough is three miles away, Whernside and Gragareth are some six miles off, and beyond them lie Leck Fell in Lancashire and Barbon and Middleton Fells in Westmorland. Where the three counties meet is the County Stone, that may be approached by an old quarry road from the head of Kingsdale. The valleys of the Doe and the Twiss—Kingsdale and Chapel-le-Dale—lie on either side of Whernside.

Within a mile or two of Ingleton, Thornton-in-Lonsdale, with the hamlets of Masongill and Westhouse, brings us to the borders of Lancashire and Yorkshire. Thornton church, with the stocks and whipping-post outside it, and the whitewashed Marton Arms Hotel opposite, once called the Church Stile, make a scene that waits to be peopled with a meet of the old Ingleton Hunt or for the arrival of coaches, gigs, and chaises.

The shallow limestone valley of Kingsdale, some three miles long, is approached over a moraine, so that you top a rise to see heather reaching down to the beck and oases of meadow land round two farmhouses, Braida Garth, partially used as a shooting-lodge, and Kingsdale Head House. At the latter we spoke to the farmer, who was born at the farm, and whose seven hundred sheep graze to the top of Whernside.

When we were there a few men with a steam-roller were finishing their day's work on the road. This road down Kingsdale over the watershed to Deepdale and Dent was built in 1952 as an experimental route over bogs. The undertaking achieved success through the use of modern machines and the dogged persistence of the men on the job; but its chief interest lies in the use of a substance called cold emulsion instead of tar to bind together the many tons of stones involved.

A grey sky threatened rain. The whole valley seemed deserted,

Whernside from Chapel-le-Dale

seldom visited.   But below the apparently plain surface are the
caves.   We climbed a pasture towards a coppice, and topping a
brow found a party of some fifty schoolchildren in the hollow near
the mouth of Yordas Cave.   A large fire glowed from within, and
acrid wood smoke stung the eyes as if the place were inhabited.
In *A Tour of the Caves* (1781) the Rev. John Hutton, when visiting
Yordas, his first cave, procured 'a guide, candles, lanthorn, and
tinder box,' and a basket of provisions at the Church Stile public-
house at Thornton.   He describes the cave, the waterfall, the
stalactite formations, called the Chapter House and the Bishop's
Throne, and says that his guide told stories of fairies and giants
and even of a madman living in it, and of a poor wayfaring woman
with a new-born child found dead there.   On the other hand,
when Lord Torrington passed through Craven in 1792 he engaged
'a jolly shoemaker' in Chapel-le-Dale as a guide to Yordas.

With Chapel-le-Dale we complete the circuit of Ingleborough.
On this side the hill's precipitous slopes on the one hand and
Whernside on the other lift to grandeur what would otherwise
appear to be a featureless small dale.   It takes its name from the
sequestered little church, until 1864 a chapel of ease in the parish
of Ingleton and sometimes called Ingleton Fells chapel; near this
the valley's community life centres with school, post office, the
Hill Inn, and near by Weathercote House and Cave.   Through
the dale ran the Richmond to Lancaster turnpike road.

Across the river from the inn, in a wooded corner starred in spring with anemones, violets, and primroses, the church hides from the passer-by on the turnpike.   In it is a wall tablet to the men who lost their lives in the construction of the Settle to Carlisle line between Settle and Dent Head.   During the railway-building era the dale witnessed a fantastic sight.   An engine was pulled up it from Ingleton to Ribblehead by forty horses.

One of Robert Southey's chapters in *The Doctor* takes for its setting a house that stood on the site of the present Weathercote House 'about a bowshot from the church,' where the poet pictured the home of Daniel Dove, a mid-eighteenth-century yeoman. But it is not so good a description as Adam Sedgwick's of similar houses in Dent.

Many motorists halt at, and walkers start their climbs from, the Hill Inn; and many famous visitors have stayed there—amongst others Lord Tweedsmuir, Tom Stobart when a boy, Edith Summerskill, and Geoffrey and Eleanor Winthrop Young.

The inn naturally takes its name from Ingleborough, whose dominant shape, so close now, irresistibly draws the eye.   Here we can never look long enough at the looming mountain, its sides so steep, and its top sloping as if the whole great mass were falling backwards.

Three generations of Kilburns have kept the Hill Inn and farmed the land that belongs to it.   Their story goes back to the building of the Settle to Carlisle railway when John Kilburn taught at a school at Bruntscar across the valley.   As he only earned 8s. a week, his wife suggested that he should take a shop and sell goods to the navvies.   This he did.   Later he was the first licensee of the Station Inn at Ribblehead, then a wooden hut, and he also taught at a school held in a barn at a turn of the road near Far Gearstones.   In 1897 his son came to the Hill Inn, and the family bought it in 1955 but left in 1963.

The names of the lonely farmhouses on the north side of Chapel-le-Dale, houses that stand with their backs to Whernside, breathe of Norse settlement: Winterscales, Gunner Fleet, Ivescar, Broadrake, Bruntscar.   Winterscales derives from *skali*, a shepherd's hut, and it means the winter house.   Bruntscar Hall has an elaborate door-head with initials of the Procters and the date, PP MP 1689, now difficult to decipher.   Alongside it a ruined house has a beehive oven, and at the back of the hall, within arm's length of it, is the chill low entrance of Bruntscar Cave, where a tame trout lived for many years. At the lower end of the dale the wild and forlorn ruin of Long Chimney, so called because of a tall chimney, now fallen down, was once a farmhouse, rebuilt in 1714.

Geologists often cite Chapel-le-Dale as an example of a U-shaped glacier-scoured valley, and they point to a more unusual phenomenon, the thick wide exposure of the same rock that we saw at Thornton Force, the greenish-grey grits and slates belonging to the Pre-Cambrian period, to be seen some two hundred yards below the natural limestone bridge, called God's Bridge.

But it is limestone that is most evident in Chapel-le-Dale—limestone in clints, in walls, in pot-holes, in caves, in quarries, in boulders strewn in the fields, in sudden rocky outcrops out of which streams trickle, in scars with gnarled yews and hawthorns growing on them. The Twiss, flowing over limestone, plays hide and seek along its course, and disappears and reappears many times. A limestone landscape is incorrigibly romantic. It is impossible to tidy it up and streamline it. It stays firmly entrenched in the eighteenth-century picturesque.

On the sides of the dale are some eighteen caves and fifteen pot-holes, counting those near the head waters of the Twiss, of which the most easily seen are White Scar and Weathercote.

White Scar, on the roadside a mile and a half from Ingleton, has been open to the public since 1924. The guide lives at the entrance, where café and car park proclaim a popular resort. On Bank Holiday week-ends parties led by guides constantly file in and out.

The cave was discovered by C. F. C. Long, a Cambridge undergraduate, in 1923. Since then other explorers, chiefly the discoverer himself, Colonel G. H. Swift, and the guide, T. G. Greenwood, who died in 1947, have penetrated almost a mile of difficult passage and underground lake. About half a mile of cave is accessible to anyone by easy walking; and by special arrangement the hardy, who are prepared to wade in ice-cold water, may reach the first lake. The entrance, a tunnel blasted through rock (it was necessary to crawl in at the original entrance), is dreary, but soon magnificent formations of stalactites and stalagmites are reached, and considerable waterfalls splash away inside the mountain.

Weathercote, Jingle Pot, and Hurtle Pot concentrate along the river-bed near the church. Connoisseurs of limestone landscape should not miss this corner, in particular Weathercote. It is exposed to view as a pot rather than a cave, first a craggy hole of mossy-brown limestone, then a crater down which a waterfall pitches veil-like seventy feet into the gloom below. Yew and garlic, bird cherry, wood anemone, and London pride luxuriate over tumbled rocks. The Rev. John Hutton describes the scene at the bottom where it is possible to scramble: 'The sun happening to shine very bright, we had a small vivid rainbow within a few yards of us, for colour, size, situation, perhaps nowhere else to be equalled.' Weathercote is one of the loveliest limestone spectacles in Craven.

Almost to be classed as another sport besides caving is botanizing on the clints, especially on Sleights Pasture Rocks above the Hill Inn. On them care must be taken: the flat pavements are smooth, sometimes topped with loose rocks, and the fissures deep. Here, particularly in May and June, the clints make a notable hunting ground for rare flowers, a natural rock-garden in the wilderness. Dells filled with bluebells and lilies of the valley remind us of the one-time woods that flourished where now the soil has been eroded. Stunted bird cherry, ash, hazel, guelder rose, and honeysuckle, their roots deep in the cracks, and some bushes bitten by sheep level with the surface, make miniature glades. There is heather on hummocks of peat, and troughs of swampy ground are hazed over with the pink of bird's-eye primrose. Globe-flowers, violets, wild strawberries, and thalictrum blossom in sunny corners; and raising their heads to the light from sunless depths grow hart's-tongue fern, herb Paris, and herb Christopher.

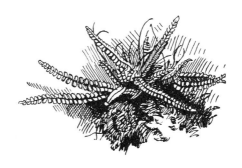

VII

DENT

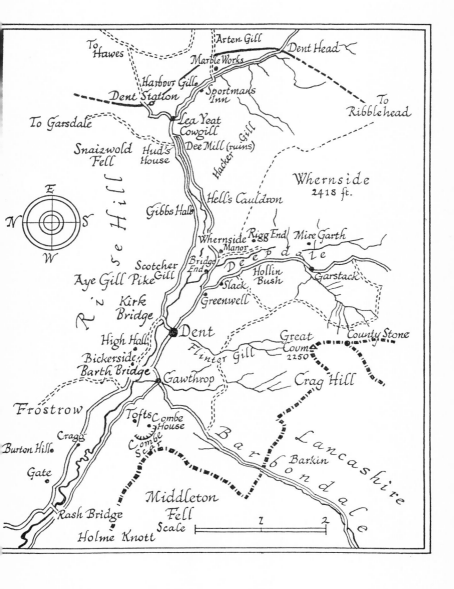

To Hawes
Arten Gill
Dent Head
Marble Works
To Ribblehead
Harbour Gill
Dent Station
Sportmans Inn
To Garsdale
Lea Yeat
Cowgill
Snaizwold Fell
Hud's House
Dee Mill (ruins)
Hacker Gill
Whernside 2418 ft.
Hell's Cauldron
Gibbs Hall
Rise Hill
Whernside Manor
Rigg End 88
Mire Garth
Scotcher Gill
Bridge End
Deepdale
Hollin Bush
Garstack
Aye Gill Pike
Slack
Greenwell
Kirk Bridge
High Hall
Dent
Great Coum 2250
County Stone
Bickerside
Flinter Gill
Crag Hill
Barth Bridge
Gawthrop
Frostrow
Tofts
Combe House
Barbondale
Cragg
Combe Scar
Lancashire
Burton Hill
Barkin
Gate
Rash Bridge
Middleton Fell
Scale
Holme Knott

1. DENT: PAST AND PRESENT

Late on a wet November afternoon we met half a dozen farmers leading saddled ponies down the road at the head of Dent. As we passed them, an express train with lighted windows rushed into sight three or four hundred yards up on the hillside; the train had just emerged from Blea Moor Tunnel and crossed Dent Head Viaduct on the way to Carlisle. Down below the men might have been returning from a horse or sheep fair of a hundred years ago, but instead they and their ponies had been out with a shooting party on the moors. None the less, as so often happens in the dale, the old and the new seemed for a few seconds to draw very close.

The small secluded valley of Dent is approached at its foot from Sedbergh, or at its head from Widdale and Ribblesdale, or over narrow roads through Deepdale and Barbondale. Dent, besides being the name of the one village, describes the whole dale; Dent-dale is a modern term not used by the inhabitants. We shall distinguish between the two by using the old name, Dent Town, for the village. As old people will tell you, Dent is ten miles long by five miles wide; but only where the one branch dale, Deepdale, strikes off south does it measure as much as five miles from hilltop to hilltop. The valley itself varies from half a mile to a mile in width.

Dent begins as a little narrow dale amongst vast treeless wastes of moorland, and taking a bend westwards opens out into a trough of fertile country scored by a multitude of wooded gills and backed by Great Coum, Crag Hill, and Barkin and Holme Fells. Patterned with walls, dotted with farmhouses, and with the one village, Dent Town, in its midst, it looks, as was said of it long ago, 'a terrestrial paradise.'

Dent, like Garsdale, from which it is divided by Rise Hill, lies on the west side of the Pennines; the waters of its river, the Dee, flow eventually into the Irish Sea. The climate is milder and the rainfall higher than in the dales on the east. In fact, the dale is situated at a comparatively low altitude. Dent Town is 480 feet above sea level. We live at Askrigg in mid Wensleydale at 800 feet. Its connections, too, are with Lancashire and Westmorland rather than with Yorkshire; the architecture of its farmhouses and the banks topped by hedges for field boundaries resemble those in Westmorland; and even the Women's Institute belongs to the federation of that county.

Below Dent Town the valley narrows; its floor is flat, and the hills, instead of following the smooth lines of the dale hills, appear gnarled and humpy like the fells of the Lake District. At this point alongside Barkin Beck the Dent Fault crosses the dale. On one side of it lies the familiar limestone country, but on the other, west of the fault, the Silurian Rock of the Lake District is found: the change is striking. At this end of the dale approach must have been difficult before the flat swampy valley floor was drained. Indeed, tradition relates that Scots raiders never found Dent.

But most of all the traveller is struck by the number of small whitewashed farmhouses, each with a porch, spaced along the sides of the valley. Sometimes ruins of old houses adjoin them. A few are unoccupied, and some, now turned into barns, were once houses. Rather than striking architectural features—only three or four have dated door-heads—they have a rustic charm that is enhanced by their names: Helks, Coventree, Dockle Syke, Hollin Bush, Rivling, Greenwell, Butterpots.

These small holdings ideally divide up the land; and each could tell a story of the human lot. Nowadays in many cases more than one are thrown together; but in the past, combining occupations such as knitting with farming, people lived comfortably on them. In 1778 there were 416 houses, but in 1951 there were only 257. Dent's story is the familiar one of a self-sufficient, productive, industrial, and farming community disrupted by the Industrial Revolution.

Adam Sedgwick, Woodwardian Professor of Geology at Cambridge, born at the parsonage at Dent in 1785, died in 1873. The dale's most famous son, he saw in his lifetime the waning of the prosperity of the countryside of his youth, and he left a record of his recollections in *A Memorial to Cowgill Chapel*. The story of decline only varies in detail from that of other dales, but none possesses a contemporary account to give it such poignancy.

Although Sedbergh is included, Dent does not appear in Domesday Book. Nor are there signs of the ranes of an early open

Dent Town

field system; yet corn was grown quite extensively in both Dent and Deepdale up to about a hundred years ago and again during the two world wars.

A church was first built at Dent Town in the twelfth century, and the village was early established as a centre with a market and fairs. Throughout the Middle Ages the FitzHughs of Ravensworth Castle in North Yorkshire owned the manor; and the people occupied their farms by the custom of tenant right. A serious crime took place on one of the lonely passes out of Dent in 1375, when the king's bailiff was shot and plundered of gold and silver; and in late August 1553, long remembered as the great 'sweat' time, plague broke out in Dent.

Old people will tell you that there were once five mills in the valley: corn mills at Deepdale, Gawthrop, and Rash, a marble mill at Stone House, and a woollen mill near Cowgill church. It is an interesting recollection, for it harks back to a much earlier time when there were five corn mills built one after another as the population increased.

In Elizabethan times there were three corn mills—Gawthrop Mill and two on the Dee, the Over Mill at the foot of Deepdale and the Nether Mill near Kirk Bridge. But shortage of water and damage by floods often caused difficulties, so that a new mill was built lower down the river at Rash. Immediately the other millers raised an outcry, and a lawsuit followed. In early Stuart times, when the manor was Crown property, lawsuits again arose over the mills, then fallen into neglect; and finally in 1698, when a fifth mill was built, more trouble and lawsuits resulted. This time the millers declared that little corn was grown, much had to be imported, and there wasn't a living for four millers, never mind five. To-day only Rash Mill, a saw-mill now, is left to remind us of the five and the disputes they once caused.

At the beginning of the seventeenth century the population had increased to such an extent that houses and land were in keen demand. At that time many were the Chancery suits in which people claimed property in Dent and in Deepdale without legal title, perhaps from a widow or a minor. During this century the great change of the transference of the manor to the tenants of Dent, attended by the usual quarrels and confusion, took place, and the estatesmen, or statesmen as they were called, obtaining full possession of their lands, came into being.

The stage was set for the full exploitation of the natural resources of the valley. The knitting industry, which had been developed in the reign of Elizabeth I, so fitted the local economy that it became the mainstay. Both home-produced wool and large quantities of imported dressed wool were made into thousands of pairs of stockings and gloves. Horses were bred and tons of butter and cheese produced. 'Dent was then a land of rural opulence and glee.'

Adam Sedgwick pictured life in the valley: the houses with their orchards of plum-trees, the interiors furnished with long settles and cupboards of carved oak, the 'simple primitive economical habits' of the people. He described Dent Town with a market cross, swinging inn signs, and overhead galleries from which sounded 'the buzz of the spinning-wheel, and the hum and songs of those who were carrying on the labours of the day.' He pictured in fact the dignity and charm of a happy and contented community in a remote place.

By the mid nineteenth century poverty and depopulation had overtaken the fortunes of the people. Most of the farms had been mortgaged and then sold; their former owners occupied them as tenants. Many holdings of perhaps seven or twelve acres were altogether too small to live off without a supplementary source of income; these were joined with other farms and the houses fell into ruin. But so long as the rent could be paid the people, deeply attached to their home land, hung on. They bartered their produce for necessities, and, as the knitting trade waned, worked at it for a pittance for 'shopping money.' The Stone House marble works provided some work throughout the nineteenth century, and again, as the old people will tell you, the enclosure of the commons by walls in 1859, and the building of the Settle to Carlisle line across the head of the dale from 1869 to 1876, by providing employment, saved Dent. Many people lived off the land, and scraped along on a shilling or two a week. A familiar saying is still used in the dale, and indeed in neighbouring ones:

> Do as they do i' Dent,
> If you can't get tobacco, chew bent.

It epitomizes the philosophic outlook still evident in the people to-day.

Many of the farms are small, and the process of amalgamation goes on. Some people work on the railway as signalmen, plate-layers, and so on. Others find work in Sedbergh. The number of old family names that remain in Dent, some surviving from the fourteenth century, is surprising: Mason, Cragg, Middleton, Sedgwick, Haygarth, Capstick, Burton, Thistlethwaite, Staveley, and Hodgson.

Although the story has been told in our book *The Old Hand-Knitters of the Dales*, the knitting industry deserves a brief mention. It developed rapidly in the seventeenth century, and though diminishing throughout the last continued into the first years of the present century. The trade, centred on Kendal, was carried on by factors who distributed wool for carding, spinning, and knitting, and later by hosiers who ran small mills, Hebble-thwaite Hall Mill and Farfield Mills near Sedbergh, Rash, Stone House, and Dee Mills, where crude machines carded and spun yarn for knitting and for the weaving of coarse cloths.

In the seventeenth century stockings of fine quality were made, and in the next the hosiers supplied enormous quantities of stockings for different ranks of the army; and in the last century a coarse, oily yarn called bump was knitted into jackets, long stockings, mittens, and caps, for which sums such as 1s. for a jacket and 3½d. for a pair of mittens were paid to the knitters.

Robert Southey in his miscellany, *The Doctor*, recounted in dialect the adventures of Betty and Sally Yewdale, who as children in about 1760 were sent from Langdale in the Lake District to the head of Dent to learn to knit. The story contains the well-known phrase, 'the terrible knitters e' Dent,' that really means 'the great knitters in Dent'; but doubtless the terrible knitters will always be associated with Dent.

Besides Southey, William Howitt, who visited the dale with his wife in the 1830's, described in *The Rural Life of England* how men, women, and children knitted at work and at the dame schools. He wrote of how they employed a belt round the waist with a knitting sheath tucked into it, and bent needles of which one was affixed into the sheath; and how working with a rhythmic movement, they knitted with 'unremitting speed' and sitting by a peat fire looked like so many 'weird wizards.'

Good knitters of a past generation had sometimes to put down their work because the needles were red-hot; and one of the last of the knitters whom we know said to us: 'My mother's needles fair made music.' A story that dates back well over a hundred years tells how a little boy used to go to church with his grandmother. Sitting in the high-sided box pews, from which he could see nothing, he was bored, so that one Sunday he bethought him to take his knitting, which he brought out during the service to the consternation and wrath of his grandmother. There was no 'laikin'[1] for children 'i' them days.' When they returned from school knitting awaited them.

Nowadays only one or two elderly people remember knitting for the industry as children. The recollections are chiefly of their parents' prowess in the craft. A few treasure the patterned gloves with the owner's name and the date round the wristband that were made up to the 1920's.

A phase of past life about which vivid tales have been handed down is the enclosure of the commons in 1859, a late date for enclosure in the dales. Before that time the farms were noted for their dun-coloured fell ponies; as described by William Howitt they must have very much resembled fiord ponies seen round the Hardanger Fiord in Norway to-day. An annual horse fair, held at Kirk Bridge, took place the day before Hawes Fair, that itself was followed by Cowper Day at Kirkby Stephen and finally by Brough Hill Fair in Westmorland.

What is chiefly remembered about the enclosures is the ill

[1] Playing.

feeling that marked the period before them. Fights were common; overstocking of the land and the unrestrained dogging of sheep prevailed; wrapped in their plaids, men sat up on the fells in little stone huts with their knitting to occupy them, and saw to it that their flocks kept to the best land, or were driven by the dogs over the boundary into Westmorland territory. Sometimes stags (young horses) were chased to their deaths over the Combe, a sinister cliff of rock above Gawthrop. This is no tale told for effect: horses' bones have been found at the foot. The story goes of two young men fighting at the top of the Combe, and of their dogs fighting 'an' all.' The dogs, still fighting, fell to the bottom.

The wages for walling helped to eke out a living, but they were no more than 3s. for a rood, that is seven yards, a good day's work. It is remembered that at Tofts Farm, near Gawthrop, they used to bake a pie, and at dinner-time take it hot from the oven, 'lap it in a cloth, and away on to t'fell' to the farmer walling there.

2. DENT HEAD TO DENT FOOT

To FILL in some of the details of the dale's story let us take a closer look at the valley. Beginning at the head, crossing bridges, deviating up Deepdale, stopping at a farm or a mill and at Dent Town, we shall find it full of interest. We shall be accompanied by the sound of running water and a harmony of colour as of old tapestry work. In spring the tang of peat fills the air on the fells; in summer the scent of hay lingers in the dale.

The moorland road from Newby Head plunges steeply down by Fell End Gill to cross under the railway, to pass Dent Head Viaduct, and to meet the infant River Dee. The viaduct stands on a quarry of black marble from which the huge blocks that built Arten Gill Viaduct a little farther on were hewn. Out of sight in the gill is the first farmhouse in the dale, whitewashed, like many more that we shall see, and once two houses; but unlike most Dent Head is a large farm of 850 acres that carries a flock of 700 sheep.

The Dee, cascading down a rocky wooded ravine, is as yet no more than a mountain beck. At Deeside youth hostel, originally built as a shooting-lodge, the road and the river meet to run side by side for a mile or two. The bright stream crosses flat, water-worn pavements of limestone, trickles over ledges, disappears underground. From little bridges whose sides bristle with ferns we look down to deep brown pools or up to vistas of clear rippling waters between tree-lined banks.

Just below the hostel, at Studley Garth, a barn on the roadside was once a dame school; and a cottage called Scow was, during the railway-building era, a licensed house, the Wonder Inn. A little farther on at Arten Gill a green-walled track drops down from Widdale and Wensleydale to a wooded overgrown corner where a group of houses and ruined buildings marks the site of the marble works.

As old people will tell you, Stone House Marble Works were 'a gey busy shop i' them days.' They came to be established here from the use of two kinds of limestone quarried on the hills of Dent and Garsdale, black marble, as one is called, and a grey fossil limestone. Besides these, white and coloured Italian marbles

Dent Head

were imported. The works flourished throughout the period when marble was the fashion for monuments, chimney-pieces, and staircases, and they were linked with marble works at Carlisle through George Nelson and Paul Nixon, who were Cumberland men and well-known sculptors in their day. Paul Nixon (1765–1850) actually owned the works with a partner and lived at Stone House.

Of the two mills, the High and the Low, the High was built originally in the late eighteenth century as a carding and spinning mill, but it had changed to marble by 1812. It is remembered that saws in sand and water ground away at the marble night and day at the High Mill, and that the polishing was done at the Low Mill. Both had water-wheels; that at the High Mill in particular was remarkable for its size—60 feet in diameter. Dams and a system of underground culverts fed from three sources, one of them Widdale Great Tarn, supplied water. In dry times an old man walked up in the morning to turn the water on and went up again at night to turn it off.

A romantic story with profound consequences is connected with the marble works. In 1835 William George Armstrong, then aged 25, whilst on holiday fishing in the Dee, explored the elaborate arrangements for the use of water-power at the works, and this casual visitor to the dale was so deeply interested that he changed his career from solicitor to inventor of hydraulic machinery. Eventually he founded Armstrong's engineering works on Tyneside.

Stone House, the largest of the three houses at Arten Gill, has obviously been the owner's house. The firm of Nixon & Denton was followed by Blackmore & Co.; but the Blackmores lived at Broadfield House farther down the dale. These firms made fire-places, tombstones, fonts, staircases, marble-topped tables, and many small objects such as mortars, inkstands, and painters' palettes. They had connections with firms of monumental masons in London, and they employed some forty men, including thirteen skilled marble masons. The story is told of a workman delivering goods in London, where, as the people did not pay him, he found himself without money. He soaped his feet and walked home. In those days carts carrying marble along the dale road, and after the railway was built carting the fragile blocks to Dent station, were familiar sights.

Staircases at the Inns of Court, Owen's College, Manchester, and the Cartwright Memorial Hall at Bradford still display the beauty of Dent marble. Many marble chimney-pieces are to be found in the dale—the vicarage at Cowgill has five and Broadfield House has a pink one; and on the fire-places in station waiting-rooms on the Settle to Carlisle line you may study the patterns made by the fossil crinoid stems on the grey polished surfaces.

There are still in the dale at Stone House and Greenwell two chess tables skilfully made by William Baynes, the owners' great-grandfather. Alas, like the marble chimney-pieces they are no longer fashionable. Towards the end there were only eight or nine men employed, and finally, because of the removal of the import tariff on Italian marble, the works closed some fifty years ago. The two mills were pulled down about 1928, and the show-room near the roadside, where up to the last war little plaster casts and moulds could be seen in an upper storey, has fallen into ruin.

Hand in hand river and road course on down the valley. On the left we pass a friendly landmark, the Sportsman's Inn, kept during the early part of the nineteenth century by the Morland family, and later for many years by the Burtons.

One of the charms of Dent is its many gills: Arten Gill, Harbour Gill, Spice Gill, Hacker Gill, Scotchergill, Blackstone Gill, and Flintergill. Less than a mile below the marble works we see, across the river, Harbour Gill House, once the home of the Quaker family of Thistlethwaite, with 'WT 1700' on the porch. It suffered severe damage from a 'gill brack,' an engulfing mass of water and snow, caused by heavy rain and a rapid thaw in January 1752; and farther up the dale, when their house was submerged, seven people perished in the same terrifying storm.

A junction of roads and the little cluster of houses at Lea Yeat seem to call for a short halt. Cowgill Institute here was once a Friends' Meeting House, and a meeting for worship is still held once a year. At Lea Yeat, during the building of the railway, blacksmiths' shops, a saw-mill, and stores temporarily transformed the place. The row of houses called the Weaving Shops, once connected with the dale's main industry, was used for brewing; and on the north side of Cowgill church near by are many un-marked graves of the victims of the smallpox epidemic of the railway-building era.

From Lea Yeat an ancient road, called Galloway Gate, marked

on modern maps as 'coal road,' turns up the hillside to Dent station, whence it continues as a green track past Garsdale coalpits to Garsdale station.   A drovers' and a pack-horse route, it was the main road to Hawes up to about a hundred years ago.

The first half-mile of this road used notoriously to be a steep rough ascent to the station, until it was repaired and tarred in 1954. Dent station at 1,150 feet, the highest station in England, offers fine views of the valley with the summit of Whernside visible, and trains with plumes of white smoke frequently dashing across the hillside.   Above and alongside the line rows of sleepers, reared on end, give some protection from snow; and the platelayers' cabin contains a canteen of emergency stores for men working to keep the line clear in storms.

From Ewegales Bridge just below Lea Yeat two roads on either side of the river—the main one on the north bank—lead to Dent Town.   Here is a lovely river scene: the waterfalls of Hud's Foss, Ibbeth Peril, and of Hell's Cauldron, with its limestone gorge, beetling crag, and wide pool like black treacle.   When compared with the falls on greater rivers than the Dee they may not be spectacular, but they have a miniature grace that suits the landscape of Dent.

Every farmhouse that we pass has something of interest to tell. Seventy years ago, when Lamb Parrock was rebuilt, the family lived for several months at Scales Barn, which had once been a house, near by.   The beds occupied the booses,[1] and sledges with bedding over them were put up to keep lime from dropping on to them from the roof.   Except for flies they managed very well. Lower down, Dee Cottage, now a shop, is said to have been the dower house for Hud's House that is distinguished by a huge old chimney; and on the opposite side of the river near the cottage are the foundations of one of the old woollen mills, Dee Mill.

It is time to jump from 'the sunny side' to 'the money side' of Dent, and to look at Deepdale, 'Dibble' as it is pronounced. Little more than two miles long, it is tucked between the precipitous flanks of Whernside and Great Coum at right angles to the main dale.   We remember a view of it in the evening from the brow of Whernside: long tree shadows fell down the sloping fields, smoke curled up from whitewashed houses, and haymakers worked in an isolated meadow at the top where hills abruptly shut in the

---

[1] Stalls.

dalehead. The formerly rough road, now tarred, is still narrow, and mounts by hairpin bends to reach Kingsdale for Ingleton.

In former days the carding and spinning of wool in particular were undertaken in Deepdale. Elderly people remember as many as forty church-goers setting out from the dale to Dent Town on Sunday mornings; some of them to save a second journey carried their week's knitting to leave at a depot in the town. One farmer kept a donkey to carry sand from the tarns on Whernside, with which to sand floors. Some sixty years ago a firm from Newcastle ran a marble mill in Deepdale for a short time; and Binks Quarry on Great Coum was one of the sources for the fossil limestone.

Like Dent, Deepdale is remarkable for the number of farmhouses. But nowadays many of the 'lile spots,' such as Parkers, Blake Rigg, and White Acre, are untenanted. High up at the head at Garstack Beck a barn at a bend of the road marks the site of three houses, one occupied within living memory. Deepdale Head is now the last farm. Near it was Tongue End, a house that never had a kitchen range. The cooking was done in a frying-pan with a lid on; and as we were told, when the buns rose they burnt! Butterpots is a dignified farmhouse that derives its name from the limestone outcrops on its land. It is remembered that a Christopher Oversby of Butterspots, who was a mason, helped to build Dent Head Viaduct. Leaving his wife and children to run the farm, he set out each day to walk to work at three o'clock in the morning.

Back in the main dale the Roman road, the Craven Way, which we traced in Ribblesdale, drops down over Whernside to the foot of Deepdale. The bleak moorland track, although not easily discernible at this point, makes a fine walk, and contrasts sharply with the bosky sheltered lane on this the south side of Dent. Near by, where Deepdale Beck crosses the road, is Bridge End; and close to it once stood the Over Mill, or Deepdale Mill as it was called.

At West House, a little east of Bridge End, was born Miles Mason, a member of an ancient Dent family, who was the founder of the firm of Mason's Ironstone China. Recently the name of the house has been changed to Whernside Manor by Sir Albert Braithwaite, the new owner of it and several farms in Dent.

This Georgian house, larger than most in the dale, was built by the Sills, themselves an old yeoman family, who formerly lived at Deepdale Head and Rigg End. Some of the Sills early migrated to the West Indies, and owned plantations in Jamaica.   In 1758 Edmund Sill of Dent advertised 'a handsome reward for the return of a runaway negro man aged twenty,' and stories, still told, concern the slaves and a deep pool, Black Dub, in the beck below Rigg End.   Here they were supposed to have bathed; and one slave who fell in love with one of the daughters is said to have been drowned.   A memorial in Dent church records the tragic deaths in their thirties of Edmund Sill's three sons.

Half way between the manor and Dent Town is Greenwell, a charming whitewashed farmhouse that was once an inn.   Greenwell and its surroundings illustrate the many supplementary occupations of former times.   There were dye-vats in what is now the orchard, and a field, still called Tenter Garth, where cloth was stretched to dry.   On the roadside at one side of the farm are limekilns and at the other is a marble quarry, and down a lane to the river a railed-off mound marks the site of a small copper-mine worked seventy years ago.

In its lovely setting of fertile dale and lofty hill Dent Town looks to the discerning eye a place springing from industrial rather than agricultural growth.   From a distance the huddle of roofs and the squat church tower give no hint of the narrow cobbled main thoroughfare, its unique feature.   The wooden galleries that darkened the streets and formed the workshops of the town have all gone; only a house here and there is old; and in recent years some houses that hemmed in the street have been pulled down, thus opening it out: yet the village is still unusual and one of the sights to be seen without fail in the Yorkshire Dales.

Dent Town was once more important than Sedbergh.   Until 1863 it was the polling station for the district, and in the eighteenth century the Archdeacon's Consistory Court had an under-office here.   Records of the archdeaconry show that there were five hundred communicants at Dent church early in that century. The Methodist chapel was built on the site of a Quaker meeting-house in 1834.   The grammar-school, founded in 1604, was closed in 1897, and the old school building stands in the churchyard.

The market at Dent Town had dwindled by the 1830's, but elderly people remember it being held up to sixty or seventy years ago.   Many carts converged on the town, and farmers' wives laid out butter on tables covered with white cloths in a barn of the George and Dragon Hotel.   Promptly at half past twelve the bellman crying 'Draw up! Draw up!' toured the town. It is remembered that in lieu of a newspaper the bellman, standing on the mounting block of the George and Dragon, announced the week's events as the people came out of church.

Eighty years ago Dent Fair, held on the Saturday after Whitsuntide, as it still is, drew large crowds. People and horses thronged the street, and stalls lined it on both sides. The crush reminds us of Hartley Coleridge's picture of Dent Town, 'Where cart with cart in cumbrous conflict meets.' In later years there were swing-boats, hobby-horses (roundabouts), shooting-galleries, and donkeys for rides for the children. As soon as it was over people began talking about the next year's fair—'It was a Dent i' them days.'

Sports were started at the fair at the time of Queen Victoria's Diamond Jubilee, and the event, moved into a field, took on a different character. Nowadays horse trotting and foot-races attract people from far and wide to attend Dent sports.

To-day you will not see those ancient carts of the dales called tumbrils or tumble-carts. Their crude construction depended on pegs that held the body to the axle and wheels, which revolved together. This peculiarity serves to explain a Dent dialect word. If a peg broke the vehicle came apart; so before starting a journey you might be advised to 'take a peg anthers.' Anthers means 'in case of.' Similarly if it looked like rain, you would be told to 'take your sagathy [coat] anthers.'

Adam Sedgwick portrays delightfully some of the Dent tradesmen, the wig-maker, the cooper, the tailor. The cooper's trade, especially the making of small barrels for butter, was considerable. Rakes and butter boxes were made for sale and sent all over England some fifty years ago, and within recollection the dale supported four or five blacksmiths and six or seven bootmakers. At the present day Dent Town has two shoe shops, a smithy, a garage, builders' and a joiner's workshops, provision, drapery, ironmongery, and butchers' shops, and even an antique shop.

The most important development of this century has been the opening of the cheese dairy of Messrs J. Dinsdale & Sons. Started in 1926 at Dent Town when times were bad, it grew out of the Dinsdales' grocery business almost of necessity. Butter was fetching so little that the old system of the barter of produce for groceries was breaking down. In 1950 the dairy was moved to

Sedbergh where we shall continue the story in the next chapter. Suffice to say here that the economy of the dale pivots round it.

Personal stories vividly illustrate past hard times. We remember talking to a woman born in Dent. She was one of a family of fourteen, and had seven brothers older than herself, all of whom were hired as farm servants. She was hired at the age of twelve to work for a schoolmaster with many children at Burton-in-Lonsdale. 'I was only a child myself,' she said. She earned 3s. a week and stayed eighteen months with no holiday. When she returned home her parents were almost strangers to her.

Boys used to be hired at Kirkby Stephen, Kendal, and Long Preston. A Dent farmer told us of how when he was about fifteen he went to Kirkby Stephen Hirings. A prospective employer, looking him over, said he was 'lile and blue,' and inspected his hands for 'segs' (callouses) made by hard work. He then clinched the bargain by giving the boy 1s., his erles, as the money was called in Dent. A lad usually had only the clothes he stood up in, and one pair of boots that he rubbed with a little fat for Sunday wear. Once a servant was hired for six months at Mill Beck Farm near Gawthrop for a 'par o' fustian breeches.'

From Dent Town the walker may climb Whernside, Crag Hill, Gragareth, or Great Coum, or strike off in many directions: up Flintergill and on occupation roads to the County Stone where Yorkshire, Lancashire, and Westmorland meet, up Scotchergill to Garsdale, or between Helm's Knott and Frostrow Fells to the west of Rise Hill to Garsdale.

The hamlet of Gawthrop on the hillside at the foot of wild uninhabited Barbondale is said to be more ancient than Dent. Old houses and cottages are spread round a little green or straggle near a gill. The green once formed the dam of Gawthrop corn mill, which was pulled down some sixty-five years ago. On this side of the dale a by-road, narrow but negotiable, leads towards Sedbergh.

At this end of the dale the precipice of Combe Scar stands out as a prominent landmark. If you climb up to it you reach a great hollow of meadow land backed by the lofty semicircular wall of blue-black rock, the blue rag as the Silurian Rock is here called. It is not difficult to picture violent events; and the foot of the scar is said to be haunted. Rowan-trees and aspen find root-hold on its sheer face, and a clump of hollies grows near its foot. A bull and herd of cows grazing there look like James Ward's picture of the white bull at Gordale Scar, perfect miniatures of animals against an impressive background.

A pair of peregrine falcons regularly nest on Combe Scar, and ravens are not rare. Amongst the vermin whose destruction was paid for by the churchwardens of Dent the ravens fetched only 2*d*., as against 4*s*. for foxes. A story is told of the great-grand-father of the present owner of Tofts Farm near by. He used to sit out in a hiding-place to shoot ravens with an old muzzle-loader. Once the birds pulled the roof off. 'Couldn't you shoot 'em?' people asked. 'Nut sae weeal,' the farmer replied. 'T'gun doesn't load seea fast.'

Near to the scar is the farmhouse called Combes with a copse and one or two old damson-trees growing beside it. Unoccupied now for over twenty years, it was once the glebe for the parson of Seathwaite in Cumberland. Many more people used to live up here. Tofts Farm, with two porches, was two dwellings. Both it and Combes have beef-lofts, where salt beef was placed to dry for the winter's supply of food.

The most important of the farmhouses of Dent are High and Low Halls and Bickerside Farm on the north side of the valley, approached by the partially cobbled lane (marked 'Floods') that runs alongside the river between Kirk Bridge and Barth Bridge. Bickerside has three of the massive round chimneys similar to ones that often ornament Westmorland rather than Yorkshire farmhouses. Low Hall has lost all its original features in altera-tions. High Hall preserves two of the round chimneys, and a huge arched fire-place in an outbuilding at the back. Standing in a commanding position reached by a bridge over a deep gorge, it was originally the chief house in the dale. 'WTI 1626' and 'RTD 1665' can just be deciphered on a weathered stone on the house front. Here lived Richard Trotter, whom the last set of initials represents, and who led the statesmen in the negotiations with the Crown for the sale of Dent in the seventeenth century.

When little traffic passes on a late autumn or a winter's day, Barth Bridge below Gawthrop on the main road out of the dale is a place to linger. The Dee flows smoothly on its way to join the Rawthey near Sedbergh four miles away. Perhaps one of the flat meadows is black with fieldfares, or quarrelsome magpies flutter amongst the trees of a gill. Lonely lanes enclosed by tall hedges lead off to farms. Whernside and Combe Scar seem very near across the

Barth Bridge

valley. Salmon come up the river as far as this point; and the ruin by the roadside was once a smithy where the gates of Dent church were made.

As we start down the dale, at first we still see many farmhouses. Up the lane from the bridge is Barth Farm, for generations the home of the Craggs, who possess what are now rare, the furnishings of older times, three court cupboards with the initials of the family on two of them. Lower down Cragg Farm, once owned by the Sedgwicks, has a fine oak balustrade and staircase; and at Burton Hill it is told that during a Scots raid a prized black mare was hidden in a stall cut out of the hay mew. But unfortunately the mare, hearing other horses in the yard, whinnied and gave her hiding-place away.

The valley narrows. Colourful plantations clothe the slopes of Holme Fell, down which pours Bracken Gill waterfall. We pass Gate, a long, low, Victorian-Tudor house with many windows, built on to an older house by Robert Burra in the last century. In the woods on the opposite side of the river is Rash Mill. First a corn mill, then a carding and spinning mill, now a joiner's shop, it represents the story of Dent.

SEDBERGH
AND HOWGILL

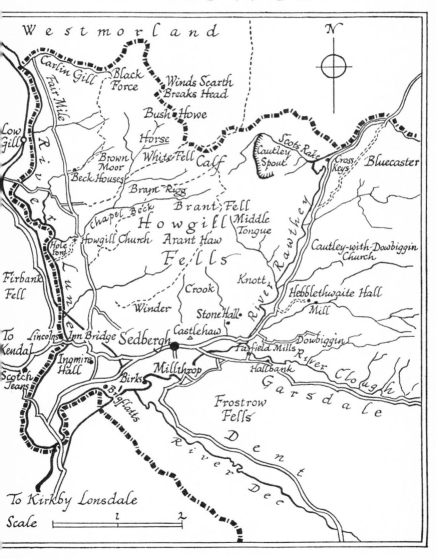

Westmorland

N

Carlin Gill
Fair Mile
Black Force
Winds Scarth Breaks Head
Bush Howe
Low Gill
River
Horse
Scots Rake
Cautley Spout
Cross Keys
Bluecaster
Brown Moor
White Fell
Calf
Beck Houses
Brant Rigg
Chapel Beck
Brant Fell
Howgill
Middle Tongue
River Rawthey
Howgill Church
Arant Haw
Cautley-with-Dowbiggin Church
Firbank Fell
Fells
Knott
Hebblethwaite Hall
Crook
Mill
Winder
Stone Hall
Castlehaw
To Kendal
Lincolns Inn Bridge
Sedbergh
Fairfield Mills
Dowbiggin
River Clough
Ingmire Hall
Millthrop
Hallbank
Scotch Jean
Birks
Garsdale
Briggflatts
Frostrow Fells
Dent
River Dee
To Kirkby Lonsdale
Scale   1   2

VIII

SEDBERGH AND HOWGILL

IN THE north-west corner of the West Riding of Yorkshire, in the remote border country that marches with Westmorland, is the bunched mass of hills known as the Howgill Fells; and at their feet lies the small market town of Sedbergh, eleven miles from Kendal, and between ten and fifteen miles from Kirkby Lonsdale, Kirkby Stephen, and Hawes in Wensleydale.

Leaving Yorkshire for a moment, climb out at the side of the Howgills up the road to Kendal and look back to the tremendous panorama that unfolds. Sedbergh is not easy to find in the vast green bowl of billowing meadow and pasture land, scored with hedgerows and groves of trees. On all sides hills and dales radiate into the distance. On a sunny evening in early summer, when the scene glows a warm green and the distant dale heads merge into an opalescent horizon, it looks idyllic, a land of peace and plenty.

The country we see before us is contained almost wholly in the ancient parish of Sedbergh, an area of 52,665 acres, one of the large moorland parishes of the Pennines, out of which have been carved the four parishes of Dent, Garsdale, Howgill, and Cautley, the valleys in fact that we see. Dent and Garsdale are separated by Rise Hill, and Howgill and Cautley by the Howgill Fells. Down them flow the Dee, the Clough, the infant Lune, and the Rawthey, which all meet in the neighbourhood of Sedbergh, and as the River Lune make 'their final escape,' as Adam Sedgwick put it, into Lancashire.

Geologically this wedge of country, only annexed to Yorkshire, as we have seen in the first chapter, in the twelfth century, is alien to the dales. Instead of the familiar limestone and millstone grit that are left behind where the Dent Fault crosses the end of that dale and Garsdale, we now have the Silurian Rocks of the Lake District.

The 'naked heights' of the Howgills, as Wordsworth called

them, are composed of this slaty rock, and dome-shaped they rise up one after another covered with herbage, smooth and plushy like giant seals: Winder, Crook, Knott, Arant Haw, Brant Fell, the Calf (the highest, 2,220 feet above sea level), and many others.

Leaving our view-point, we descend the hill to Scotch Jeans, once a public-house, distinguished by the black horse on the front, the crest of a local family, the Uptons. We cross Lincoln's Inn Bridge, so called after a person of that name who kept an inn near by; pass Ingmire Hall, once the home of the Otways and the Uptons, but partially destroyed by fire and the remnant turned into flats; and approach Sedbergh.

Situated at a crossing of ancient routes from Kendal to York and from Lancaster to Newcastle, the town spreads over the lower slopes of Winder. In 1818 Benjamin Newton, diarist and parson of Wath, near Ripon, writes of Sedbergh as 'the narrowest town I ever saw, the street in no place exceeding 8 to 10 feet except for about 20 yards opposite the shambles,' a description that still partially holds good.

If it is Wednesday the market will be in progress. Over a hundred years ago this had almost vanished, and now it consists only of the van of a nurseryman from Appleby. Yet the town is busy with farmers on their way to the auction mart and their wives come to shop. For a small town of 2,330 inhabitants there are many shops. People pass and repass on the narrow pavements, amongst them a schoolmaster in flying gown and schoolboys in navy blue shorts and white sweaters. In fact, Sedbergh would be a vastly different place but for the large and progressive public school, whose buildings and playing-fields dominate the town and its outskirts.

The name Sedbergh derives from the Old Norse *setberg*, meaning a flat-topped hill, and this and many other names such as Branthwaite, Settlebeck, Dowbiggin, and Bland speak of the over-whelming Norse settlement of the district.

Long before the Norsemen arrived the Romans brought their road down Dent; and carried another up Howgill to Borrow Bridge. But there is no evidence to connect with the Romans the fortified mount, Castlehaw Tower, one of the small lower spurs of the Howgills near Sedbergh. This awaits full-scale excavation; it is worth climbing to the top if only to see the view.

At the time of the Domesday survey Sedbergh was an isolated

Sedbergh

village in the Manor of Whittington, and in medieval times the Staveleys were lords of Sedbergh. They obtained a charter for a market and fairs for the town in 1251, and they gave pastures in Garsdale and half Sedbergh Mill to Easby Abbey. Coverham Abbey held the advowson of the church, which after the Dissolution was given to Trinity College, Cambridge.

The important date in the story of the town is 1525. In that year Roger Lupton, a native of the parish, canon of Windsor and provost of Eton, founded a chantry school, and endowed it with scholarships and fellowships at St John's College, Cambridge. He primarily established the school for his own kinsmen and for 'theym of Sedber, Dent, and Garstall,' places described as without elegance or culture. Masters were to be appointed by St John's College, and, at the time of the suppression of the chantries, it was owing to the intervention of the college that the school was refounded in 1551.

In company with other ancient grammar-schools, Sedbergh experienced varied fortunes: quarrels broke out between the governors and the fellows of the college; and masters either failed in their duties, or brought fame to the school. After the long and successful mastership of Posthumous Wharton a new school was built in 1716. This, on the Dent road, is now a library and museum. In the 1860's the numbers of scholars had so diminished that a new constitution was drafted; and in the following years the school grew under progressive headmasters, and the buildings we see to-day were erected.

The school, and especially the foundation scholarships and later endowments, without which the old grammar-schools made little mark, nurtured a long cultural influence. Several local men, not counting the many other famous old scholars, rose to fame, and their names and achievements are to be found in the *Dictionary of National Biography*.[1] Some were Quakers in a district with a strong Nonconformist tradition and where people came under the direct influence of George Fox.

The meeting-house at Brigflatts, built only a few years after

---

[1] John Bland, *d.* 1555, Marian martyr; John Duckett, 1613–44, Catholic priest; Francis Howgill, 1618–69, Quaker; Samuel Bownas, 1676–1753, Quaker; Anthony Fothergill, 1732?–1813, physician; John Dawson, 1734–1820, mathematician; John Haygarth, 1740–1827, physician; Edward Tatham, 1749–1834, scholar; Robert Willan, 1757–1812, physician; James Inman, 1776–1859, writer on nautical science; Adam Sedgwick, 1785–1873, geologist.

Fox's second visit to the district, is a mile west of Sedbergh down a lane off the Kirkby Lonsdale road. The little whitewashed building is one of the oldest meeting-houses in use in England, and in the garden is a piece of the town's market cross broken down by the mob when the Quaker, William Dewsbury, preached at it. This corner offers to the wayfarer a few moments of quiet, either in the secluded garden or in the interior, with its white walls, oak forms, and little balcony.

In 1761 a turnpike Act led to the improvement of all the roads that converged on Sedbergh, and in the coaching era two coaches, the 'Lord Exmouth' and the 'Old Lord Exmouth,' plied from Lancaster to Newcastle (the former twenty-five miles away and the latter seventy-seven); and in the 1840's a coach ran through Wensleydale, Garsdale, and Sedbergh, to Kendal for passengers to the Lake District. These were the days of early morning starts, especially for the carriers' carts, of which many went to Kendal and met on Waterside, as indeed their modern counterparts still do.

Along these roads the cotton trade spread into a countryside already partially industrialized by the knitting industry centred at Kendal; and cotton mills, whose buildings remain to this day, were built at Birks, Millthrop, and Howgill. Here, too, following the invention of machinery, woollen mills, driven by water-power, were built at Hebblethwaite Hall in 1792 and at Farfield, which replaced Hebblethwaite, in 1837. What a tale of enterprise these two mills have to tell! The story of the mills, the Dovers who ran them, and the craftsmen and women, the knitters, is told in our book, *The Old Hand-Knitters of the Dales*.

Benjamin Newton gives a picture of industrial Sedbergh in the early nineteenth century: 'In this place all the boys and girls are knitters employed in knitting not stockings but blue woollen caps of yarn which make all the children look as if they came out of a dyeing factory.' He adds: 'A good knitter knits 12 caps per diem which on examining must be worn by convicts and prisoners, they are knit very loose on wooden pins.' (He did not realize that the caps were milled after being knitted.) At that time the houses in the yards behind the main street were crammed with people who lived in upper storeys with wooden balconies, sometimes called spinning galleries, and who left the lower floor for use as store-rooms and stables. Weaver's Yard commemorates by its name the occupation pursued there, and Railton's Yard has one of the old spinning galleries.

As elsewhere the cotton mills soon failed and became bobbin- and later, saw-mills.   At the present day, Birks Mill, which stands on a fine site above the Rawthey, is an egg-packing station, where over 80,000 eggs are dealt with each week, and Millthrop Mill, run by a West Riding manufacturer, is the only one that by spinning carpet yarn keeps up the traditional connection with wool.

Farfield Mills, sold by the Dovers in 1937, were used by Arm- strong Siddeleys during the last war, and after various changes the dairy of James Dinsdale & Sons, moved from Dent, opened here on 1st January 1950 for the manufacture of Wensleydale cheese.   Originally beginning in a small way with 50 gallons of milk, the dairy deals with some 3,000 gallons daily; and in 1953 over 6,000 cwt. of cheese was made from milk largely collected from the farms of Dent and Garsdale.   So instead of the rattle of carding engines and spinning-jennies there is either the clatter of milk kits or the silence of airy upper rooms with their tiers of shelves filled with cheeses.

We talked with Miss M. E. Sedgwick and Mr Christopher Askew, both elderly Sedbergh people, who described to us old times.   A hundred years ago on fair days the street was packed from end to end with stalls, while hobby-horses and shooting- galleries filled the market square.   Boys started to work at Far- field at the age of nine, and beginning at 6 a.m. finished at 7.30 p.m.   In those days the general wear of the women was bedgowns, a kind of short cotton coat.

They spoke of the poverty within their own recollection: shoe- makers sold good hand-sewn boots at 18s. 6d., and worked long hours to make a living; and people walked to Kendal, where they could sell their butter for 1d. a pound more than at home.   One of the chief recreations of the men was to drink themselves into a stupor.

In the main street some of the threads of Sedbergh's story may be picked out.   The large Georgian house at the west end is one of the school houses, Evans House, built by James Wadeson and named after one of the most famous nineteenth-century masters, who lived there.   Another house, Brackensgill, is the bursar's house, and was the town house of the Burras of Gate in Dent.

Similarly the chemist's shop with the massive chimney backing into Weaver's Yard was the town house of the Uptons. At the east end, Thorns Hall is an early seventeenth-century house occupied by Posthumous Wharton and enlarged for his boarders.

If it is December you will see a lifelike clockwork monkey eating an apple in a shop window, a signal of the approach of Christmas for Sedbergh children and grown-ups for over fifty years. At any time a familiar sight is a bus almost elbowing its way through the street; for the cross-country routes are still used: motor-coaches run either way once a day from Newcastle to Blackpool, and many more pass through at the time of the west coast illuminations.

In this stock-rearing countryside farming life centres round the auction mart. Started by Richard Harper in 1903, the mart has been run by three generations of the family, and was moved to new premises in 1951. Each year 20,000 sheep, Dalesbred, Swaledale, and Rough Fell, and over 2,200 dairy and store cattle are sold, and important sales for the pedigree Northern Dairy Shorthorns are held in the autumn. Nor is romance absent; for nowadays the girls often bring stock to the mart, and meet their future husbands.

Recently a farmer showing a poor heifer in the ring boasted of the beast's parentage. 'Nay,' said the auctioneer. 'Thoo had a good muther, but luke at thee, thoo's naywher near her standards, neither is thy heifer.'

During the hundred and fifty years up to the last war, the population of Sedbergh increased, and after the arrival of the railway in 1861 many houses were built in a style borrowed from the Lake District. Since the war, in spite of a decline in population, 100 council houses have been erected to rehouse the dwellers in the yards and in wartime huts. Many people work in Kendal, and others find employment in Liverpool for part of their lives. We met an old farmer who had gone there as a young man to run a milk-house. 'Ivvery year when spring came round and t'sun shone,' he said, 'I allus heerd t'blayting o' sheep and lambs; only i' my mind yer knaw, I cud hear 'em blayting.'

In this well-wooded vale of hedgerows rather than stone walls some farmers make their own lamb sticks from suitable hazel or ash branches. At Sedbergh two men have brought this little craft to a pitch of perfection, and they compete in classes for sticks at northern shows. A branch with a thick piece of root attached is the raw material, the root forming the handle. The shaft, whose merit is straightness, remains brown with the bark left on, and the handle is shaped and polished to reveal the light colour of the wood in attractive contrast.

The hills of Sedbergh, the Howgills, seem lone outriders between the rolling Yorkshire hills and the rocky mountain peaks of the Lake District. From the summits are to be seen extensive views—from Helvellyn to Ingleborough, from Morecambe Bay to Cross Fell. White bent with some bracken, rush, and heather clothes them; becks in deep slacks cleave one from another, and sheep trods, like ripples on sand, furrow the precipitous slopes.

On them we find the Rough Fell sheep, which thrive on the herbage and the dry hillsides, and whose short legs and long coats make them better adapted to the terrain than other breeds. 'We think them bonny,' said one farmer to us; and in fact they are bonny sheep with their black mottled faces and long thick wool.

At the foot of the western slopes of the hills, Howgill is worth seeking out along twisting roads between high banks. A narrow lane, only suited to local traffic, either ends so far as the motorist is concerned, or branches to cross Crook of Lune Bridge into Westmorland; and through this sequestered vale is to run a great modern trunk-road, which is planned to pass up the west side of England.

In two miles from Sedbergh the lane crosses Chapel Beck, near which cluster the little church, the school, the derelict mill, the mill manager's house, and a few cottages—a charming rural corner. Amongst the mill buildings is a stable used when this was a baiting place for the pack-horse trains on the route from Kendal to Kirkby Stephen. The route, having crossed Hole Ford on the Lune and passed the mill and the church, followed Chapel Beck up White Fell over the Calf to Ravenstonedale and Kirkby Stephen.

Near the source of Chapel Beck on Bush Howe the track passes one of those large figures of horses cut out on some of the hills of England. In this case the animal is misshapen through neglect; but a lively horse, probably eighteenth century in date, made up of stones on bare ground, shows up as a dark patch on the green hillside. It is well seen from Firbank on the opposite side of the valley.

A little farther up the dale Beck Houses, a solitary farmhouse,

The great chasm of Cautley

marks the site of three farmhouses and a cottage, of which one was the last straw-thatched house in Howgill. In it lived Tommy and Betty Shepherd, who eked out a living, the one by doing odd jobs, and the other by keeping a little school. Bet also sold the goose-berries from her garden, and sometimes, with heavy baskets of berries slung over each arm, journeyed twice a day to Sedbergh.

Other characters were the Sedgwicks, of whom Bill, who lived to be over ninety and died in 1941, could boast that his father, Thomas Sedgwick, who married rather late in life, was born in the eighteenth century. Old Thomas used to go to bed early, and round him collected the boys of the neighbourhood to listen to his tales of Scots raids and stirring events in the past.

When we were in the Howgill valley in late spring, the lambs were being marked preparatory to being driven on to the fells, and the cries of sheep and lambs, 'mothering up' after being separated, sounded from the crofts and folds by the lonely farm-steads. Formerly on these holdings the farmer would take the plough round the farm, whereas now only one or two ploughed fields are to be seen.

On the other side of the Howgills, Cautley might be just such a remote valley as this, but instead a main road busy with traffic, the turnpike from Sedbergh to Kirkby Stephen on the route from Blackpool to Newcastle, passes through it. Few trunk-roads in

England have a finer setting than this at Cautley. The Rawthey, that resembles a Scottish burn, splashes over mossy rocks in a deep channel below the road. Across it the hills soar towards the sky, and every now and again part to reveal a vista of a secret dale. They loom out dramatically, especially in the evening, as shafts of light tilt across their shadowed sides.

Here is the small church of Cautley-with-Dowbiggin, and off the road up narrow winding lanes are remote farmhouses such as Stone Hall with large round chimneys, and Hebblethwaite Hall, once a seat of industry with the mill deep in the gill near by. At Hollin Hill, next to Stone Hall, we sat for a while in the farm kitchen and talked to the stalwart old farmer, by name Woof. 'Ay,' he said, 'there's a deal o' Woofs i' Cautley, all part akin.'

Five miles from Sedbergh on the roadside appears the white-washed building of the Cross Keys Hotel, and beyond it a view of the great chasm of Cautley with the Spout pouring down black rock. On the north side of the chasm a green track along the fellside is called Scots' Rake, and along it part of the army of the Pretender is said to have retreated in the '45 Rebellion.

A mile beyond the hotel, Rawthey Bridge spans a wide and deep ravine; in 1584 the breaking down of the bridge caused hardship to travellers, and in 1822 it was again rebuilt for the stage-coach traffic. Before the latter date a circle of stones, probably a Bronze Age monument, stood alongside it, and on each side of the bridge is to be seen a carved head that may well be medieval. Here, where the Rawthey turns eastwards towards its source on Baugh Fell, Yorkshire ends and Westmorland begins.

GARSDALE

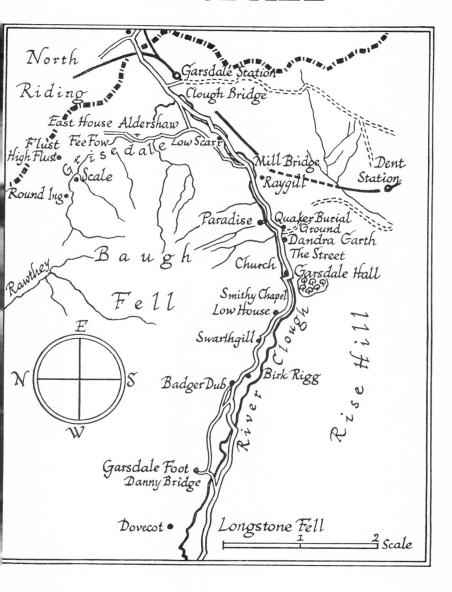

North
Riding

Garsdale Station
Clough Bridge

East House Aldershaw
Flust Fee Fow Low Scarr
High Flust
Scale
Round Ing

Mill Bridge
Raygill

Dent Station

Paradise Quaker Burial Ground
Dandra Garth
The Street
Church Garsdale Hall

Baugh

Smithy Chapel
Low House

Fell

Swarthgill

Badger Dub Birk Rigg

Garsdale Foot
Danny Bridge

Dovecot Longstone Fell

Rise Hill

River Clough

Rawthey

2 Scale
1

IX

GARSDALE

LASTLY, of the dales that radiate from Sedbergh, Garsdale strikes off eastwards from the town. Cautley and Garsdale are in fact separated by the great bulk of Baugh Fell, one of the highest and least known of the Yorkshire hills; and Garsdale's river, the Clough, rises on the fell close to the Rawthey, but flows in an opposite direction. The two rivers actually encircle Baugh Fell.

We reach Garsdale from Sedbergh over Longstone Fell. Harrison's *Description of Britain* describes it as 'an uplandish towne, wherein are seene manie times great store of red deere that come down to feed from the mountains into the vallies.' In those Elizabethan times Garsdale, with its long slopes of forest land, must have been a wild remote place. Earlier Easby and Coverham Abbeys had pasturage in it for large herds of cows and a stud of horses. But through it at the present day runs a road that is part of a romantic long-distance if not main route for travellers from the Plain of York to the Lake District.

Formerly, before the road was improved as a turnpike, it ran from Longstone Fell steeply down to Danny Bridge, and continued for a mile or two on the opposite side of the valley from the modern road. Farther up the dale, the straight stretch from Mill Bridge to Clough Bridge was made in 1825, and there again the narrow old road can still be followed on the other side of the river. Badger Dub Cottage was a gate-keeper's house at a toll-bar on the turnpike.

Near Danny Bridge over the Clough may be seen a section of the Dent Fault, along which the Great Scar Limestone is thrown against the Silurian Rocks. Below the bridge in Dovecote Gill on the line of the fault, the limestone ravine ends in a cave through which it is possible to scramble and emerge at the other end.

We remember once visiting Garsdale on a brilliantly fine day in early August, a hay day in a wet summer. The hillsides were alive with people. Groups of men, women, and children armed with wooden rakes strewed and turned the hay, rhythmically raking backwards and forwards across the steep meadows. The whole dale was astir with feverish activity.

In the eighteenth and early nineteenth centuries the same pattern of life was observed in Garsdale as in Dent. Many small farmhouses dot the slopes of the hills, and where the land of some has been thrown together to make one farm, houses have fallen into ruin. People made a living on these small holdings by working at secondary occupations such as knitting, quarrying, and coal-mining.

Most of the houses in Garsdale are old. East Rackenthwaite has a massive chimney buttress and marks the site of a grange of Coverham Abbey. Dandra Garth, a three-storeyed house in what was originally a cobbled yard, now a garden and surrounded by a high wall, stands as a kind of monument to the statesmen of Garsdale. In what was the parlour is a plaster panel depicting a lion rampant and with rose and pineapple motifs. Birk Rigg figured in proceedings in Star Chamber in 1610. On the death of its owner, Elizabeth Nelson, a widow, several Wensleydale men kidnapped her child aged nine 'against her will and likinge,' and took possession of the house by armed force. Whitewashed Low Scarr, at the roadside near the head of the dale, looks like a bit of rural Westmorland strayed into Yorkshire.

Other houses are linked with some of the famous people already mentioned at Sedbergh, of whom Garsdale claims a large share. At Garsdale Foot was born James Inman, who devoted a distinguished life to navigation and naval matters. The Inmans were also connected with Low House, a charming old building, which still contains an oak court cupboard carved with their initials. John Haygarth, who inaugurated the isolation of infectious fevers in hospitals, was born at Swarthgill; and at Raygill was born John Dawson, who by dint of his own endeavour and ability acquired remarkable mathematical knowledge and taught many brilliant students from Cambridge University, who stayed at Sedbergh with him during vacations.

Every now and again the road crosses bridges, and others lead across the river to farms or barns: Garsdale might be called a dale of bridges. Those with iron railings instead of stone parapets were built after a cloud-burst struck the dale on 8th August 1889.

Low House, Garsdale

It is remembered that the men rushed out with nets to catch the fish in the water sweeping down the road.

In the days when the dale was an isolated community with few connections outside, it used to be a custom that if a 'foreigner' came to court a Garsdale girl the men drummed on a tin can until the man paid a fine.

In the centre of the dale the houses draw together into a small community. Although the church was rebuilt in 1861, as long ago as the thirteenth century the canons of Easby Abbey maintained a chaplain at St John the Baptist's Church in Garsdale in return for pasturage. The school was founded in 1634 by Thomas Dawson, and over a hundred years ago the whitewashed farmhouse, Garsdale Hall, at a sharp bend of the road was an inn. At this corner, seen unexpectedly on clear days as if through a magic key-hole, is a view of Bowfell, Scafell, and Scafell Pike, over thirty miles away.

George Fox stayed in Garsdale on his way northwards. A little east of Dandra Garth a croft enclosed by a high wall is a Quaker burial-ground, but all signs of the meeting-house that stood a little farther up the road have gone.

In the last century Methodism secured a firm hold in the dale, largely owing to the ministry of Jonathan Kershaw who came from Lancaster. He took the lead in the building of Smithy Chapel in 1830, and lived in a cottage adjoining until his death in 1846. Between Grisedale and Sedbergh there are six small Methodist chapels, all in use; and here the old-fashioned camp meetings and love feasts are kept up.

The Clough, as Grisedale Beck, runs from its source through the small upland valley of Grisedale, slung between Baugh Fell and Swarth Fell. The few scattered farmhouses, set in a chequer-board of small meadows, have lovely names such as Nettle Brow, Flust, Fee Fow, and Aldershaw; and their occupants, easily cut off by snowstorms from the main valley, stock up well with necessities before winter begins. Recently farmers from the Sedbergh neighbourhood have bought up some of the holdings, and houses are left unoccupied.

Grisedale means 'pig valley,' from the Old Norse *gris*, a pig. In the Middle Ages Jervaulx Abbey owned the larger part of the valley, and Easby the rest; and in 1225 disputes became so frequent that the abbots and convents met together and came to a decision as to how the pasturage should be apportioned. Scale, a little group of buildings by the beck at the head of the dale, has obviously been the site of one of the monastic lodges.

Back in the main dale Garsdale station, a row of railway cottages, and even a little post office and shop give more life to the dale head than is usual. Here we may continue on the turnpike to cross over the watershed at about 1,100 feet to Wensleydale and the North Riding; or for the walker an old drove and coal road to Dent offers a high-level route with fine views, and Iron Age village sites to be seen on the left-hand side.

The railway is again the Settle to Carlisle line that has emerged through Rise Hill Tunnel from Dent, and the station, once known as Hawes Junction, is in fact still a junction where a local line branches off to Hawes. Here passengers for Wensleydale dismount, and woe betide the traveller who in the dark mistakes his station. We know two cases of people, bound for Wensleydale, who dismounted at Dent instead of Garsdale, and while the two stations are only three miles apart, a large mass of the Pennines lies between Dent and Wensleydale by road, only overcome by a circuitous and expensive taxi ride. An even better true story relates how a very tired Wensleydale man, returning home for Christmas, fell asleep on the train, and awoke to find himself beyond Garsdale at Appleby. He boarded a south-bound train and woke up at Settle, and boarding another found himself at Carlisle. He had passed Garsdale three times.

The station has its special features and links with life around it. It has its own water supply obtained from springs on the fell and purified by a plant in one of the buildings, and in a waiting-room a library once given by two sisters stranded there. Three-quarters of a mile away down the line are the troughs, the highest in the world, we were told, where engines take in water without stopping, and which in this bleak place freeze and coat the rails with ice in winter.

Underneath the enormous water-supply tank at the station is the Tank Room, once an engine repair shop, but now Garsdale Welfare Institute where anything may take place from a concert to a christening. It chanced to be a moonlit evening when the station-master took us to see the long lofty room warmed by a big stove, lighted by oil lamps, and decorated with gay paper streamers. It is a wild, lonely place where people forgather to enjoy a social evening. Outside a train, its smoke lit up by flames, rushed past; an owl quartered the moor for prey, and all around the fells merged into the dark of night.

X

WENSLEYDALE

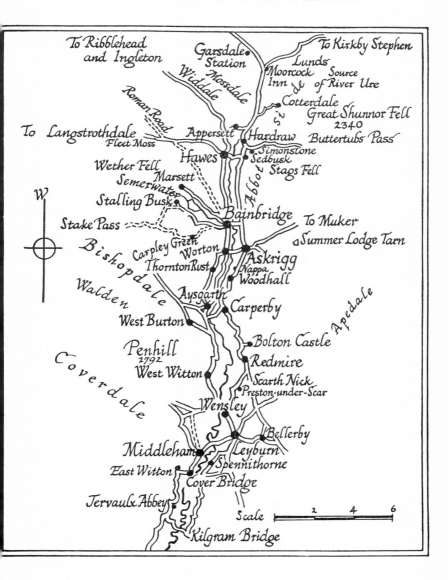

To Ribblehead and Ingleton
Garsdale Station
To Kirkby Stephen
Lunds
Moorcock Inn
Source of River Ure
Widdale
Mossdale
Cotterdale
Roman Road
Great Shunnor Fell 2340
Fleet Moss
To Langstrothdale
Appersett
Hardraw
Buttertubs Pass
Wether Fell
Hawes
Simonstone
Sedbusk
Marsett
Stags Fell
Semerwater
Stalling Busk
Bainbridge
To Muker
Stake Pass
Summer Lodge Tarn
Bishopdale
Carpley Green
Worton
Askrigg
Thornton Rust
Nappa
Woodhall
Walden
Aysgarth
Carperby
Apedale
West Burton
Bolton Castle
Penhill 1792
Redmire
West Witton
Scarth Nick
Preston-under-Scar
Coverdale
Wensley
Bellerby
Middleham
Leyburn
East Witton
Spennithorne
Cover Bridge
Jervaulx Abbey
Scale
2 4 6
Kilgram Bridge

W

1. WENSLEYDALE:
PAST AND PRESENT

'WENSLEYDALE in Yorkshire is one of England's green valleys,' wrote Ella Pontefract. 'Many of the dales which intersect these moors are very fertile, of which Wensley Dale may be ranked the foremost, both for extent and fertility,' said Tuke in *General View of the Agriculture of the North Riding of Yorkshire*. 'Wensleydale is generally esteemed one of the most beautiful spots in the world,' wrote Dr Pococke.

Look for a moment at some of the views in Wensleydale: near views such as those at Aysgarth Lower Falls and Hardraw Scar; but above all distant views: the woods round Bolton Hall flaming with colour in the autumn; the view with Lady Hill in the middle distance looking westwards from Aysgarth; the vista from the summit of the Buttertubs Pass to where away beyond the confines of Wensleydale Ingleborough, seemingly chiselled out of the sky itself, raises its head; the sudden view from Widdale Foot of the spacious valley unfolding below Hawes, which looks like a vision of a promised land; or the view above all views from Scarth Nick, with the great bulk of Penhill rising up terrace after terrace to the flat top, the long corridor of Bishopdale, and the wooded vale curving between Nab End and Addlebrough towards the head.

From its source on Lunds Fell the River Ure flows down Wensleydale some twenty-five miles before it leaves the hills at East Witton; ever widening it curls along between emerald meadows that fan out and, gently rising, give place to rolling pasture land beyond which stretch the fells; and overlooking the valley like guardian outposts placed at strategic points, isolated hills with flat weathered tops give it individual character.

Beyond the gaps in the sentinel hills lie many hidden side valleys, branching off mostly on the south side of the dale— Coverdale, Walden, Bishopdale, Semerdale, Widdale, Mossdale, Cotterdale, and many other smaller dales. Wensleydale is a family of dales, which like members of a family exhibit different

179

characteristics; and some, independent members, which we shall describe in later chapters, are large enough to have a life of their own.

At the end of the Ice Age many of these side valleys held great lakes, of which that in Coverdale, over six miles long and two miles wide, was the largest, and of which Semerwater, covering about ninety acres, is the sole survivor; and that lakes once filled the main valley near Hawes and Aysgarth is plainly to be seen from the presence of acres of flat fields.

What we call the Ice Age is of particular interest in Wensleydale. Although the dale itself and the hills, if with sharper contours, were there before that era, glacial debris shaped the face of the dale as we see it.

As the Wensleydale glacier rapidly retreated towards the Plain of York, it left behind vast trails of debris, of which boulder clay covers the hills up to 1,200 and 1,600 feet above sea level, and moraines and drumlins (large oval mounds) cumber up the valley floor.   In the twelve miles of dale above Aysgarth may be counted over eighty large drumlins: Lady Hill is one, and the Romans chose another as a strategic site for their fort at Bainbridge.

Formerly the dale was called Yoredale, as witness early monastic charters, but 'Wensleydale' was already in use in the mid twelfth century.   Leland wrote: 'There is no vall, as I here, in Richmontshir that is caullid Uresdale, but the dale that Ure first rennith [to] is caullid Wensedale . . . Wensedale, as some say, taketh name of Wensela Market.'   The dale, as is well known, takes its name from what is now a small village, but was once a market town.

Although the western boundary at Hell Gill, adjoining Westmorland, is well defined, the eastern boundary was and still is a matter of choice.   In Leland's time Wensley Bridge appears to have been reckoned as the boundary; he wrote of Wensley that 'straite on the farther side beginnith Wensedale.'   Cary's road book of 1791 says that the dale starts at Cover Bridge, and other writers give the ruling as Kilgram Bridge below Jervaulx, a choice that embraces all the hill country.

Wensleydale in past centuries was never easy of access.   When in 1751 plans were under way for the making of the Richmond to Lancaster turnpike road, which passed through the dale, it was said that Wensleydale had never before possessed a road worthy of the name. Many roads that may well be Roman meet and cross at the fort at Bainbridge: one of these, approaching from Richmond, coming down Scarth Nick for Bainbridge, and leaving over Wether Fell, is shown on the fourteenth-century Gough Map, which marks a route from Richmond past Bolton Castle to Kirkby Lonsdale; the same route was roughly followed by the turnpike.

The most difficult angle of approach in former times was from the south-east. Between Leyburn and Middleham we have to picture the scene without Middleham Bridge, which now carries the traffic from Ripon and the West Riding. This iron bridge, slung between two pairs of sham medieval towers, was only built in 1829. Prior to that the traveller forded or was ferried across the river there if possible, and if not he continued across Middleham Low Moor to join Hollin Lane that drops steeply down to Wensley Bridge; or he could go forward across the lower slopes of Penhill above Capplebank for West Burton, Thornton Rust, and Hawes, a road that still exists but is only partly in repair; an eighteenth-century milestone can be seen near it on Penhill where a road branches off to West Witton.

In modern times the railway, first brought to Leyburn in 1856 and completed to Hawes in 1878, ceased to provide a passenger service, that had existed for less than a century, in March 1954. At the present day transport is provided by a public bus service.

Because it is broad and open, it is not often realized that even to-day the upper half of Wensleydale is as remote from industrial towns as any part of the Yorkshire Dales; Swaledale links up with Durham, and Wharfedale with the West Riding, leaving Wensleydale in between; and in consequence people who take houses here use them as permanent residences rather than as week-end cottages.

Man has settled in Wensleydale from early times. Tumuli and stone circles of the Bronze Age are well represented, to be found at Castle Dykes, near Aysgarth, and round about Bainbridge and Askrigg, and to be seen at Nab End and on East Witton near Braithwaite Hall. Sites of Iron Age villages lie on Nab End, the western face of Penhill, and the slopes of Addlebrough near Stone Raise, a burial mound of the same date; and a sword of this era (La Tène period), found in Cotterdale, is in the British Museum.

Later the Angles and Danes, coming from the east, established the villages we know to-day as far up as Askrigg, whilst the Norsemen, arriving from the west, colonized the head of the dale. Every village up to Askrigg appears in Domesday Book; and several small places—Fors, Dentone, and Burg—then existed round Bainbridge. But that village was established in the twelfth century as a centre of the forest government, and Hawes is an even later settlement, first found in documents as 'Le Thouse' in 1307. In 1086 East Witton, with many hamlets, including West Witton, connected with it, was the largest place in the dale. (Domesday Book, not distinguishing between the two, says 'Witun.')

The development and decline, the fluctuating fortunes of the many villages of Wensleydale, are full of interest for the economic historian. Who would think of a market being held at Carperby (although it has a cross); yet so it was. Indeed Carperby, Askrigg, Wensley, Middleham, and East Witton, now comparatively small villages, have all at one time or another been market towns. Leyburn and Hawes, the first granted a charter for market and fairs in 1684 and the second in 1700, are both newcomers.

During the Middle Ages the dale was roughly divided into three great properties. Firstly, the Lordship of Middleham included most of the south side of the valley from Middleham westwards, and contained various parks, Bishopdale Chase, and the great Forest of Wensleydale reaching to the head; secondly, Abbotside on the north side of the Ure from Askrigg up to the dale head belonged to the monks of Jervaulx; and thirdly, the north side of the valley from Carperby to Leyburn was built up during the fourteenth century as a vast estate by the Scropes.

These were great days in Wensleydale when the deer grazed in the parks and the hunting-horn rang out in the forest, when the castles of Middleham and Bolton were built, kings stayed at Middleham and Mary Queen of Scots was imprisoned at Bolton, when the abbey buildings with 'ye fairest church in Richmond-shire' grew at Jervaulx, and monks and many priests were familiar figures in the dales; but when also poverty was rife, passions unbridled, murders frequent, and the homes of humble people miserable hovels.

That 'whole country of people,' the Lordship of Middleham, was broken up by Charles I, who sold it to the citizens of London,

The market-place at Leyburn

who in turn, not without trouble, sold it in lots to the yeomen of the dale during the mid seventeenth century. The dalesmen were reluctant, indeed in many cases unable, to put down the money for their farms instead of paying the small rents with guaranteed possession as had been the custom for many preceding centuries. Although after the Civil War Bolton Castle fell into ruin, the estates of the Scropes descended to the Dukes of Bolton, and eventually to the Orde family, of whom Lord Bolton still owns much of the property.

In 1780 Thomas Maude wrote: 'The commodities of the valley for home and foreign consumption, which last is not inconsiderable, are fat cattle, horses, wool, butter, cheese, mittens, knit stockings, calamine, lead.' The list breathes of a rich and fruitful vale, of lush feed for cattle, grass 'hard and sound' for horses, fells for sheep, and hills with hidden mineral wealth.

Many of these industries have come and gone, and almost all are of great age. The mining of lead, the making of cheese, and the breeding of horses go back at least to the monks of Jervaulx Abbey, who dug for lead probably in Forsdale in the twelfth century, who made cheese from ewes' milk, and who at the Dissolution owned a stud of horses that were 'the tryed breed in the northe.'

Though to a lesser extent than in Swaledale, lead-mining was once important (although even in the heyday of mining it used to be said that the weight of butter, cheese, and bacon exported from Wensleydale was greater than that of lead). As many as fifty mines have been worked in the main and branch dales. In 1294 lead merchants lived at Redmire, Preston-under-Scar, Leyburn, and the Forest of Wensleydale, and in the seventeenth century the London Lead Co. leased ground for mining in the upper dale.

In this latter period a bitter dispute over boundaries between the Marquess of Winchester, who afterwards became the first Duke of Bolton, and a group of Askrigg yeomen, including Thomas Metcalfe of Nappa Hall, raged for several years. Another later episode that marks Wensleydale history was the bread riots of miners in the neighbourhood of the market town of Askrigg, a pitiable affair that resulted in men being sent to the gallows, and one that gives us cause to think of the conditions of the poor in the eighteenth century.

During the nineteenth century the mines on the Bolton estate were pre-eminent. Keld Heads, Apedale, Bolton Gill, Virgin, Cobscar, and Cranehow Bottom all produced thousands of tons of ore, made huge profits for the companies that worked them, fortunes for the royalty owners, and gave lucrative employment to many men for two or three generations.

Twenty years ago a few old miners, in particular Kit and Tommy Peacock living at Redmire, used to recall the hard times when the mines were failing. They spoke of how they started work on the surface when they were boys, of how they joined partnerships and went underground, of pay days and of the money being divided by the simple process of sharing out the coinage; of how Keld Heads mine was flooded by water from the River Ure, and of how the mines, their prosperity diminished by the falling price of lead, ceased. On Preston Moor the short chimney of Cobscar smelt mill still makes a landmark; the ruins of Keld Heads smelt mills and their two-mile-long surface flue can be seen, as well as a fine collection of mining tools in the museum at Bolton Castle.

As for the mittens and knit stockings—the knitting industry— it dwindled away throughout the last century and ended altogether early in this. When it began in Elizabethan times it concentrated round the market towns of Middleham and Askrigg, and travelling hosiers distributed wool for spinning and knitting by people in their own homes.

In about 1784 three cotton mills were built at Aysgarth, Askrigg, and Gayle, but they soon ceased to spin cotton, and by spinning wool for yarn for knitting and for coarse cloth turned to the traditional industry. At one time Aysgarth and West Burton were centres for wool-combing, but throughout the last phase Hawes with Burtersett and Gayle became 'a seat of the knit hosiery trade.' Most of the people who knitted have gone; and in general what was remembered up to a few years ago was the extreme poverty of the old knitters. A character such as old 'Molly i' t'Wynd' at Gayle would be 'wapping away' the whole day long to eke out a living; and it was she who once showed the doctor the jersey she was knitting and asked: 'How would you like to knit yan o' them for a groat?'

Horse-breeding is, however, a very different story. As we shall see at Middleham, the breeding and training of racehorses flourish. In the twelfth century the monks of Jervaulx had folds for horses in the Forest of Wensleydale, and at the Dissolution Sir Arthur Darcy said: 'The stallions and mares [are] so well sorted that I think in no realm should we find the like to them, for there is high and large grounds for the summer, and low grounds to serve them.'

In later years every big farm had its horse park or paddock; and the gentry and the yeomen kept studs, sometimes large, sometimes small.   Sir Christopher Metcalfe in Elizabethan times rode to York with his small army of kinsmen on three hundred horses, and Adam Middleham, steward of the Lordship of Middleham, who lived at Gill, near Aysgarth, in 1622 possessed, amongst other stock, eighteen mares, fifteen of them greys.

The present-day prosperity of farming holds for dairy produce. But there has been a radical change: instead of every farm, however small, making butter and cheese, milk is now sold to the dairies at Leyburn, Hawes, and Coverham, which either distribute it or manufacture from it Wensleydale cheese.   A dairy at Askrigg closed in 1953.

In the old days the farms were run so that the cows calved in the spring, and from May to October or November, whilst they were grazing in the fields, cheese was made.   Almost all the butter was made in the early spring, when as much as 7,000 pounds was sold on a single market-day.   The work fell hardly on the women, who were constantly tied to their daily arduous work, but who, when it ceased, in many cases mourned the loss of a craft in which they took great pride.

In consequence of this change white farmhouse cheese (grass cheese) is a rarity and Blue Wensleydale is treasure trove.   When it exists the latter sells for 11s. a pound.   Factory cheese-making differs in that the milk of many herds is of necessity mixed, salt is added to the curds instead of the cheeses being pickled in brine, and often recipes differ.   Yet a good factory-made Wensleydale is excellent, and for its creamy taste it ranks amongst the best English cheeses.

This emphasis on the sale of liquid milk has had the effect of turning Wensleydale into a milk-producing instead of a stock-rearing area, a position that is being readjusted at the present day.   In this fertile vale where every drop of milk leaves the farm every morning it is often difficult to buy milk if not ordered beforehand, and not easy to buy separated cream.

Two new industries replace some of Maude's now vanished commodities of the valley. Both cause singularly little damage to the beauty of the dale. Behind Leyburn, Redmire, and Preston-under-Scar limestone is quarried for the blast-furnaces of the steelworks on the north-east coast. The other industry, the tourist trade, is new since modern means of transport in the last eighty years introduced many more people to the dale.

So in the wake of the railway trippers and the charabanc parties and with the cyclists, walkers, and motorists of the present day, it is time that we set out to explore the pastoral land, where in summer the country is green from valley bottom to hilltop, where very few scenes are spoilt by the hand of man, and where stone-built houses clustered in many villages and grey stone walls melt into the unrivalled harmony of colouring of the Yorkshire Dales.

Old cheese-making utensils: copper cheese kettle, a 'brig for t'sile' (bridge for the sieve), and two chesfords (cheese vats)

2. KILGRAM BRIDGE TO
WENSLEY BRIDGE

WITHIN a few miles of each other three of the oldest and finest bridges of the dales—Kilgram, Ulshaw, and Wensley—span the Ure in Lower Wensleydale. They cross a river broad and wide, swelled by the innumerable rills, becks, and small rivers of the dale. We take leave of the low lands at Kilgram, and start in earnest for the high lands at Wensley.

With tall beeches, oak, and sycamore overshadowing it, autumn is the time of year to visit Kilgram Bridge. According to Warburton, the cartographer, this crossing of the Ure lies on a Roman road from Catterick to Ripon; Leland spoke of 'the great bridge of stone on Ure, caullyd Kilgram Bridge,' and it seems likely that the present bridge has stood since early Tudor times. There is a tradition that, except for one stone, which is visibly missing yet, it was built by the Devil in a single night. Its six arches with four square ribs rise high above the river; and nowhere can we think of a richer texture of stone-work.

A mile west of the bridge are the ruins of Jervaulx Abbey. The Norman–French name means, of course, Yore valley, and is usually pronounced as it is spelt; although 'Jarvaulx' is often said, the old form 'Jarvis' has passed out of use. One of us as a child remembers the porter at the station calling out in harsh flat tones: 'J-a-r-vallix! J-a-r-vallix!'

The abbey, although nothing like so large a monastery as Fountains, but comparable with Rievaulx and Byland, is one of the famous Cistercian houses of England. Alas, despoilers have almost razed the church to the ground, and few interesting remains are left.

But if the architectural features disappoint, the ruins are a delight. They are privately owned and in the grounds of Jervaulx Hall, the property of Mr W. L. Christie, who has himself written a short book on the abbey. Here are no guides, notices, cemented stone-work, and all the other paraphernalia of the useful and often necessary Office of Works. Instead the grass grows long, and nettles abound, and the red gravel that covers the area of the church is mossy and weedy. Wild flowers root, jackdaws and blackbirds nest in the walls. In the north transept of the church is a vignette of the picturesque: forget-me-nots and ground ivy flower at the foot of a stone altar, and ferns sprout from surrounding walls hemmed in with the blackness of yews and laurels. Jervaulx is in a state of perfection of neglect.

In the first years of the last century the Marquess of Ailesbury, to whose family the estate had come in the seventeenth century, transformed the neighbourhood of Jervaulx. At this time the hall, then a farmhouse, was built, and under the direction of the agent, John Claridge, the ruins, buried under mounds of soil in a 'close of pasture full of bushes,' were excavated. The grounds were laid out, and the woods and avenues which we enjoy to-day planted. The present houses of East Witton, then thatched and small, together with a school, were built by the marquess, and to mark the jubilee of George III the church was re-erected on a fresh site.

East Witton, with its small houses and long green, and Witton Fell above it are the first landmarks for the traveller entering the dale from the east. In 1307 the abbot of Jervaulx was granted a market that continued after the Dissolution, until in 1563, when plague swept the village, the market was temporarily moved to Ulshaw Bridge; it eventually ceased in the eighteenth century. Witton was for long noted for its quarries and for its grindstones hewn on the fell above it. It was to Witton Fell that the ill-fated Abbot Sedber fled for refuge during the Pilgrimage of Grace. The historian of Wensleydale, W. G. M. G. Barker, was born here, as was also Mrs Holtby, the mother of the writer, Winifred Holtby.

The site of the old church is worth seeking out, especially in the autumn. Then the sheltering arms of lofty beeches in the walled-in churchyard drop a carpet of leaves over the scattered table-tombs and headstones: an ideal place in which to meditate or to see ghosts at dusk.

Nor should the traveller miss Braithwaite Hall a mile and a half along a lane to Coverdale. This fine seventeenth-century hall with massive chimneys of an earlier date was left to the National Trust by Jane G. Topham of Middleham in 1940.

Braithwaite was a small manor, and in 1301 is listed as a grange of Jervaulx Abbey, though it does not appear amongst the abbey's properties at the Dissolution. In 1541 a cousin of Sir Christopher Metcalfe, Thomas Metcalfe, of St Nicholas, near Richmond, presumably owned Braithwaite. He had there ten score wethers, twenty-five oxen, sixty cows, two bulls, and forty head of young cattle. During Elizabethan and early Stuart times the Wards owned it; and in the mid seventeenth century, according to Barker, Benjamin Purchas built the present house. He was steward to the Bathursts in Arkengarthdale and also to Thomas Wood, Lord of the Manor of Middleham, and he died at a great age in 1718. Tradition relates that the three gables at the front of the hall were built in memory of three sisters.

The front door opens into a fine stone-flagged hall with a large open fire-place recently uncovered. Eighteenth-century panelling and an oak staircase and floors are features of the house, which has been furnished with taste and care by the present tenants of the house and farm, Mr and Mrs Duffus.

The spoil heaps of lead workings and coal-mines are numerous round Braithwaite and on Flamstone Pin, the hill above it. Up Red Beck Gill is an Iron Age hill-fort, which we shall mention again in the chapter on Coverdale, and which is best reached by an old sunken road from the hall.

Half way between East Witton and Middleham we approach Cover Bridge and the inn adjoining it along an avenue of ancient elms. Within a few hundred yards is Ulshaw Bridge over the Ure, once an important crossing on the route from York to Kendal. The date, 1674, on a sun-dial records the year of its building. Near by was the village of Ulvishowe, one of England's lost villages, a place with nine persons paying tax in 1301.

From the bridges we shortly reach Middleham's tall, grey, Georgian houses lining a hilly market-place up to the castle. Few places in Yorkshire can show a richer story than Middleham, once the head of the Honour of Middleham, the centre of forest government for Wensleydale, a market town with important fairs, the shopping and administrative centre for Wensleydale, and a starting place for coaches. In early centuries the Musters of the Wapentake, when local men were summoned for training and for inspection of arms, took place on Middleham Moor, as did the great sporting events of later times.

At the present day Middleham is a village of 644 inhabitants, kept alive and prosperous by the industry, if so it can be called, of the breeding and training of racehorses. Besides this, many people travel by buses provided for them to work at Catterick Camp.

In 1845 Charles Kingsley, who paid a short visit to the town to be installed as honorary canon in the collegiate church of Middleham, wrote to his wife: 'Really everyone's kindness here is extreme after the stiff south. The richest spot, it is said, in all England is this beautiful oasis in the mountains.'

His contemporary, Bulwer Lytton, however, did not come to Middleham, and in *The Last of the Barons* he contrasted the peaceful seclusion of the medieval town with what was evidently the southerner's idea of Yorkshire. He writes of a Middleham where rise 'a thousand factories . . . foul and reeking with the squalid population . . . where now around the gin-shop gather the fierce and sickly children of Toil and Discontent.'

Lastly, Lord Torrington, who stayed at the White Swan, enjoyed his explorations. Amongst other employments he went to church, and he describes 'a decent well-dressed, well-behaved congregation,' and the choir, accompanied by two bassoons, attempting 'And the Trumpet shall sound.' He continued with a description of dinner: a boiled fowl, cold ham, loin of mutton roast, Yorkshire pudding, gooseberry pie, cheesecakes; 'a better dinner, and better dress'd, I never sat down to; but fear that the charge will be heavy—1s. 6d. at least: We shall see.' (It was 1s. 3d.)

Middleham, an Anglian settlement—the middle village between East and West Witton—rose to importance after the Norman Conquest. Ribald, younger brother of Earl Alan, built the first castle on William's Hill, south of the present castle, to guard the road from Richmond to Skipton through Coverdale; and Robert Fitzralph built the present keep in about 1170. In the thirteenth century the castle and honour came to the Nevilles of Raby through the marriage of a daughter. This daughter, Mary Neville, the Lady of Middleham as she was called, was a kind of medieval Lady Anne Clifford, a widow for nearly fifty years, managing large estates that were her inheritance by birth.

In 1471, after the death of Richard Neville, Earl of Warwick and Salisbury—Warwick the Kingmaker—at Barnet in the Wars of the Roses, the Honour of Middleham reverted to the Crown.

Middleham

Ten years previously the youthful Richard, Duke of Gloucester, the future Richard III, had joined the household of Warwick at Middleham, and after Barnet he was granted the honour, partly by right of his wife, Anne Neville, co-heiress of Warwick's estates. Middleham became Richard's home and in effect the seat of government for the North.

'With a veil of darkness upon him,' many vile deeds have been attributed to Richard III, yet before he ascended the throne he enjoyed the trust of his brother Edward IV, and by acts of simple kindness and the creation of a council, precursor of his great Council of the North that he set up in 1484, whose justice became famous, he won the devotion of the people of Yorkshire. This period was undoubtedly the climax of the story of Middleham.[1]

The castle fell into ruin after the Civil War, and feudal times ended when the manor was sold by the citizens of London to Thomas Wood in 1661. The Woods sold it to the Cunliffe-Listers, and in 1925 the parish council bought the manorial rights from Lady Swinton.

In 1389 Ralph Neville, Earl of Westmorland, had obtained a charter for markets and fairs. Some three hundred years later, in spite of the opposition of Thomas Wood and the people of Richmond and Bedale, the Marquess of Winchester obtained a market charter for Leyburn. New toll shops and shambles were built at Middleham in 1688; yet the market was irrevocably damaged, and it died out altogether in the first quarter of the nineteenth century.

In the 1890's people came from far and wide to Middleham Moor Fair that lasted three days. Cattle were sold on the first, sheep on the second, and 'nags and odds and ends' on the third. Drovers strode about in their Scots plaids, dogs barked, unbroken colts reared in fright, shaggy ponies were raced up and down at breakneck speed, gipsies in their bright clothes lent colour, and a troop of jockeys originality. In the market-place a huge bonfire was kept alight day and night for the drovers who could not find lodgings and who slept round it on the cobbles.

It is noticeable that in 1794 Lord Torrington, always keen of eye and candid of comment, mentions Middleham Moor and horse-training; on the other hand, fifty years later Kingsley says: 'This is quite a racing town—eighty horses standing here.

[1] See *Richard III* by Paul Murray Kendall (1955).

Jockeys and grooms crowd the streets, and I hear they are the most respectable set, and many of them regular communicants.' The first trainer of any standing at Middleham was Isaac Cape (1720–90), who trained at Tup Gill in Coverdale; and at the present day there are in all twelve training stables, six in the town and six outside, mostly in Coverdale at the opposite side of the Low Moor.

The trainers rent what are the common pastures of the town—Middleham Low and High Moors and Busks Pasture—and they use the High Moor in summer and the Low Moor in winter. Strangely the High Moor, Old Penhill Park, is in the township of West Witton, and was assigned to Middleham long ago by one of the Lord Scropes.

Rights on the Low Moor, which we cross on the way to Coverdale, and Busks Pasture, the open common by the river, are shared by three lots of people—the lord of the manor who owns the mineral and sporting rights, the gait-owners who have the summer pasturage, and the freeholders (householders) who have the winter grazing. If people do not want their gaits, as frequently happens, an auction of them, with the by-lawmen in attendance to mark the stock, takes place in the market-place in May. The freeholders let their rights to the trainers; and if you live in Middleham you partake of a share, 10s. a year.

Part of the rent is devoted to the employment of four full-time men, the gallopmen or beaters, who look after the moors by flattening down the footings with pompoms, as they are called locally, and by blocking off some of the gallops to rest them and making jumps with broom that grows there.

On Middleham Moor is still to be seen the old racecourse, where races were run, though not every year, from 1676 (very probably earlier if records were found) until 1873. In 1688 thirty-three subscribers, including names such as Darcy, Wyvill, Lowther, Scrope, Millbank, and Danby, put up £38 0s. 6d.— easily £400 of present-day money—for prizes for the races. Middleham and even more so Richmond Races were fashionable and popular resorts for two centuries, and were competed in by the best horses of the times. At Middleham a gold cup was introduced in 1805.

After noon not a horse is to be seen in Middleham for the rest of the day; the strings start out for the gallops in the early morning, the long-legged elegant horses in their carnival-mask hoods, held by their diminutive mounts. Perhaps they will finish fresh up the two miles of the Nailer's with its hard three furlongs' climax, which tests their stamina for the mile and a half.

Many are the famous trainers, jockeys, and horses of Middleham: Dr Syntax was trained by John Lonsdale at Tupgill, and Flying Dutchman by John Fobert at Spigot Lodge. At the present day Dante, winner of the 1945 Derby, was trained by M. J. Peacock at Manor House, owned by Sir Eric Ohlson of Scarborough, and ridden by W. Nevitt of Patrick Brompton Hall —a real Yorkshire win, as they say in Middleham. Others we shall find in Coverdale.

The eccentric Lord Glasgow, racehorse owner, gave his name to the training stables, Glasgow House, where in the garden is a memorial tablet recording the feat of James Croft, who trained all the first four horses of the 1822 St Leger. The horses walked the seventy miles to Doncaster; and, it is said, won the race in the same order in which they had left the stable. Warwick House, a conspicuous Georgian house with bay windows, is the training stables of Captain N. F. Crump, who has recently won the Grand National twice in four years with Sheila's Cottage and Teal. Horse-racing is a world of its own that touches us who are outside it only occasionally. When Dante won the Derby the news flashed from Middleham up Wensleydale with the speed of bush telegraphy.

As we have said, a bridge between Middleham and Leyburn, built by public subscription, has existed only since 1829. It collapsed the next year whilst cattle were crossing. However, it was reopened for traffic in 1831. The house alongside was the toll-house and the Bridge Inn, closed in 1856. Neither the tolls nor the shaky manner of passage was popular. The tale goes of a sweep who put his boy in a sack and carried him over to save the 1*d*. due;[1] and hordes of children used to dash across in a body and thus defeat the demands of the gate-keeper. I thus defeat the demands of the gate-keeper.

In 1864 the woodwork had decayed, and the following year a committee spent £1,500 on a substantial new bridge. In 1880,

[1] It seems worth noting that this story of the sweep and his boy, members of a gang of sweeps who lived in part of the castle ruins, appeared in the *Wensleydale Advertiser* a month before Kingsley stayed in the town.

having repaid the initial outlay from the toll money, the committee handed over the bridge to the county council. Trouble continued: after an appeal by local people in 1905 the northern approach, subject to serious flooding, was raised, and in 1949, when extensive repairs were made, the bridge would have been rebuilt but for post-war restrictions.

At the top of the long slope from the bridge Leyburn stands at a junction of roads from Middleham, Bedale, Richmond, Reeth, and Hawes. On wild days the wind swirls round the three squares, the old Grove Square, Commercial Square, and the new market-place—all, especially the last, large open spaces.

The town serves Wensleydale as a centre of local trade, jurisdiction, pleasure, and as a jumping-off point for visitors. Here buses converge, and here each Friday farmers attend the auction mart, and their wives the market. Until 1836 the town was that anomaly a market town without a church. Here is the County Home for the Aged, and here are held petty sessions; the town has two cinemas, and is the venue for the Wensleydale Tournament of Song and the Wensleydale Agricultural Show. Leyburn has few industries: it is a town of shopkeepers, retired people, and workers at a dairy, neighbouring quarries, and Catterick Camp.

The spacious, well-equipped depot of the Express Dairy Co., opened in 1937, to-day employs some fifty-six people, and, collecting from the dales, distributes to northern towns on an average 18,000 gallons of milk a week. Recently an egg-packing and grading station has been added; and thousands of eggs are sent regularly by road to London.

If Leyburn cannot boast a bold and colourful past, it is none the less an Anglian settlement and appears in Domesday Book. After the Conquest, Earl Alan's chief tenant at Leyburn was Wymar the Steward, from whom the de Leyburns are said to have descended. Members of the family were benefactors to religious houses, and held land in the township until the fourteenth century. One of the two manors descended to the Scropes, and, as we know, the Marquess of Winchester obtained the market charter. In 1856 the then Lord Bolton built the town hall, a good building in a Regency style.

Leyburn emerges from the immediate past as a kind of small outpost of fashionable society. Many of the local gentry patronized events such as the concerts and balls at the Bolton Arms, for which the famous Leyburn Quadrille Band was in demand, and also the Leyburn Shawl Tea Festivals that, started by some 'young tradesmen' who laid out a promenade, attracted thousands of people.   The New Theatre stood in Love Lane; and on Easter Monday 1814 Mr Brady's company gave *John Bull or the Englishman's Fireside,* followed by *The Sultan or the True-Born Englishwoman.* The Bolton Arms Hotel, a Georgian building recently restored, still has its long room with a large bay window overlooking the dale.   Here are held the dinners of the Leyburn Market Club, founded in 1832, and part of old Leyburn.

An ancient elm which once grew in the market-place was felled in 1821; on fair days cattle and sheep used to be sold in the squares, and horses shown off in the High Street.   In 1917 the auction mart was built, and about 1931 the shambles were pulled down to be replaced by the Central Garage and Café.

The development of the town is so recent as to be particularly interesting.   Half the houses, including many on the south side of the market-place, were built in the first years of the nineteenth century; from 1801 to 1831 the town more than doubled its population.   Later came developments such as the terrace near the station following the arrival of the railway from Bedale in 1856. In the inter-war years many modern villas were built, and since the last war about a hundred houses, including the Maythorne estate of council houses, have been put up.   Yet the population is decreasing.

It seems that Leyburn as a centre has great potentialities. and ought to attract to it other small factories for the employment of young people who now have to leave the dale.   A secondary modern school to serve the whole of Wensleydale is being built there, and a community centre is planned.

Lastly, picture one or two scenes in Leyburn to-day: the crowded squares on fair days, the clangour, colour, and the people thronging round the stalls.   Or look into the packed room of the town hall when the Tournament of Song is in progress: a neighbour remarks: 'I can't remember how many times I've been coming'; a men's choir from East Witton sings 'Waltzing Matilda' with great verve; and other choirs and individual performers render their long-practised pieces.

Whereas Leyburn is sited on the hilltop, Wensley, a mile away, lies in the valley on a terrace above the river.   Noted for its gracious aspect and gentle situation in contrast to the usually more bleakly situated villages of the dale, Wensley is largely built in estate style with the entrance gates to Bolton Hall at one side of the green.   In recent years the loss of trees—the old elm was blown down and other trees which were unsafe were felled—has unavoidably detracted from its looks.   The parish church is outstanding, perhaps the finest church in the dales.   Recently a new rectory has been built to replace the large Georgian one surrounded by its clipped yew hedge.

It is difficult to picture this quiet little village of only 207 inhabitants as the only market town in Wensleydale for a hundred years after 1202 when its first charter was granted.   In 1563 many died from the plague and others 'fled ye town,' and when Askrigg obtained a market charter in Elizabethan times it lost all importance.

Bolton Hall, over a mile from the village, stands in a fine wooded park and within sight of the river spanned by an ornamental bridge.   The hall was built by the Marquess of Winchester, the first Duke of Bolton, an eccentric and extraordinary individual, and it was partially rebuilt after a serious fire in 1902.   The pictures at Bolton are its especial treasures; amongst others are a collection of early Scrope portraits, and pictures by Van Dyck, Kneller, and Romney.   Lavinia Fenton, the original Polly Peachum in *The Beggar's Opera*, was mistress and then wife of the third duke, and is supposed to have sung from the ruined tower on the hillside across the valley from the hall.   The present Lord Bolton is an expert on forestry.

At Wensley the last of the three old bridges of the lower dale crosses the Ure, already a narrower river than at Kilgram.   The stone bridge was built in the late fourteenth century.   An old belief in the upper dale is that if the coroner comes over Wensley Bridge he will come twice more, and strangely this often happens. Westwards we start for the high lands and the colder climate of Upper Wensleydale. climate of Upper Wensleydale.

3. CASTLE BOLTON TO PENHILL

AT FIRST the country of a great estate lies before us. A footpath leads from Wensley through Bolton Woods to Redmire. Redmire, Preston-under-Scar, Castle Bolton, and West Witton across the valley were all industrial villages, largely inhabited by craftsmen and lead- and coal-miners who worked on the hills between Wensleydale and Swaledale; and the first three of these villages keep the ancient agricultural arrangement of common cow pastures that have not been enclosed and parcelled out amongst individual owners.

Redmire, spread round a green with its ancient oak-tree propped up by posts, still preserves a charming rusticity unaltered by the recent building of a policeman's house and several council houses. Not long ago when a building on the north side of the green was pulled down, it was found to be cruck-built. Amongst the old houses and charming corners Priory House commemorates where Coverham Abbey had property.

The name Redmire means 'reed mere,' from the lake or swamp that lay near the lane past the church. On the site of the swamp, now marked by a pond, were once clay-pits, a brick kiln, and a pottery, known as the Tile Sheds. Examples of the earlier products such as large jars are to be seen at the museum at Bolton Castle, and once the pottery supplied containers for local breweries. Latterly it was a family business, the Storeys', of whom Tiler Jim, working in the 1860's, was the last to make the bricks, bowls, and plant pots that supplied the neighbourhood.

People at Redmire have long memories. Jane Rider, who died in 1937, remembered tales of events in her mother's childhood, and her daughters still recollect much that has been handed down. It is remarkable to hear of the eccentricities of Parson Calvert, who died in his nineties in 1856. The story goes that a nephew of his closed a footpath and had either to go to jail or pay a fine. He preferred, rather than pay, to 'sit it out,' and in consequence spent two years imprisoned in York Castle. An old woman who made the beds used to bring him bottles of gin under her crinoline.

199

Redmire has a town hall built in 1862 as a drill hall for the local volunteers of that date; and for the benefit of volunteers from West Witton a bridge, called the Monkey Bridge because of the steps made up posts to mount it, was built across the river a little east of Redmire.   Though it has long been washed away, an iron post that supported it still stands in the river-bed.

The Ure at Redmire Falls is a popular resort, as in times past was the sulphur well that emerges as springs on the river bank not far from the corn mill.   Here was once a stone bath used to dip people as a medicinal treatment.   Mill Farm remains, but only the foundations of the corn mill in the gill near the river.   Once it was run by two brothers and a sister, who were so busy that they all took turns.   People used to buy a bowl of corn at Leyburn market and take it to the mill for grinding, whence it was fetched as three types of meal—bran, seconds for everyday bread, and white flour to make bread for Sundays.

If you come towards Redmire in the dusk of a late September evening, you will find a little crowd clustered round a few booths— a coco-nut shy, darts, and shooting-galleries—the celebration of Redmire Feast that a hundred years ago, beginning on the first Sunday after 19th September, continued until the following Saturday with 'foot-races, leaping, hunting, wrestling, and other gymnastics.'

Closely linked with Redmire, the village of Castle Bolton lies high up on the hillside, its houses and church dwarfed by the great ruined castle that looks boldly over the dale.   From here to Carperby the river bending southwards encircles an extensive territory of land that medieval men found desirable for their arable fields and the pasturage of their stock.   In the twelfth century, before the Scropes had become dominant, Rievaulx and Jervaulx Abbeys owned considerable pastures and meadow land at East Bolton.   At Carperby Easby Abbey had a grange with amongst other stock a stud of forty mares.   The terracing of the once open arable fields west of the castle is one of the sights of Wensleydale for the agriculturist or medieval historian.   Through these fields ran the road from Richmond to Bolton and on through the dale, traversed by the ox-drawn wagons of the monks, the retinues of great lords, perhaps a Crusader bound for the East, local traffic of farmers, and the passage of labourers and beggars.

Down by the river is the site of Thoresby, a village with twelve

Bolton Castle

taxpayers in 1377, and now two farms. The discerning eye may trace amongst the hollows and mounds of this, one of the lost villages of England, the main street, houses, and the church. The place gave its name to a family amongst whom were Peter de Thoresby, a hunting parson of Aysgarth in the thirteenth century, Archbishop Thoresby, Archbishop of York from 1354 to 1373, and Ralph Thoresby, the antiquarian of the eighteenth century.

A hundred years ago many oak-trees surrounded Bolton Castle; but at the present day, exposed to the four winds of heaven except on the north side, its stone-work never fails to draw the eye from near or far, either when dark and forbidding against the black of winter trees or when blending with the yellows and greens of summer.

The builder was Richard Scrope who fought at Crécy, was knighted at Nevilles Cross, and became the first Lord Scrope. Leland tells us that the castle, begun in 1379, took eighteen years to complete and was remarkable for the construction of its chimneys. Some tenants paid their rents in kind by providing coal, valued at 10*d*. or 12*d*. a quarter to heat it. The most important episode in its story was the imprisonment of Mary Queen of Scots from July 1568 to January 1569.

The castle is open to the public and is full of interesting detail; and as a local collection the museum objects are valuable. Sometimes plays and pageants are performed here, and we remember a realistic reconstruction of the medieval kitchen with pots, pans, barons of beef, ham, herbs, and jars, and even the smells of cooking.

Behind the castle in wild and lonely Apedale (the Norseman Api's valley) is the quarry called Apedale Greets, worked to this day by the Peacock family of stone-masons, who live at Castle Bolton. It represents here the never-ceasing stream of life and the twentieth-century social revolution. From it was hewn the stone for the quoins, string courses, window jambs and so on of the castle; and nearly six hundred years later the same stone has been used by the Peacocks for the corner-stones of the new council houses at Carperby and West Burton.

Up here to this little village of magnificent views, massive ruins, the beautiful Bolton Gill, and the hinterland of wild moor came Fred Lawson, the artist, first on a day trip with a friend, George Graham, in 1910, and the following year to settle permanently. Since then Fred has interpreted Wensleydale for very many people, and made its landscapes known far outside the bounds of the dale. He has gathered round him a nucleus of the arts. His wife, Muriel Metcalfe, artist and native of Leyburn, expresses herself in drawings of the utmost sensitivity. Here too comes George Jackson, artist, writer of a history of the castle, and editor of the *Wakeman* magazine published in Ripon; and with them is linked Dorothy Una Ratcliffe, poet and writer, who has for long identified herself with Wensleydale. The strength of the group lies in its unity with the people and places round it.

Two miles west of Bolton Castle, the long street village of Carperby, stretching for half a mile, lines the main road. Behind it can be seen the many ranes of the townfields. It has a Friends' Meeting House, a seventeenth-century market cross, and a well-known inn, the Wheatsheaf. A little corn is still grown round about. A fire in 1810 destroyed twelve houses, an event that has almost passed out of recollection. Not so the stick of incendiary bombs which was dropped on the village in 1941, damaging a few houses.

One of the large farms of the Bolton Hall estate, Manor House Farm, Carperby, is remarkable for the long tradition of progressive stock-breeding carried on by the Willises, who have lived in the neighbourhood for three centuries and have farmed at Manor House for four generations. Their flock of pedigree Wensleydale sheep and the herd of pedigree Shorthorns, both started in the early years of the last century, are nationally famous.

The breed of large, hornless, blue-faced, long-coated sheep to which Wensleydale gives its name originated in this part of the dale; mugs they were once called.   Not so hardy as other local breeds, they live on lower ground and are valuable for crossing with the Swaledales to produce the half-bred lambs called Mashams.   At present there is a tendency for the Teeswater breed, an ancestor of the Wensleydale, to replace the latter.

West Witton, on the opposite side of the valley on a terrace of Penhill, straddles, like Carperby, on either side of a long main street.   A place of great antiquity—a fragment of an Anglian cross is to be seen in the church vestry—its story is linked with Penhill whose summit lies in the township.   It was a centre of the dyeing trade, as witness the token of Henry King, dyer, issued in 1667.   John James, famous as the writer of *The History of the Worsted Manufacture in England*, published in 1857, was born at West Witton, and memorials to him may be seen in church and churchyard.

In Victorian times Witton Feast lasted three days.   Many stalls lined the streets, and at night were lit with naphtha flares. The children would be given a fairing from the favourite stall of sweets, toffees, and china near the Star Hotel.   Ribbon and copper kettles, the prizes for the races, were hung from upper windows, and the chief event was a dog trail: 'Baxter's coming!' rang out from the churchyard, one of the vantage points; and ribbon dances were held at the inn at night.   As many as twenty-five friends and relations might be asked to come and partake of a huge joint of beef—'a fine lump o' Bartle' they called it, meaning the meat.

The feast is now a one-day sports event, the end of which is crowned by a ceremony known as the Burning of Bartle.   Briefly it means the carrying of an effigy down the village street, and at various points, usually outside the inns, the reciting of the following verse:

> In Penhill Crags he tore his rags;
> At Hunter's Thorn he blew his horn;
> At Capplebank Stee he brake his knee;
> At Grisgill Beck he brake his neck;
> At Wadham's End he couldn't fend;
> At Grisgill End he made his end.
>   Shout, lads, shout.

No satisfactory explanation of its origin can be found.   It certainly

is part of the folklore of Wensleydale, but whether it reverts to a
fertility ceremony at harvest time is open to doubt. The rhyme
evidently refers to a chase and may well record a recollection of the
destruction of a local terrorist, perhaps linked with the legend of
the wicked Giant of Penhill related in J. Fairfax-Blakeborough's
The Hand of Glory. The name Burning of Bartle does not refer
to the burning of the patron saint of the church, St Bartholomew,
but no doubt means the burning *on* the feast day, St Bartholomew's
Day.

Penhill is a generous, great-hearted kind of hill, comparable with
Ingleborough, although nowhere near so high. It is a triangular
island, surrounded on two sides by Walden and Coverdale and on
the third by Wensleydale itself, and its huge bulk is a landmark to
be picked out from the summits of distant peaks and passes.

Old roads cross it—that up the dale already described, and a fine
lofty route from West Witton to Coverdale. Up here the racehorses train, where deer 'once roamed the high pastures of the
mountains,' and where people have dug peat and quarried
building stone since time immemorial. Leland saw a little
tower on Penhill, and many old maps picture a beacon on it. At
1,500 feet above sea level on the western face of the hill may be
seen an important Iron Age settlement with extensive remains of
dwellings and field walls comparable with that not far away on the
southern side of Addleborough; and besides this, stone coffins and
the foundations of a Knights Templars' chapel are to be found on a
lower slope above Temple Farm.

From the old road across Penhill a track drops down to Temple
Farm past the Templars' chapel. Just before the chapel is
reached, near a gate, is a boundary stone with the double cross of
the Templars; a second is to be seen on the north side of the main
road where Stony Stoop Lane leads down to Slapestone Wath, and
a third is set on a stone in the wall on the south side of the road
between Swinithwaite and Temple Farm.

The interesting old house, Temple Farm, stands on the site of
the Templars' secular buildings, and it was for long called Temple
Dowsker, from Dovescar, a boundary of their lands. Parts of the
present house appear to have been built in 1608 by Peter Atkinson
and his wife, whose initials appear on an inscription over the backdoor. The house was enlarged in the eighteenth century.

Opposite Temple Farm a high wall surrounds overgrown and

disused pleasure grounds with a summer-house set on a knoll in their midst. The summer-house and Swinithwaite Hall, a mile east, were built for T. J. Anderson in the latter half of the eighteenth century by John Foss, architect of Richmond. Both are good examples of Georgian architecture. The summer-house is built in 'rustic' style of freestone brought from Penhill, and is octagonal and two-storeyed, with a decorated plaster ceiling, a superb stone floor, and over the entrance the carving of a pointer and the date 1792. Round the upper storey runs a balcony from which, with the ghosts of past romantic picnickers, we may look out in all directions—down the dale to Leyburn, across to Walden and Bishopdale, and up to Hawes.

4. THE PARISH OF AYSGARTH

FROM the tops of any of the prominent hills of the mid valley of the Ure—Ellerkin, Nab End, or Addlebrough—it is possible to see almost all of the original parish of Aysgarth, the largest ancient parish in England, 81,033 acres in extent, in fact the whole of Upper Wensleydale. Sometimes on wild and stormy days we have looked down to the tempestuous contours of the head of the valley surrounded by dark unfriendly hills, and marvelled that man may live comfortably and make a reasonable living in such country.

Aysgarth, with a population of 259, is one of the smaller villages of Wensleydale. Its name, meaning 'an open space marked by oaks,' hints at the once wooded terrain. It lay on the coaching route through the dale; in 1815 a diarist wrote: 'Met new coach tolerably well loaded; it runs from York to Lancaster by means of two coaches which meet and change horses at Aysgarth three days a week.' But it was when the falls became popular in the railway era that the village achieved fame.

At the present day Dr W. N. Pickles, who has won an international reputation for his work on infectious diseases, lives at Aysgarth, where he has practised for some forty years; and here as a central point in the valley the meetings of the Wensleydale Society, a historical and cultural society founded in 1952, are held.

The church, almost a mile from the village, stands above the river, the bridge, Yore Mills, and the famous upper falls. Unfortunately it suffered extensive restoration in Victorian times, but it still retains the magnificent screen, and pews with poppy-heads of the Ripon carvers, poppy-heads that some consider finer than those at Wensley. The churchyard measures five acres, and in former times the vicar paid rent for it, 'a thing scarce ever knowne,' as he said. Although the great parish has long ago been divided up, as churches have been built at Askrigg, Hawes, Hardraw, Stalling Busk, and Lunds, it is still legal for people in Upper Wensleydale to be married at Aysgarth church as if they were residents in the parish.

Yore Mills, now a modern flour mill owned by Yorkshire Farmers Ltd, stands on the site of one of the three cotton mills built in Wensleydale in 1784. Here a partnership of eight people—John Pratt of Askrigg, John Harrison of Hawes, and the rest from Settle—bought a field called Bridge End Close or Bull Ing in order to build there a mill for cotton spinning. Unfortunately it failed and fell into ruin; it was burnt down in 1852, and the present building dates from the rebuilding in the following year. The mill, changing from cotton to wool, spun woollen yarns that made red jerseys for Garibaldi's army and Balaclava helmets for the soldiers in the Crimean War.

It is a lovely scene, this wooded hollow by the mill and bridge. Of the three falls at Aysgarth the upper, splashing over mossy rocks, is our favourite, but the lower falls, a mile lower down the river, are the most spectacular. They all have that quality that deserves the overworked epithet—beauty-spot. Arthur Young, who came up Wensleydale specially to see them, says: 'Upon the whole, these falls are great curiosities and sufficient, I should apprehend, to entertain the least scrutinizing traveller.'

In the mid nineteenth century temperance galas under the auspices of the Carperby Improvement Society took place on the banks of the river by the upper falls; on those occasions 'addresses on temperance, teetotal melodies, etc. were the order of the day.' Aysgarth Flower Show and Gala still carries on an open-air summer gathering and is a popular event.

Such was the fame of the falls that in the 1880's the proposal to build a brick railway bridge across them to link a line from Skipton with the Wensleydale line on the north side of the valley raised a national outcry. A Defence Association with Lord Wharncliffe as president, and supported by John Ruskin, William Morris, Alma Tadema, Walter Besant, Ouida, Edmund Gosse, Jessie Fothergill, and others, was formed. Lord Wharncliffe gave evidence before the House of Lords, and Turner's painting of the falls was specially exhibited at Agnews in Bond Street. The railway project was eventually abandoned.

At one point in the controversy Ouida wrote prophetically to *The Times*: 'If science have any of the skill it pretends to possess, so ugly, noisy, clumsy, and dangerous a method of locomotion as railways offer will, after 50 years more have passed, be superseded by some other invention.'

From Aysgarth the upper reaches of Wensleydale lie ahead, the valley still broad and green round Bainbridge and Hawes, but gradually narrowing as it rises higher and higher to Lunds on the watershed. One by one we reach the peaks of Addlebrough, Wether Fell, Dodd Fell, Widdale Fell, and Cotter End; and villages and hamlets: Thornton Rust perched on a hill terrace and Worton below it, Bainbridge, Askrigg, Burtersett, Sedbusk, Hardraw, Gayle, and the market town of Hawes.

The open space of Bainbridge green calls for a halt. The village has many remarkable features—the Roman fort, dating from the first century A.D., on Brough Hill, the River Bain, flowing out of Semerwater, the shortest river in England, and the forest horn, blown every night at nine o'clock from Holyrood, 28th September, to Shrovetide, or, as the hornblower may tell you, from Hawes Back-end Fair to Pancake Tuesday.

The Bainbridge horn has a little history all its own. It goes back to a time when a horn was blown to guide travellers through the forest. An old horn is preserved at Bolton Castle Museum, and the present one, kept at the Rose and Crown Hotel during the summer, was presented in 1864 amidst the kind of rejoicings—a grand fancy-dress carnival event—in which Bainbridge excels to this day. For many years the Metcalfe family have been horn-blowers. The present member, Jack Metcalfe, times his duties by waiting for Big Ben to begin striking the hour on the wireless; and immediately he goes out on to the green and gives three long deep-toned blasts into the night air. It has become a custom recently for the horn to be blown at wedding receptions. A visitor once asked Jack if the horn could be heard three miles away, to which he replied: 'I don't know. I'm at this end.'

As we have said, many roads meet and cross at Bainbridge; and the Roman road crossing Wether Fell as straight as an arrow is one of the sights of the dale. The Stake Pass, the Roman road to Ilkley, runs along Raydaleside, and from it is seen Semerwater, one of Yorkshire's few lakes, some eighty acres in extent.

Although providing a tamer scene than those of the Cumberland lakes, nevertheless Semerwater has many charms and a traditional story. The legend of a city sunk beneath its waters has probably a basis in fact. Here were Iron Age lake dwellings, some of which may well have been submerged by a sudden flood. A causeway leads out into the lake from the strange rocks near the enormous limestone boulder of glacial origin called the Carlow Stone, and a Bronze Age spearhead was found some years ago on the north shore.

Three small villages lie around Semerwater—Stalling Busk, Marsett, and Countersett. At Stalling Busk is the church built in 1908 to replace the old church whose ruins stand not far from the lake margin. Countersett has Quaker associations: George Fox slept there in 1652; and at Carr End lived the Quaker family of Fothergill, perhaps in the last few centuries Wensleydale's most distinguished family. Two members made missionary journeys to America, Dr John was an eminent doctor in London and the founder of Ackworth School, Alexander surveyed and super-intended the making of the Richmond to Lancaster turnpike, and kept a fascinating diary, alas partially lost, and Jessie Fothergill wrote Victorian novels, of which *Kith and Kin* is still an out-standing work.

Semerwater is a place of many moods. Sometimes under a black lowering sky waves ruffle it, sometimes it is so hot in the deep hollow that cows wade far out in its placid blue waters. It is most entrancing in winter when in a white world it is frozen over and the honking of whooper swans echoes on the still air as they fly in to settle on the ice. Whitaker gives a remarkable list of birds found at Semerwater, and although many, such as the osprey and bittern, are not seen to-day, the lake is still interesting for its wild life.

In striking contrast to the village of Bainbridge, Askrigg, on the opposite side of the valley, presses its houses into a main street, itself wedged between two hillocks. Here from 1587, when a market charter was granted, until the beginning of the nineteenth century, when the market lapsed, Askrigg was the centre of trade in Upper Wensleydale. Here people from far and wide came to buy their weekly needs, and here was a centre of the trades of dyeing, knitting, brewing, cotton spinning, and lead-mining. Almost every yard behind the tall three-storeyed houses of the main street contains old dilapidated cottages, now used as out-buildings, but once the homes of industrial workers.

Askrigg was a comparatively large place at the time of Domesday Book, and its church, the first chapel of ease in Aysgarth parish, was built about 1175. The village has a long story of a turbulent independent people, and until it was destroyed by fire in 1935 the Old Hall enriched the scene in the market-place. We have told the full story in our book *Yorkshire Village*. Before leaving we would point out the superb view of it, so completely harmonious and unaltered since the eighteenth century, seen from across the valley from between Worton and Bainbridge.

Near Askrigg is Nappa Hall, until 1756 the home of the Metcalfes, the huge clan who overran Upper Wensleydale in the sixteenth and seventeenth centuries and whose name is still common. The hall, now a farmhouse, was built about 1459, and is one of the finest examples of early domestic architecture in Yorkshire.

On the other side of Askrigg is Yorebridge Grammar School, housed in a fine new building, but founded in 1601. Farther along Colby Hall, built by John Colby in 1655, graces a green hillside, and below it at Dale Grange is historic ground, the site of Fors Abbey, the forerunner of Jervaulx, and close to it the monks' little bridge, Bowbridge.

West of Dale Grange to the head of the dale stretches for six miles the commons called High and Low Abbotside, the abbot's side of Yore, a valuable pasture belonging to Jervaulx Abbey until the Dissolution. Along it are strung farms and hamlets. At the village of Hardraw is the famous scar, a waterfall pouring down from an overhanging crag; and through Simonstone near by runs the Buttertubs Pass linking Wensleydale with Swaledale.

On the north side of the valley is the market town of Hawes. T'Hawes you may hear it called, and so it is, the hause or pass between mountains, a place not mentioned in Domesday Book, and one that grew up as people became more numerous and settled farther up the dale. It obtained its market charter in 1700, and in the last century wholly absorbed the trade once centred at Askrigg. At Hawes and the surrounding hamlets, Gayle and Burtersett, there were, in the last century, small textile mills and stone quarries that gave employment to large numbers of people.

Until the turnpike to Lancaster was made through it in 1795 only pack-horse traffic connected Hawes with the outer world. See it nowadays on market-days with the farmers' cars lining the streets and filling every open space, and the goods of drapers, greengrocers, and fishmongers displayed on stalls in the market-place. In the autumn thousands of sheep, pedigree Swaledales and fat lambs for the butcher, are sold at the auction mart; and in summer coach-loads of people stop for meals, and visitors staying in the town or the neighbourhood stroll here and there. As Ella Pontefract said: 'Hawes is the Mecca of the upper dale.'

Hawes

In Gayle Lane at Hawes is the dairy of the Wensleydale Creameries Ltd, opened in 1953, not as a new venture but as an enlargement of the first cheese factory in the dale, started by Edward Chapman in 1898 and then housed in the old woollen mill at Hawes. At the present day the dairy employs some twenty-five people who in 1954 made over 404 tons of Wensleydale cheese from 880,975 gallons of milk.

Above Hawes the first streams of the Ure flow down many little branch dales, all inhabited valleys with farms or hamlets in them. In Fossdale was a grange of Jervaulx Abbey; in Cotterdale were many miners' houses and a tiny Methodist chapel, still in use, built for the miners; in Mossdale are the falls painted by Turner; and up Widdale is the turnpike to Ingleton.

In these once almost trackless wastes where guides through the forest were needed we reach the Moorcock Inn, a junction of roads that fork the one for Sedbergh, the other for Kirkby Stephen. Once a fair took place at what was then called the Guide Post Inn. To-day in September a small show is still held in a field behind the Moorcock for the Swaledale sheep and the attested cattle bred on the wide moorlands of the watershed, where the West Riding and the North Riding and Westmorland meet.

COVERDALE

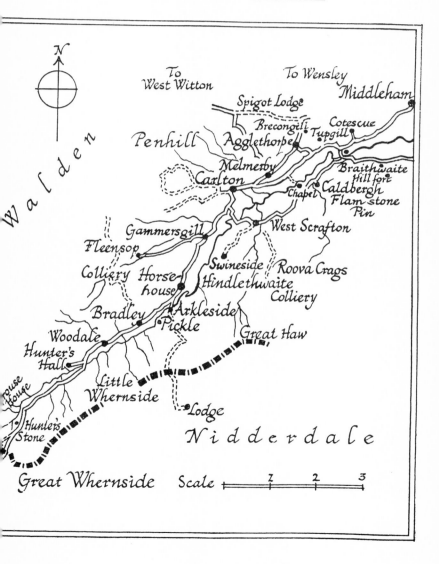

N

To West Witton

To Wensley

Middleham

Spigot Lodge

Brecongill

Cotescue

Walden

Penhill

Agglethorpe

Tupgill

Melmerby

Braithwaite Hill fort

Carlton

Chapel

Caldbergh

Flamstone Pin

West Scrafton

Gammersgill

Fleensop

Swineside

Roova Crags

Colliery

Horse-house

Hindlethwaite

Colliery

Bradley

Arkleside

Pickle

Woodale

Great Haw

Hunter's Hall

Little Whernside

rouse house

Lodge

Nidderdale

Hunter's Stone

Great Whernside   Scale   1   2   3

XI

COVERDALE

AMONGST Wensleydale's family of dales Coverdale, Bishopdale, and Walden form a trio related to each other yet with varied characteristics; and the three find their sources in the lofty hills that divide Wensleydale from Wharfedale—Buckden Pike, Great Whernside, and Little Whernside. Coverdale is the largest of them, twelve miles long from its head to where its river, the Cover, joins the Ure below Middleham.

Whichever way we approach Coverdale, we reach it by devious routes. At its head the formidable steep road, Park Rash, makes access from Wharfedale adventurous; and from Wensleydale four routes—from East Witton, Middleham, Wensley, and West Witton—either follow ancient winding lanes or cross high open moor into the dale.

If we take the last of these routes, that from West Witton over a shoulder of Penhill to Melmerby, a dramatic view of Coverdale unfolds. Immediately ahead a long barrier of hill rises up to two points, Flamstone Pin and Roova Crags. Looking westwards a great sweep of dale curves away in the distance under the eaves of the Whernsides to the dale head. Perhaps it is summer with many trees in full leaf and herds of cows in the meadows; or perhaps the misty grey landscape is brushed everywhere with frost, and the setting sun streaks the sky red.

What lies before us is the parish of Coverham, an area of 20,564 acres, 'a whole country of people' as its inhabitants described the Lordship of Middleham, of which the dale formed a part. It contains Coverham church with chapels of ease at Carlton and Horsehouse, seven townships, many hamlets, and 685 inhabitants. In this most secret and hidden of dales, with its self-contained life, old customs lingered long after they had vanished elsewhere.

Secluded it may be, yet Coverdale, cleaving the Pennines, has provided an important cross-country route in past times.

A great sweep of dale curves away

Through it came Bronze Age men, as three tumuli in Carlton village testify; and in the Iron Age it apparently formed a line of retreat for peoples defending themselves from invaders from the south-west, as witness the fortifications on the summit of Park Rash and the hill-fort on Red Beck Gill near Braithwaite Hall. In the Middle Ages a road through it connected the castles of Lancaster and Skipton with that of Richmond. Up it marched Richmondshire men to join battle at Blore Heath in the Wars of the Roses. To Hunter's Hall at the head of the dale rode the lords of Middleham for deer-hunts in the forest; Sir Arthur Darcy, carrying news of the rebels in the Pilgrimage of Grace, hurried through; and in his seventeenth-century road atlas John Ogilby gives a route through Coverdale from London to Richmond. Scotchmen, packmen, monks, robbers, drovers: the dale has seen the passage of all sorts of people.

In historic times Coverdale was settled by Angles and Norsemen, who came to share it between them with Carlton as the point of division and the Norsemen in the High Dale, as the upper half was called. Place-names reveal the kind of landscape that these people found: Caldbergh means 'cold hill,' Bradley 'broad clearing,' Hindlethwaite 'forest clearing for hinds,' and Woodale 'wolves' valley.' Mentioned in the Domesday survey, Coverham, Melmerby, Agglethorpe, Caldbergh, Carlton, and Scrafton were all comparable in size with the Wensleydale villages of the same date.

For the stranger the pronunciation of some of these names holds pitfalls. Coverdale is correctly pronounced to rhyme with hover, and the hamlets of Bradley and Woodale are respectively 'Bradely' and 'Woodle.' 'Cover' is an ancient British name, and means 'a brook running in a deep ravine.'

One fine autumn day we walked on to the bracken- and heath-clad summit of Flamstone Pin, whose strange name means 'a waste open place,' in search of prehistoric remains, and finding nothing we were rewarded instead by as fine a view of medievalism as may be found anywhere in England, in as grand a setting of moor and fell. From it may be seen Middleham and Bolton Castles, Middleham and Coverham churches, Coverham Abbey down by the river, the purlieus of Jervaulx with the ruins hidden in trees, Cotescue Park, once a deer park, and Braithwaite Hall, once a grange of Jervaulx Abbey.

It is said to be possible to see the seas on either side of England from the summit and from other hills near by, but except from Great Whernside the feat seems unlikely. The story, however, goes that a Coverdale man built the cairn on Flamstone Pin so that from his ship on the North Sea he might pick it out and picture his mother's cottage just below in the hamlet of Bird Ridding.

In autumn the amphilopsis on the front of the house, Cotescue Park, shines out a brilliant red in the dun landscape of woodland and rough pasture. About the middle of the fifteenth century the park for deer was made here for the lords of Middleham, and in 1526 the office of Keeper of the Park was given to George Lawson for the maintenance of the garrison at Berwick. It has been a racing stables, a boarding-school for girls, and is now a private house.

The scenes of medieval glories in Coverdale concentrate in a small area in the lower dale. Grouped round Coverham Bridge are to be found the abbey ruins, Coverham church, the ancient abbey mill, and an eighteenth-century miller's house, the two latter greatly renovated. The lovely hump-backed bridge, with its single pointed arch and unusual structural features, is a place on which to linger and dream of those strange past times of medieval England, while below the waters of the Cover, 'brown water clearer than crystal,' as Kingsley described it, ripple over 'bright white stones.'

The few ruins of Coverham Abbey, approached through the inner gateway, lie in private grounds. The canons were granted lands in many villages and hamlets of the dale, and advowsons of the churches at Sedbergh, Downholme, Coverham, and a mediety of Kettlewell. In 1388, when the abbot complained that fourteen of his oxen yoked to two wagons had been driven off by robbers as they were passing through Melmerby, he recorded for us a glimpse of the kind of traffic on the roads of that day: a sight still to be seen on the Tuscan hills in Italy.

Near a ford a mile and a half up-stream from the abbey ruins, the canons maintained a chapel founded by Ranulph Pigot in 1328. Only the foundations of what was the chapel of SS. Simon and Jude are left in this hollow by the river; but they are worth visiting for the atmosphere of antiquity. A footpath beyond a wicket and also an ancient lane lead down to them from the road near East Scrafton; and an iron bridge (out of sight of the chapel) carries the path over to Melmerby and Carlton.

No more than half a mile from the chapel, the small village of Caldbergh straggles up a steep hillside. The hall, now a farmhouse, was the supposed birth-place of Miles Coverdale, one of the most distinguished of clerics, who translated the Bible and the Apocrypha from German and Latin versions at Antwerp, and was concerned with the printing of other Bibles. Lastly in this brief glance at the Middle Ages in Coverdale, at the manor-house at Swineside farther up the dale lived the family of Loftus, of whom Edward Loftus, bailiff for Coverham Abbey, was the father of Adam Loftus, Archbishop of Dublin and Lord Chancellor of England, and the grandfather of the first Viscount Loftus of Ely, who held equally distinguished positions.

Worth seeing in this neighbourhood is the little pack-horse bridge, Ulla Bridge, below Caldbergh, between the village and a new road bridge. It shows the original width of four feet, and has been widened twice.

Cross to the other side of the river, where is a different aspect of life in the dale. Between Coverham and Carlton we come to what was Rowntree's cheese factory, now owned and run by Cow & Gate Ltd. This most up to date of cheese factories, with two pairs of houses built for members of the staff, makes up a small new community. One of its buildings, now used as store-rooms, is, however, historic: a seventeenth-century house, once the Lady Bab Inn, so called after a racehorse of local repute, and for long the resort of the racing people of the neighbourhood.

At the factory between thirty and forty employees handle some 2,000,000 gallons of milk a year, milk that is collected from all over Coverdale and from as far afield as Masham. Although liquid milk is dispatched to the towns during shortages in winter, the factory produces 18,000 cwt of Wensleydale and Cheshire cheese annually; and both types of cheese from this factory have won first prizes in recent years at the dairy show at Olympia.

At this lower end of Coverdale are to be found the racing stables of Tupgill, Ashgill, Brecongill, Ferngill, and Thorngill: groups of houses and outbuildings, many of them as large as hamlets, all of which can tell of the triumphs of horses, trainers, and jockeys. For instance, the fine Georgian house at Brecongill was built about 1800 by John Mangles, who trained there seven winners of the St Leger, and in the last century it was the home of John Osborne.

Perhaps of all these past figures of the racing world in the neighbourhood of Middleham, John Osborne, 'Honest John' or 'The Bank of England Jockey,' is the most picturesque. He competed in thirty-eight successive Derbys, and set up as trainer at Brecongill in 1869. In those days they used to kill a cow each week to feed the many stable-boys. Horses were walked to meetings: the journey to Newmarket took a fortnight and that to Manchester via Park Rash, Kettlewell, and Skipton several days. John Osborne with his wife (and six sons and three daughters as they grew up) regularly attended services at Coverham church for fifty-four years; and he went to York races the week before he died in his ninetieth year in 1923.

To-day Brecongill, the stables of S. Hall, with boxes for forty horses and a farm of fifty to sixty acres, is a ranch in miniature. It is the centre of a highly organized community of about twenty people, most of them stable men and boys, of whom nine live in the house.

We were taken round by Mrs Hall and her daughter. Intelligent-eyed horses poked their heads over doors for sweets—during the last war the boys saved their rations for them; from a field came the rhythmic thrump, thrump of hoofs as four or five yearlings galloped towards the fence; hens cackled in what were once the bothies, and a pig waddled under the lofty stone arch that joined the house to its outbuildings. We were shown a young foal just parted from its mother. An animal like this is worth hundreds of pounds, and may have been entered for races before it was born. Valuable horses are fed like babies: the horse dentist from York and the blacksmith from Middleham pay regular visits. Indoors pictures of past winners hang on the walls, and Tearaway, which we had seen, had just won the last flat race of the season, the Manchester November Handicap.

The factory and the racing establishments are the present industries of Coverdale. In past times considerable lead- and coal-mining was carried on on the hills of the dale. There was a 'ledebeter' at Coverham in 1301, and collieries existed at West Scrafton, Fleensop, Woodale, and Coverhead. Here, too, were several noted slate and flag quarries, in particular at Gilbert Scar.

Features of the dale are the excellent masonwork and the fine-grained sandstone used, which, as at Appletreewick in Wharfedale, give pleasure to those who appreciate stone.

One of the most ancient families of Coverdale, connected with it from at least the fifteenth century, is the Tophams, who lived during the seventeenth century at Agglethorpe Hall, not far from the racing stables. Although it has been rebuilt and is now a farmhouse, this large old hall still retains an air of faded glory, and a huge ancient wall surrounds its one-time garden.

On a slope of Penhill at about 900 feet above sea level the houses of Carlton line either side of a mile-long street. Here is the school for some ninety children brought daily from all over the dale by bus, and adjoining it is the small chapel of ease. The oldest building in the village is the barn of Old Hall Farm, with a dated door-head inscribed 'WFS 1659.' Two other houses catch the eye, one with an enormous old pear-tree trained up it, its trunk protected from the scratchings of cats by corrugated-iron sheeting, and the other with three yews of great age trimly decorating the house front. There are two inns, the Foresters' Arms and the Moorcock, once the Hare and Hounds and the XYZ. The latter was so called after a famous north country racehorse that won the Richmond Gold Cup three times in succession in the early years of the last century. Notice too the charming Georgian vicarage, and the house where lived Henry Constantine, local poet, who before he died fixed a stone tablet, inscribed with his own epitaph, on the front of his house.

The three Bronze Age barrows are to be found off the village street, the largest behind the Foresters' Arms, the second in the garden of Manor House Farm, and the third in a field at Town Head on the left as the road turns to leave the village. At one time elm-trees, now much decayed, were planted on them, and under the tree on that in the garden at Manor House people used to sit and smoke their pipes on summer evenings.

Coverdale is a stronghold of Methodism, and, together with Gunnerside, Garsdale, and Arkengarthdale, is one of the few places that keeps up the love feasts—celebrations with testimonies of faith. These, held annually in the summer and following a specified round, begin at West Scrafton, continue on to Horsehouse, and end at Carlton.

Should you pass up the dale on Wednesday in the second week

of June, you may find the biennial walk of the Coverdale Foresters' Friendly Society in progress. This local society, comparable with the Friendly Society at Askrigg, was originally formed in 1816 as the Banks of Cover branch of the Ancient Order of Foresters. Later the branch broke away; but officials in the procession wear the traditional green coats, green sashes, peaked hats, and black belts, and some carry staves surmounted by figures of the forest animals. The day is taken up with a church service, processions, a dinner, tea, and children's sports at Melmerby.

Across the valley from Carlton we can see the terracing of the ancient arable fields of West Scrafton between the river and the houses of the village, and open common stretching away to Roova Crags. Here and there amongst the farmhouses of West Scrafton are several cottages, once occupied by quarrymen and colliers, and the house with a tall chimney was formerly the Moorhen Inn.

In the deep limestone gill that runs through the village and down to the Cover is to be found the cave called Tom Hunter's Parlour, after a highwayman who is supposed to have been captured there, and a second cave, Otter's Hole, is entered from the riverside between Scrafton and St Simon's Chapel.

From Carlton along the road that slips out of the village we set out for the fastness of the High Dale, for Coverhead and the top of Park Rash, seven and a half miles away. Above the green meadows and brown pastures the Whernsides crown all our views; and in summertime wherever we go cows are to be seen, cows wending homewards from open commons or waiting in crofts and yards at milking time. One by one we pass through hamlets and see others on the opposite side of the river. These, first the farms of the Norsemen, next the farms of the lords of Middleham or the canons of Coverham, then occupied by yeomen, farmers, or colliers, were larger a hundred years ago than at the present day.

At Gammersgill a group of four farms, the cawing of rooks in the tall trees, and perhaps the bleating of lambs from the farmyards greet us. The hamlet is more wooded than most, but keeps only a vestige of its hundred-acre wood, enclosed in 1740. Riverside Farm is an interesting seventeenth-century building, and Hall Farm, with a door-head inscribed 'GR 1737' (George Rider), stands up boldly.

From Gammersgill northwards a by-road runs up Flemmis Gill

to end at Fleensop, where in the seventeenth century lived four yeomen, and where coal was extensively mined. In 1738 Fleensop was acquired by the Pennymans of Ormsby, who worked lead-mines and planted clumps of trees on the commons.

At the present day the hamlet is a single model farm, planned by William John Lister who, born at Fleensop, bought it in the early 1920's. After building the road up to it he set about reclaiming the land. Eventually the amount of meadow and pasture was doubled, all old grass land reseeded, the allotments improved, several new byres built, including a round one to hold 24 cows, a herd of Friesian cattle for milk production introduced, and about 1933 a grass-drying plant set up. Thus a farm of approximately 100 acres has been converted to a large-scale enterprise that, with a herd of 100 cattle, 450 breeding ewes, and a staff of five, contrasting with the usual dale practice of small holdings, reminds us of the great cattle runs of the monks.

Continuing up the dale we reach Horsehouse with the church, chapel, and school, and although the latter is closed the village is the centre for the High Dale. The road descends past old houses and the Thwaite Arms to the little church, a chapel of ease under Coverham and remarkable in that it has a rare dedicatory saint, St Botolph, and a fine weeping beech in the churchyard.

We talked with Mr Dawson Yeoman, retired farmer, who spoke of the former two inns when the village was a baiting place for the pack-horses that passed through to Wharfedale or turned off here through Arkleside to Nidderdale. His great-grandfather used to travel with a cart-load of oatmeal, fetched from Yore Mills in Wensleydale, to Kettlewell market, and bring back a load of besoms made by the Ibbetsons of Threshfield. He remembered that in his youth it was possible to stay at the house which had succeeded the notorious inn where the packmen were murdered on Dead Man's Hill near the track to Nidderdale. He told us that formerly the High Dale postman walked to Coverham for the letters. One postman announced his arrival at a village by blowing a horn, and on May Day he wore ribbons that people gave to him.

After passing through the few farms of Bradley, where a hundred years ago there was an inn to cater for the pack-horse traffic coming over from Walden, the road rises out to open common and shortly arrives at Woodale, three farms and a shooting-lodge and the last hamlet in the dale.   Here the bridge was overthrown and devastation wrought by a cloud-burst in August 1949.   A similar storm struck Great Whernside in 1872.

At the opposite side of the river we have already passed Pickle, now an unoccupied farmhouse, but once a large enough place to deserve the title of hamlet, and Sod Hall, a barn now called West Close, where potatoes were last grown in the High Dale.   These little forsaken dwellings remind us of the former larger population and of other cottages once scattered alongside the river at Coverhead.

A mile beyond Woodale across two moorland bridges, one only of which, dated 1799, withstood the recent cloud-burst, stands Hunter's Hall, nowadays more often called Coverhead.   In its remote situation this is a large farm with a flock of 1,000 sheep, and a comparatively modern and recently restored house.

By now the dale has narrowed to a mere gill, where the curlews call and sandpipers whistle by the beckside; and the road, leaving all habitation behind, winds on and on to as wild and bleak a dale head as any in Yorkshire.   We reach Hunter's Stone, a gaunt pillar, incised with a small cross, a guide post on the monastic route from Coverham Abbey to Kettlewell.   The story goes that every time the clock at Hunter's Hall strikes twelve, Hunter's Stone turns round.

The top of the pass flattens out into a plateau that ends abruptly at a long semicircular rampart of scar, so that we look over the brink towards Wharfedale.   The natural barrier was improved for defence, probably by Iron Age peoples, by throwing up a mound on top of it and digging a trench beneath, an ambitious undertaking that was carried on at either side of the road for half a mile.   On the east side small square enclosures for stock may plainly be seen.   Recently we picked up there two Iron Age scrapers of different types made of chert.

Along the top of the western edge of the scar runs an ill-defined green road that takes a roundabout route to Kettlewell, and avoids the badly engineered corners and steep gradient of Park Rash.   Although the latter was partially surfaced in 1940 and finally tarred in 1953, it is still dangerous.

Round us are Huntersleets and Hunterstone Pastures, and off to the right a ruined house, the epitome of desolation out in a wilderness of moorland.   Marked as Grouse House on old maps, it stands at about 1,650 feet above sea level; and originating like the former houses at Tan Hill as cottages for pitmen working in the coal-mines round about, it once vied with them as the highest habitations in Yorkshire. It was last occupied by a gamekeeper about sixty years ago. Near it, amongst a sea of bronze-tufted rushes, rise the first springs of the Cover.

Hunter's Stone

BISHOPDALE
AND WALDEN

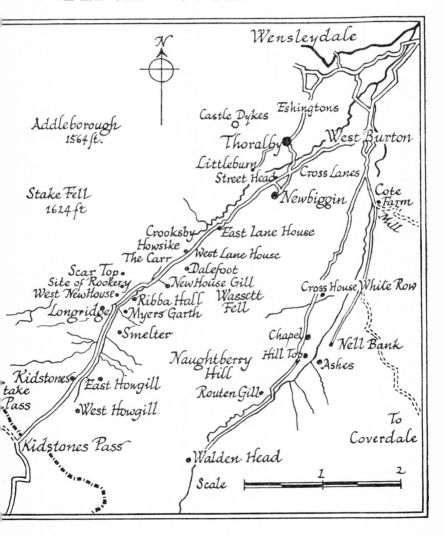

Wensleydale

N

Addleborough
1564 ft.

Castle Dykes

Eshingtons

Thoralby

West Burton

Stake Fell
1624 ft

Littleburn
Street Head

Cross Lanes

Newbiggin

Cote
Farm
Mill

Crooksby
Howsike
The Carr

East Lane House

West Lane House

Scar Top
Site of Rookery
West NewHouse

Dalefoot
NewHouse Gill

Cross House White Row

Ribba Hall
Myers Garth

Wassett
Fell

Longridge

Smelter

Chapel
Hill Top

Nell Bank

Naughtberry
Hill

Ashes

Kidstones
take
Pass

East Howgill

Routen Gill

To
Coverdale

West Howgill

Kidstones Pass

Walden Head

Scale 1 2

XII

BISHOPDALE AND WALDEN

THE two dales to be described in this chapter branch off south-westwards from Wensleydale near Aysgarth, and divided by Wasset Fell and Naughtberry Hill they run some six or seven miles into the hills to the sources of their becks on Buckden Pike.

Bishopdale is the wider of the two, with room in it for many farms and three villages—Thoralby, Newbiggin, and West Burton—whilst Walden has only thirteen farms and no space at all for villages. In Bishopdale runs the highway from Wharfedale to Wensleydale connecting the West and North Ridings, but in Walden the two narrow roads on either side leading from farm to farm come to an end, except for tracks over the fells.

The border between Wensleydale and Wharfedale is crossed at about 1,400 feet above sea level by the Kidstones Pass, a long steep hill from either side. At the summit the Stake Pass, a green road once part of the Roman road connecting the forts of Ilkley and Bainbridge, branches off over the moors towards Semerwater. This is the country for the walker, where the song of the lark and the cry of the curlew are borne away on the wind.

From the wastes of the summit of the Kidstones Pass go forward to the brow of the hill and look down to the green oasis of Bishopdale. The valley resembles the inverted half of a mussel shell, narrow and curving with its sides slanting upwards. Down these sides, sliced by narrow gills, stride little plantations. Trees mass where the beck piercing downwards rushes impetuously to the valley bottom, and trees spatter the fields and the hedgerows, except where far down lies the flat, rush-strewn, boggy land called the Carr.

Roofs glinting in the sunlight show where barns perch precariously on fellsides or cling to road edges. Isolated farmhouses, of which we see only a few, here and there reveal their whereabouts by a pale wreath of smoke from a kitchen chimney, or

229

remain invisible behind copses or tucked into hollows. Bordering the horizon, the sweeping far side of Wensleydale, with the gash of the quarry above Redmire and Bolton Castle, fragile as a fortress in a fairy-tale, near it, rounds off the picture.

Like so many other dales, Bishopdale is a U-shaped valley hollowed out by the scouring action of a retreating glacier; and the Carr is all that remains of a lake formed by an overflow from Semerwater, and also by the damming up of the end of the valley by the Wensleydale glacier at the end of the Ice Age. In those ancient times the lake was some five miles long and two and a half miles wide; and alluvial drift, reaching to an unusual height up the fells, has made Bishopdale a rich and fertile valley. In the days of farmhouse dairies it was renowned for its butter and cheese.

Part of the Lordship of Middleham, Bishopdale was preserved as a chase for the deer. Leland said of it: '. . . yn the Hilles about hit be Redde Deere. In faire Winters the Deere kepe there, in shrap Winters they forsake the extreme Colde and Barennes of them. . . . There is a praty Car or Pole in Bishops Dale.' In 1621 a butcher and two labourers from Newbiggin were brought before the quarter sessions 'for breaking the King's Park at Bushopdale, called Bishopdale Chase, and there shooting a doe younge with fawne with an arrow shot out of a crossbow.'

One of the appointments of the Master Forester of Wensleydale was 'Keeper of the Carr,' and in 1605 wages were paid to the Paliser of Bishopdale Carr, described as a 'frith' (enclosure) for the deer; it was later parcelled out amongst the farms, but in 1677 we read of Robert Ryder being given 9s. 8d., and 6d. for ale, for making half the hedge of the Carr.

Here as elsewhere the hunting of deer and the inevitable poaching of game gradually ceased. In 1654 the citizens of London sold most of Bishopdale to William Norton of St Nicholas, near Richmond, and thirty years later it passed to the Purchas family. Some of the yeomen, who had lived on their holdings for generations by the custom of tenant right, bought their farms, and built houses with dated door-heads, such as Longridge, Smelter, West New House, and Dalefoot, which remain largely unaltered to this day. At that time small tenements were absorbed in large farms. In 1605 the houses in the township numbered twenty-six compared with the ten or eleven of to-day.

From the mid seventeenth century we no longer read of deer and 'affrays' in the dale, but of orderly agriculture, of rules regulating the keeping of horses in the common pastures—Kidstones, Chapel, and Newhousegill—of the cutting of turfs, and of the hanging of pasture gates.

This road over the Kidstones Pass and down Bishopdale is little better than a lane. All the year round it carries considerable traffic: cattle lorries, tradesmen's vans, farmers' cars, and on summer week-ends the burden of pleasure cars and buses that sometimes form queues of anything up to a mile long. Yet the lane, so inadequate for its present-day usage, makes much of the charm of Bishopdale, and if it were widened and the tall trees growing in the hedgerows cut down, most of the beauty of the dale would go.

Like Bishopdale Beck, that runs beside the road for much of its route, the lane plunges down the dale, sweeping on until, having spent its force, it meanders along into Wensleydale. It has been part of a route from north-east to south-west for centuries, and it once continued directly across Wensleydale as a narrow pack-horse lane, Stony Stoop Lane—still there, if overgrown—to ford the Ure at Slapestone Wath.

Starting down from the head of the dale, we pass first one then another farmhouse, those on the south side turning their backs on us so as to face the sun, and most lying well back from the road. Dalehead, the first, has an eighteenth-century doorway and the inscription 'IL 1747' scratched on one of the stone steps of the staircase. Howgill, an empty house near it, was the home in Tudor times of the Fryers, one of the oldest Bishopdale families. In 1587 the grand-daughter of John Fryer of Howgill, after being deprived of the farm when a child, was granted possession, but she had to pay over certain sums of money at the Guildhall at York.

Stories could be woven round any one of these farmsteads. At Kidstones were three farms, of which two old houses used as outbuildings remain; the present house is comparatively modern. Here, in 1301, lived Robert and Alan Kidderstanes. We think of a later tenant, Giles Fawcett, and the sad life of his daughter Jane, who in the early seventeenth century married a ne'er-do-well, Peter Thornton of Askrigg.

The front of the next farmhouse, Smelter, with an elaborate dated doorway inscribed 'IH 1701,' is a period piece, even though the original small leaded lights of the windows have gone, and the cobbles and flags of the garden walk have been replaced by concrete.   Several interesting features, including a plaster panel and deep closets in the thick walls, remain in the interior.

By its name the farm records a place for the smelting of lead. Here, perhaps, lived Peter and John Smelter and John's son William, who were three of the men brought to justice by the Percys for digging for lead in Buckden ground in 1369.   On the farm are one or two disused levels, and several patches of bellaned ground [1] where grass formerly would not grow.   On one still bare patch in a pasture behind the house we picked up charcoal and lumps of slag from the smelting of lead.

Across from Smelter, high up on the hillside, Longridge commands a magnificent view of the valley.   The farmhouse, built by George Dodsworth in 1653, again shows a wealth of architectural detail, including arched fire-places, a plaster frieze of acorns and thistles, and a two-storeyed porch with inner and outer inscribed doorways.   Longridge, with 995 acres and a stock of 500 sheep, is the largest amongst the comparatively large farms of Bishopdale.   On the steep hillside behind the house Foss Beck rushes down a series of seven waterfalls in a particularly lovely gill.

Below Longridge, West New House faces us on the flat fields of the valley bottom.   Dated 1635, it is the oldest house in the dale, and with a central chimney-stack and adjoining buildings it has the oldest plan.

Near by, built on the site of New House proper, stood a house called The Rookery until it was pulled down and sold piecemeal in 1952, and whereas West New House has survived over three centuries this Victorian mansion only lasted between seventy and eighty years.   It was the home of the Lodge family, who at one time owned almost the whole of Bishopdale, and who sold off the estate, mostly to the tenants, in 1922.   The Rookery was used later as a farmhouse, during the last war as a private school, and finally as a youth hostel.   To-day only the entrance gates, stables, and drive remain; and on the south side of the dale the plantations spell LODGE, although the felling of trees has spoilt the shape of the letters.

A pleasant footpath on this north side of the dale leads past Howsike Farm to Thoralby.   Opposite West New House is Ribba

---

[1] Ground made poisonous by particles of lead ore.

Hall, so called after field names, Ribholeynge and Ribhalholme, that figure in an early rental when the farm appears to have been called Brokanrigge. Myers Garth near by was then called Mirehous; and many farm names that have since disappeared were variations of Scales—West, Middle, and East—which derives from the Old Norse *skali*, a hut.

The last of the old farmhouses of Bishopdale, Dalefoot, perched on the hillside, was built by George Fryer in 1640. It is again a period piece with its cobbled yard, an oak beam supporting the original open hearth, a spiral staircase, and a fine carved stone fireplace in a bedroom. Dalefoot, Smelter, and Longridge all had hearths in large alcoves with small, round-headed windows to light them; and these, including West New House, are beautifully kept and treasured by their owners.

One September day we walked with a dalesman friend across the Carr beyond Howsike Farm to the fields called Crooksbys and Crooksby Barn, an ordinary laithe with a spring of water behind it. Yet these names commemorate one of the lost villages of England, Crocsbi, as it was spelt in Domesday Book, meaning the Norseman Krok's Farm. No foundations remain of this village that disappeared in the latter half of the thirteenth century; perhaps the site was subject to flooding, but the terraces of early arable cultivation extend on either side.

At Dalefoot, which stands half in the township of Bishopdale and half in Newbiggin, we officially leave Bishopdale so far as the township is concerned, and past the Street Head Inn and Cross Lanes we approach the villages of Thoralby, West Burton, and Newbiggin.

Of these three villages West Burton is the largest, and Newbiggin, first mentioned in documents in about 1230, is the only one not to be found in Domesday Book. In that survey Ecinton appears as a hamlet under West Burton, and like Crooksby it is a lost place remembered in the name Eshington Bridge between West Burton and Aysgarth.

Here again, especially between Newbiggin and West Burton, are to be seen many ranes of the open arable fields, grassed over now, but strikingly seen from the Aysgarth to Thoralby road. Tithe barns for the collection of tithe corn existed at all three villages; but these, presumably neglected after the Dissolution, had fallen into ruin by the end of the sixteenth century. The marks of rigg and furr on Forelands Rigg are not so ancient but show where land has been ploughed in wartime.

Thoralby and Newbiggin face each other across the valley, the one poised on a warm southern slope, the other in a pleasant backwater. Both villages straggle up long streets, yet Thoralby in particular gives the feeling of being a homogeneous community with its inn, the George, a Methodist chapel, and a new village hall. Town Head farmhouse is again old, and on the lane beyond it is Littleburn Hall, a Georgian house with a fine front, if in disrepair, the home of Matthew Lord Rokeby in the last century. Note also the inscribed stone on the bridge near by.

At Thoralby was a chapel of All Hallows in which in 1316 Mary Neville, Lady of Middleham, founded two chantries and gave land in Crakehall to the abbot of Coverham for the maintenance of two chaplains. The chapel disappeared at the Dissolution: Adam Middleham, the last chaplain, was then being paid 100s. a year by the abbot.

Hugging the foot of Wasset Fell, Newbiggin straggles along a narrow lane that ends as a green-walled track on to the moor, a route to the township peat pots, quarries, and lead-mines on Wasset Fell. The township contains sixty-seven inhabitants with ten farms, counting small holdings, and several cottages, including a shop. The school is at Cross Lanes, now a primary school for the children of Thoralby, Newbiggin, and Aysgarth, founded originally for Newbiggin children by Elizabeth Whithay in 1748. The commons of Newbiggin are unstinted, and together with the shooting rights they are the property of sixteen gait-owners.

Again we find dated houses; one with a door-head 'ICD 1636' has been rebuilt, and was a pack-horse baiting place. Some eighty years ago many cottages were thatched. The white house in the centre was the Bishopdale Heifer Inn. Here, it is remembered, lived George Hesletine, innkeeper and cattle dealer, with his wife and thirteen children. George regularly bought up local cattle, and taking three days on the journey, drove them to York market, where they were sold for fattening on the stubble for Christmas. Another man who dealt similarly in geese was known as the Gosling King. The geese were shod with tar and sand, but latterly were sent by train.

We talked with Mr Thomas Hesletine, whose family have been masons for generations and who is the last member to have followed the trade. He pictured for us Newbiggin in the last century when it was a busy place, with many 'daytal' workers,[1] who were employed in walling and draining, and in bringing coal from Fleensop colliery in Coverdale. The blacksmith shod horses and sharpened tools; the shepherd herded the farmers' sheep on the moor; the bootmaker, whose workshop served as a clubroom for the men, worked until after eight o'clock at night; and three tailors, sitting cross-legged on the counter in the grocer's shop, sewed suits for the men and boys from cloth woven in Bradford with wool from their own sheep.

He pictured Newbiggin Feast that ended with the First World War, and that used to last three days beginning on the first Thursday after the second Wednesday in June. The first morning was occupied with a communal sheep-washing, after which everyone tidied themselves up ready for the fun. Friends and strangers streamed into the village. It was a matter of course for households to feed fifty or sixty people. Well-known runners competed in a fell race and in races up and down the street; games of quoits and wallops and shooting-galleries vied with each other for the patronage of the grown-ups, and hobby-horses catered for the children.

Two miles from Newbiggin at the foot of Walden is West Burton, in the past variously styled Burton-in-Bishopdale and Burton-cum-Walden. With its large beautifully mown green it rivals Wensley and Bainbridge as the show village of Wensleydale. As several large houses on the outskirts testify, Burton has for centuries been a desirable place of residence. At the east end a lane slopes down to the old mill beyond which splash the Lower and Upper Cauldron Falls.

There is something warm and friendly in the way the houses and roads circle the green. At one end is a disused blacksmith's shop, and at the other a private house that was the Black Bull Inn. The central attraction is the cross erected in 1820 and restored in 1889; and at the top of the village a pair of semi-detached stone-built council houses, built by the Peacocks, well take their place with the rest.

Although Burton was never a market town, customary fairs used to be held there. The village originally lay on the highway up Wensleydale from Middleham over Witton Moor on Penhill.

[1] Labourers engaged and paid by the day.

This route, by Morphet Gate, and the pack-horse bridge that carried it over Walden Beck, still remain on the northern outskirts of West Burton. This was an industrial village with a 'coyllour' (collier) as far back as 1301 and with dyers, wool-combers, and hand-knitters.

In 1660 Samuel Watson of Stainforth Hall, the Quaker whom we mentioned in the chapter on Ribblesdale, came to hold a religious meeting at West Burton, 'when one wicked fellow with a great staff and pistol threatened to lodge a brace of bullets in his belly and with his staff struck him several blows and knocked him down so that he was thought to be killed but afterwards he was put in the stocks and thrown in the river.'

Round the green some of the buildings remind us of other details of West Burton's story. The Congregational chapel, now a coal depot, is to be converted into a village hall. We think of the congregation 'of not less than a hundred persons' who, in 1851, subscribed to build it, of the first minister, who formed a Sunday-school and founded preaching stations at neighbouring villages, and of how, in 1855, further subscriptions were raised for the buildings of a school in Walden, where the 'spiritual darkness of this valley' was such that there was 'as much need for education as for preaching the gospel.' The school at Walden, with others like it in the little dales, is closed now and the children come to Burton.

At the corner of the green where the road turns for Walden a barn with a dated door-head at the back, 'FEB 1707' (Frederick and Elizabeth Buckle), stands on the site of Burton Hall. On the roof of this barn is a weathercock that once decorated the top of the old cross.

On Burton Feast Day the cock, which is pierced with holes, was stranded with many coloured ribbons and carried from house to house by the children, a custom last performed at the peace celebrations in 1918. 'You couldn't see t'cock for ribbons,' said our informant. Remembering the gallops and trotting racing on Feast Day, he added: 'There was nothing else for 'em then. If they'd been to Leyburn they thought they'd seen all England.'

Up into Walden the two narrow roads lead two and a half miles to Nell Bank Farm on the south side and four and a half miles to Walden Head on the north, where they end for the motorist. In any case the roads are unsuitable for traffic other than local. To

Walden

make the circuit of the dale on foot is an unforgettable walk, and to
follow the pack-horse tracks up Thupton Gill or over Dovescar to
Coverdale is to savour wild ancient routes.

What a long dale it seems, this nook in the hills! Each corner
hides a farm or two below a slope or round a hillock, where a telltale
curl of smoke spirals upwards against the hill. In autumn the
fells wear as dark a hue as a ripe plum and the fragrance of moorland herbage ebbs and flows on the air.

The name Walden derives from *weala*, a foreigner or a Welsh-
man, and *denu*, a valley, and points to the antiquity of the settlement of the dale. Walden was in the Lordship of Middleham,
and the lead-mines were worked at Dovescar, Wild Garth, and
Walden Head. In past times there were almost twice the number
of houses that there are nowadays.

At the foot of Thupton Gill near Cote Farm, whose proper name
is Thupton or Thubden Cote, is a short chimney and a few ruins,
all that remains of Burton smelt mill, the mill to which lead ore
from Bishopdale, Walden, and sometimes from Kettlewell was
brought for smelting in the latter half of the seventeenth century
and throughout the eighteenth. In 1703 the mill was furnished
with a water-wheel, bellows, and a hearth, tools, and implements.
Here as elsewhere the lead ore was always smelted at the lord's

mill so that a check could be kept on royalties, either a fifth or a sixth dish of ore or piece of lead. In 1749, on account of a feud that had developed, apparently the usual boundary dispute with Wharfedale people, the smelt mill was burnt down, but it was rebuilt later.

At the present day in this quiet wooded corner it is difficult to picture pack-horses arriving with their loads of ore, or the activities of the smelters and the smoke from the chimney, or to see the horses loaded with pigs of lead starting off on the journey to Yarm or Stockton.

Always Buckden Pike forms the background of any views up Walden: vistas framed by a wind-swept tree, or from Nell Bank to the hills sloping down on either side to a narrow pathway of flat green meadow land crossed with walls. They are stern scenes in a valley warmed by a brief summer.

At Walden Head two farmhouses and two ruined houses cluster together amidst trees by the beck, and beyond them rises fold upon fold of fell. Perhaps it is a cold February evening with the Pike fleeced with snow. Across the valley a dog barks; a woman crosses a meadow to feed hens. Each homestead in the valley is a unit: the farmer and his wife, perhaps a child or two, cows, hens, sheep, and a horse or a tractor. Each one carries on life in the dale.

Smelter, Bishopdale

XIII

SWALEDALE

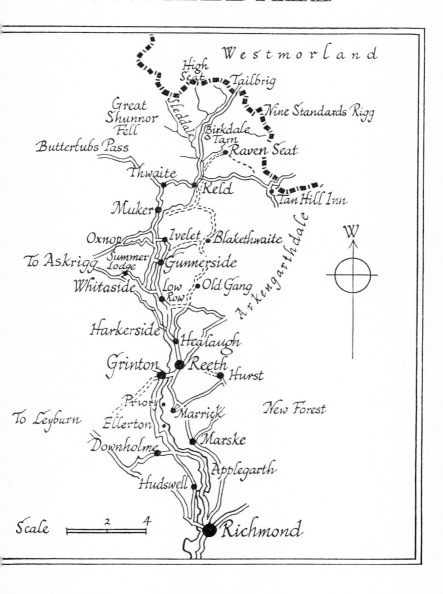

Westmorland
High Seat
Tailbrig
Great Shunnor Fell
Nine Standards Rigg
Buttertubs Pass
Sleddale
Birkdale Tarn
Raven Seat
Thwaite
Keld
Tan Hill Inn
Muker
Oxnop
Ivelet
Blakethwaite
To Askrigg
Summer Lodge
Gunnerside
Whitaside
Low Row
Old Gang
Arkengarthdale
Harkerside
Healaugh
Grinton
Reeth
Hurst
Priory
Marrick
New Forest
To Leyburn
Ellerton
Downholme
Marske
Applegarth
Hudswell
Scale   2   4
Richmond

W

1. RICHMOND TO REETH

CHOOSE, if choice is possible, a day in early spring for a visit to Richmond in Swaledale, when sunlight burnishes old stone-work, and the breeze is just strong enough to stir a flag. Walk across the market-place, pay your sixpence to the custodian of the castle, and climb to the top of the keep. Here, aloft above the town, is one of the most satisfying view-points in the north of England: northwards are the market-place and Holy Trinity Church, southwards the Castle Green and the river bridge, eastwards the white-flecked river and Easby Abbey, and westwards Bargate and the hills of Swaledale.

We look down over the stone, slate, and red-tiled roofs to the tall houses round the market-place, their variegated fronts as gay as those of continental towns. Once, in the circular market-place at Siena in Italy, a hint of the familiar puzzled us. Although, unlike Richmond, it was packed with covered stalls, suddenly the elusive likeness came into focus: exchange square keep for slender tower, northern simplicity for southern ornament, and the resemblance is there. Both places stand on hills and are country towns with ancient historical backgrounds; both market-places seem made for medieval pageantry. Richmond perpetuates no such barbaric event as the Palio, a horse-race held in the piazza; but races were run on the town moors from Elizabethan days until the end of the last century.

'Its buildings are all stone, ye streets are like rocks themselves,' wrote Celia Fiennes of Richmond in the seventeenth century. Since her day Georgian, Victorian, and twentieth-century buildings have altered the old town, and spread far and wide beyond Frenchgate, Finkle Street, and Bargate, themselves once suburbs outside the walls.

From our vantage point we see council houses and modern villas, but amongst them neither factory sheds nor works chimneys. Except for the hand-knitting and paper-making trades, now gone, Richmond has developed no industries. Once it was a great mart for corn, but other markets springing up spoilt its monopoly. If

241

it were not for the military camp at Catterick, Richmond would be a decayed market town largely dependent on the tourist trade.   As it is, in 1851 the population was 4,106, in 1931 it numbered 4,769, and in 1951, 6,166.

Richmond gave its name to Richmond in Surrey and to the ancient division of territory called Richmondshire.   It is a municipal borough, and is unique in that the town clerk's appointment must be sanctioned by the reigning sovereign.   It is the head of a parish, a deanery, and an archdeaconry.   In the seventeenth century it was the post town for a wide area stretching as far afield as Wensleydale.   It was a parliamentary borough until 1885, and on the circuit of the North Riding Quarter Sessions until 27th July 1951.   Petty sessions for Richmond and Gilling West are still held there.

The story of Richmond, like that of Middleham, divides into two parts: the first phase, centred round the castle and the religious houses of the Middle Ages, ended at the Dissolution; and the second, following the fortunes of the borough, still continues.

The first began at the Norman Conquest when Earl Alan, Duke of Brittany, built a castle near the old capital of the district, Gilling, and named it Richmond.   The castle proved to be a medieval folly, partly because the Breton Earls of Richmond, with their divided loyalties to England and France, were sometimes dispossessed of it by the English kings; and, although it provided a stronghold and a prison during the era of Scots raids and wars, most national events passed it by.   Even in the fourteenth century it had fallen into disrepair.   In 1565 it was said of the governor that he was 'too much given to pastime and would be fitter at Court.'

Under the castle's protection the Normans gave land for the founding of many religious houses: Greyfriars, a nunnery near it, five or six chapels, a college, a guild for priests, and Easby Abbey, St Martin's Priory, and the Hospital of St Nicholas in the adjacent countryside, and the priories of Marrick and Ellerton in Swaledale. Richmond was filled with the religious.   Early charters often address French and English, clerks and laymen.

The second part began in 1093 when Earl Alan Niger, reserving a feudal rent, sold the borough to the inhabitants, and thus enfranchised the town.   Markets and fairs were granted: the

Richmond from Bargate Green

medieval fairs at Richmond must have been tremendous events. Elizabeth I gave the charter of incorporation in 1576, and Charles II confirmed and enlarged it in 1668.

Look for a moment at Richmond from the Terrace, a romantic view, engraved, etched, and painted by artists who come from far and wide.   The eye, beginning with the River Swale and the bridge over it, travels to grey houses and many trees clinging to a steep hillside and topped by the curtain wall of the castle and the keep, beyond which spreads a band of dark moor.   Obscured by a morning haze, the town looks as if it dreams of a rich past.   We can see the parish church of St Mary's in its garden-like churchyard, and the old grammar-school building where James Tate, the famous headmaster, taught his 'invincibles.'

The story of the town may be read in its buildings.   There are the tower of Greyfriars, a last blossoming of monasticism; the bar on Cornforth Hill, one of the original entrances through the walls; the Georgian houses in the cobbled streets of Newbiggin and Frenchgate; and the grand-stand, built in 1775, on the old race-course.

The survey could be long, but for lack of space must end with two buildings—one religious, one secular.   From 1740 until 1923 Holy Trinity Church was so hedged about with houses and shops that it constituted a little district sometimes described as 'Round the Church in the Market-place.'   Even now, though shorn of buildings at the tower end, there are in the island of Holy Trinity two houses, ten shops, and a suite of offices.

In Friars' Wynd a building with rough windowless walls is the theatre.   It and one at Bristol make the only two remaining Georgian theatres in England.   Built by Samuel Butler, it opened on 2nd September 1788, and here Kean, Kemble, and Macready played.   In 1840 the theatre fell into disuse, and after being reopened temporarily in 1943, it has been further restored.

Although no historical event took place in the market-place, burgesses, townspeople, and children assembled there for feast days, markets, and fairs.   We picture them against a setting of the huge old cross, the Barley and Oat Crosses, the pillory, stocks, tollbooth, shambles, and maypole, all of which have now gone. Here in 1644 Prince Rupert and his men rested after their defeat at Marston Moor, and four years later Oliver Cromwell halted on his way south from Scotland.   In January 1746 Scots prisoners were billeted in public buildings, including Holy Trinity Church, and in 1757 armed horsemen gathered to quell a bread riot of miners from Wensleydale.

To-day only one market cross, the tall obelisk topped by a ball, adorns Richmond market-place, but the town preserves the cobble-stones at great expense by resetting them in concrete. On Saturdays, market-days, stalls fill part of the square; and every day hardly a moment passes without single- and double-decker buses from all parts of the North either entering or departing.

Richmond boasts several famous sons, including Henry Great-head, the inventor of the lifeboat, and Samuel Buck, the engraver; and at Hill House lived Fanny I'Anson who inspired the song, 'The Lass of Richmond Hill.'

George Cuitt, the artist, who became drawing master for the town, was born at Moulton, near Richmond, in 1743. His talent attracted the attention of Sir Laurence Dundas, who sent him to study art in Italy. When he returned he settled in London, but owing to ill health came back to Richmond. His son, George Cuitt junior, the etcher, followed him as drawing master, and was in turn succeeded in 1805 by Julius Caesar Ibbetson junior.

In modern times outstanding figures in the town's affairs are the Ropers, of whom Miss R. G. Roper has been mayor four times, and David Brooks, town clerk from 1941 to 1955, who wrote a short history of Richmond, and for fourteen years vigi-lantly upheld the traditions and beauties of his adopted town.

Richmond represents continuity. The Curfew and the Prentice Bell, and once a year on Shrove Tuesday the Pancake Bell, ring out from the belfry of Holy Trinity Church. The feudal rent, first paid to Earl Alan in 1093, is still paid with surprisingly little alteration part to the Crown and part to the rector of Melsonby. The Company of Mercers, Grocers, and Haberdashers is the sole survivor of the thirteen guilds, and it and the corporation treasure their plate—cups and insignia—given for one reason or another by local men; and Richmond's own regiment, the Green Howards, keeps a close link with the ancient garrison town.

Once more at our view-point, the east prospect takes us to Easby, about a mile from Richmond. It consists of a hamlet in the woods, the hall, and down by the river the abbey and parish church. Modern opinion suggests that before the abbey was founded in 1155 there was perhaps a small minster or college of secular priests at Easby. Both abbey and church deserve careful exploration to see in the one case the extensive lay-out of a Premonstratensian monastery, and in the other the thirteenth-century frescoes, painted in black and terra-cotta colours, crudely restored but still striking. If you wish to see the magnificent design and carving of the Easby Cross you have to visit the Victoria and Albert Museum. Here is only a cast. Although it has been spoilt by the building of a wooden bungalow and the felling of trees, Easby is one of our favourite corners of the dales; the church especially has an atmosphere of great age.

The horizon of distant hilltops, seen from the west view of the keep, draws us to Swaledale. It used not to be an easy dale to reach; and although railways through it were considered in 1882 and in 1912, they never materialized. Nowadays the motorist takes the road on the south side of the river; the walker perhaps chooses the old road on the north. The first, still called the New Road, was made as a turnpike from Richmond to Reeth in 1836, and was virtually new as far as where the Leyburn to Reeth road came in near Ellerton Abbey. It opened out a route below hanging woods with across the river the steep scars and rough wild country of Applegarth. The old road, which we are about to follow, traverses the hilltops on the north side of the Swale, dipping down to Marske and up again, and finally down to Fremington and Reeth.

About a mile and a half along the old road, a little past Beacon Hill and approached through a gate half way between a plantation and two radar masts, is Willance's Leap. Across a big field stand two stones commemorating the escape from death of Robert Willance when his mare leaped over Whitfield Scar in November 1606. From here we look down to the narrow gorge of the Swale winding between steep wooded slopes, with afar off the Plain of York and the Hambleton Hills.

In the Middle Ages Richmond Castle dominated this part of Swaledale; below us lies Applegarth, and for miles behind stretched the New Forest of the Earls of Richmond, to this day wild bleak highlands. Families lived on small manors at Feldom, Skelton, Marske, and Marrick, some followers of the earls, or the FitzHughs, or the Scropes, some fighting at the Battle of the Standard, others going on a crusade to Jerusalem. At East

Applegarth, the farm immediately below us, lived a family called Applegarth, who held their land by the service of attending the earls at Easter and Christmas processions.

A few miles farther on, Marske rests quietly in a sequestered, tree-protected hollow. When it was on the main route up the dale the village had an inn, now the Temperance Hotel, and up to the last war it had a smithy. Though Marske does not appear in Domesday Book, the ranes of a common field show up plainly as we approach it from the east. It has a church dating from the twelfth century, a fine bridge with ribbed arches of the fifteenth, and a Georgian hall. Clipped yew hedges, a magnificent lime avenue, great beeches, and ornamental grounds below the hall give the air of an estate village.

From 1598 the Huttons have owned Marske, and although they have sold the hall, which is now divided into flats, they still possess the estate. They claim the rare distinction of having had two archbishops in the family: Matthew Hutton was Archbishop of York from 1595 to 1606, and a later Matthew, having been Archbishop of York, became Archbishop of Canterbury in 1757. The obelisk on a hilltop marks where Matthew Hutton of Macclesfield, a benefactor to this district, was buried.

From Marske a small, wooded valley with a prominent limestone scar a mile or so long is watered by the Marske Beck, a stream with many tributaries finding their sources in the New Forest, the 'forest waters' let for fishing in medieval times. During the Ice Age the Stainmore glacier, overflowing into Swaledale, carved out this deep channel. Once the stranger approaching the valley saw the surprising sight of two mansions, Marske Hall and Clints Hall, less than a mile from each other; and farther on he saw yet a third, Skelton Hall, on the other side. Skelton, by far the least interesting of the three, remains, part unoccupied and part converted into three cottages. Clints Hall was pulled down by the Huttons, who bought the estate in 1842. It had had many owners, including the Willances, Bathursts, and Turners, and although it was enlarged by John Carr for the last owners, the Erringtons, it appears to have been castellated and early Stuart in date. A group of cottages and stables marks its site.

On a spring evening, when the westering sun lights up the yew-fringed scars and splashing waterfalls of the beck, the charm of this little valley is to be seen at its best. Below a footbridge and a little south-west of the farm, Orgate, you can find large mounds by the beck where stood Clints smelt mill, to which lead from Arkengarthdale was brought to be smelted in the eighteenth century; and at Jingle Pot behind Clints was once a famous racing stable of the Turners, as at Helwith Farm were the stables of the Huttons.

Soon along the old road we reach the cross-roads to Marrick and Hurst. Just before them a green-walled lane leads to the ruins of Marrick smelt mill, one of the largest mills in the dale. Marrick, a mile off the road, and three miles from a bus route, lies at 1,000 feet above sea level, a bleak, somewhat neglected village. Amongst scattered farmhouses sheltered with fine copses of sycamore are the old vicarage, the manor-house, and the White Horse Inn that when we were there looked untidily antiquated, with some fifty hens roosting on the edge of a garden-bed by the door and a cat sunning itself in the doorway.

Away down by the river and at either side of it stand Marrick and Ellerton Priories. Ellerton, a sad meagre ruin with only a small tower left, was in 1342 sacked by the Scots, who carried off several charters with the result that little is known of it. It was recorded in 1268 that a local family called Ellerton had always accompanied the prioress on journeys, taken messages for her, or when she wished to travel alone had provided a horse, and had also given her and the convent an annual entertainment in their own house.

To savour to the full the atmosphere of these medieval days in Lower Swaledale you should first read H. F. M. Prescott's *The Man on a Donkey*, published in 1952, and then approach Marrick Priory from Marrick village down the Nuns' Causey. The long flight of stone steps, over three hundred of them, overgrown and embowered in trees, ends near the purlieus of this long-forsaken Benedictine nunnery. The few ruins, the orchard, the neglected church, and the farmhouse near it cluster above the rippling Swale in an atmosphere of ageless tranquillity.

Before returning to Hurst we may glance at Downholme and Walburn Hall by crossing the river at Downholme Bridge. Both places lie far up the hillsides approaching Wensleydale, and both belong to the War Department, whose property extends here from Catterick Camp. Downholme church by the roadside, in a churchyard surrounded by tall conifers, is old and interesting, and near the village are the turfed-over ruins of the manor-house.

The inn, the Bolton Arms, by its name commemorates the former owners of the place, the Scropes. Once mineral wealth—coal, lead, and stone—made Downholme a busier place than it is to-day.

The isolated farm of Walburn Hall, seen to advantage in its setting of green meadows, arrests the attention and arouses conjecture. A fortified manor-house, largely Elizabethan in date but with many earlier features, it was restored in 1882 by the then owners, the Huttons. It has a cobbled courtyard, flanked on two sides by battlemented walls with a terrace for defenders, a ruined chapel, an enormous isolated chimney, and a bay window overlooking the road from what is called Mary Queen of Scots's room.

In Swaledale only short distances separate sheltered valley from desolate moor. The few houses at Hurst lie three and a half miles north-east of Marrick Priory at 1,250 feet on a wind-driven, drear landscape. A first view fixes on a house in green meadows, a ruined, single-storeyed, whitewashed house with barns under a long ling-thatched roof. At one end of the hamlet is a gamekeeper's house, once the mine agent's, and at the other an inn, the Green Dragon; and westwards stretches the debris of lead-mines. Hurst mines claim great antiquity and were worked from Roman times to the end of the last century. A hundred years ago the hamlet seethed with life and activity. Old men have remembered as many as sixty houses 'gone down'; and in the 1840's at Hurst races the miners and the ore and lead carriers competed with their horses.

Its former life of mining halted, Hurst keeps anachronisms in the ling-thatched buildings. The long whitewashed house, Roan Farm, was occupied until 1938. How far removed it seems from the present dale farmhouse with electric appliances and television! An ancient cowshed on the road approaching the hamlet and a barn in it are the only thatched buildings now in repair.

In times past the place was known as Red Hurst, so called from the discoloured waters of a chalybeate spring, and Hurst men were nicknamed Redshanks. A legend attaches to this well. It tells of a passing traveller who, snatched by the guardian spirit, dyed the well red with his blood; the villagers going there to pray for his soul saw a vision of the Virgin, and henceforward the Well of Roan 'flowered with blessings streamed with health.' In later years the Methodists held camp meetings at the well on Trinity Sunday, the day associated with the legend.

2. SWALEDALE:
PAST AND PRESENT

FROM the hilltop over which the old road drops down to Fremington, a fair prospect of Swaledale unfolds. What first strikes the onlooker is walls: walls criss-crossing on the narrow flat valley floor; walls that so densely stripe the green hillsides that they darken the landscape. Grey buildings, black blobs of churchyard yews, a patch of water reflecting the sky, where the river is crossed by a bridge, mark Grinton. Only just showing on the right the houses of Reeth encircle the green; on either hand the ling-clad heads of Harkerside and Mount Calva enclose the dale and a vista of overwrapping hills. As like as not a grey sky with advancing clouds caps the picture.

Nowadays Swaledale means to us the thirty miles of dale from Tailbrig on the west to Richmond on the east. But to medieval men Swaledale was a smaller area with definite dimensions: a tract of land from Stollerstone Stile, near Cogden Hall just below Grinton, to Tailbrig, or Hollow Mill Cross, by which the boundary was then marked. An old jingle perpetuates these limits:

> From Hollow Mill Cross to Stollerstone Stile,
> The extent of Swaledale is twenty long mile.

Long ago after the Ice Age when the steep slopes sank into sinister lakes, Swaledale did not attract prehistoric man. An arrow-head or two found at the head of the dale, a lead spindle whorl at Ivelet, enclosures behind Calvert Houses, earthworks at Grinton and Fremington, and Maiden Castle on Harkerside largely comprise the remains, of which Maiden Castle, a defensive structure, is by far the most interesting and awaits full-scale excavation to reveal its secrets.

Two local traditions of great antiquity say that the Romans came by boat into the dale, and that it was colonized by outlaws. Both may contain a grain of truth. Although quite unconnected with the Romans, perhaps the post-glacial lakes in the valley round Reeth were known to early man, and by outlaws may be meant the Norsemen living amongst the hills away from Norman rule. A Roman pig of lead, now lost, was discovered in old workings at the Hurst lead-mines in the last century; a large horde of Roman military scrap, now at York Museum, was found on Fremington Hagg; and although not scientifically identified, the road from Bainbridge, entering down Haverdale Gill, crossing Swaledale, and continuing by Peat Gate to Arkengarthdale and on to Barnard Castle, is probably Roman. About eighty years ago at Crackpot in the little Haverdale valley, a pig of lead with what appears to have been a Roman inscription was dug up by workmen levelling a meadow, but its historic value was not realized, and it was melted down for use.

As for the permanent settlement of the dale, place-names point to the Angles, coming from the east, establishing themselves at Reeth, Grinton, Fremington, and Healaugh, and Norsemen arriving from the west reaching down to Feetham. So far as Swaledale is concerned the Domesday survey ends at Reeth and Grinton. For two or three centuries after it most Swaledale villages were single farms.

In the twelfth century Maud, daughter of Count Stephen of Brittany, brought 'Swaledale' as dowry to her husband, Walter of Gant. The Gants gave to Bridlington Priory the Manor of Grinton, which extended on the south side of the river as far west as Haverdale Beck, and a later member of the family gave to Rievaulx Abbey a vast pasture that eventually became the Manor of Muker at the head of the dale. The Manor of Healaugh, with the hunting-lodge of the Gants at that village, covered the rest of the dale.

A last paragraph completes these facts on which the story of the dale hangs. After the Dissolution, except for the Manor of Grinton, the Whartons of Wharton in Westmorland acquired Upper Swaledale, and some two hundred years later, to pay the debts of Philip Lord Wharton, it was sold to Thomas Smith of Easby and Grays Inn. From him it descended to Captain F. H. Lyell, and it was later bought by Lord Rochdale who sold it to Lord Peel, the present owner.

Reeth is to Swaledale what Grassington is to Wharfedale, a little metropolis for visitors. It stands on the hillside above the Swale

High Row, Reeth

and Arkle Beck at the point of meeting of Arkengarthdale with Swaledale. Once Reeth was a market town with a charter granted to Philip Lord Wharton in 1695. A hundred years ago five fairs for merchandise, two cattle fairs, and a market on Fridays drew large crowds. The town served not only a farming but an industrial community: then the lead-mines were in full swing, though the knitting industry had already declined. The population numbered almost 1,500, and it now totals 588.

What a wide-flung open space is Reeth green! Many hotels and cafés mingle with the houses that surround it, and on summer Sundays cars and buses crowd its cobbled border. At the north-east corner, the old part, is an ancient well, and by the Arkle Beck the corn mill and the miller's house. The house, with small mill-stones used as lintels for its many windows, is something of a curiosity. High Row, dominating the west side of the green, speaks of eighteenth-century prosperity, when the shop fronts had decorative bow windows and the inns rubbed shoulders with each other, as to some extent they still do.

In this mid twentieth century Reeth Show and large autumn sheep sales have taken the place of the market and the fairs. On 1st September, show day, crowds, stock, and vehicles mass round two rings on the flat meadows for which the ridge of Fremington Edge makes a background. A friend said to us as he waved his arm towards the hills: 'To me this is it—just the place for a show.' And so it is. Sheep and cattle, marquees, stands, and a band playing make up a big event that preserves a vigorous local character. Spectators and competitors in family or friendly parties mingle on the ground, and enjoy the holiday atmosphere of what at this time of year is usually the end of the hay harvest.

Across the valley Grinton church, Blackburn Hall, and an hotel cluster by the bridge over the Swale, but most of the houses of Grinton straggle up a gill away from the noise of traffic. The 'Church of Swaledale,' as it was called when the Gants gave it to Bridlington Priory, stands in a spacious churchyard. Here in medieval days people from the far ends of the parish, carrying wicker biers along the Corpse Way, came to bury their dead. Grinton, besides being the parish town of Swaledale, was also once the market town. Leland says that the market was for 'Corne and Linyn Cloth for Men of Sualdale, the wich be much usid in digging Leade Owre.'

Blackburn Hall, or Nether Hall as it was once called, was the chief house of the lords of Grinton, as Swale Hall, half a mile west, was the chief house of Bridlington Priory. The first, called Blackburn Hall after the family of that name who owned it in the eighteenth century, looks shrunken with age, and even older than the date, 1635, on a chimney and fire-place.

Swale Hall, connected with the Swale family, stands well above the river and close to the lane across Harkerside. Three hundred years ago there were other houses and a walk mill near it; and in the early years of the last century it was divided into tenements occupied by miners.

The Swales, who were an ancient local family, lived at the hall after the Dissolution. In the middle of the seventeenth century they fell into debt; Richard Swale languished in fetters in York Castle; and their home was a mean place little better than a barn. About 1649 Solomon Swale, who later was knighted, restored the family fortunes and rebuilt the house. But lead-mines were the saving and the undoing of the Swales. In a prolonged endeavour to claim a manor of West Grinton, and with it the mineral royalties, a later Sir Solomon beggared himself and died a debtor in the Fleet Prison in 1733.

On this the south side of Swaledale, where only a narrow road leads on from farm to farm and eventually over the hills to

Wensleydale, Harkerside and Whitaside stretch up the dale as far as Haverdale Beck, the old limit of the priory land. On these slopes men have lived from time immemorial. Here are Maiden Castle and the ranes of arable fields that line the meadow land between road and river; here were once rich lead-mines, How groves, Birks, and Green Hills mines, over which both the Swales and the Whartons fought bitter lawsuits with a lessee of the Crown; here ling was gathered to thatch houses; and here still grows a few acres of juniper to remind us of the once huge acreage of the bush in the dale.

On the wild upland road to Askrigg are still to be seen the ruins of ling-thatched houses and barns, once miners' small holdings. In one of them, a little west of Bents Farm, lived Wartin Jinny. The story is told that if she wanted to know the time Jinny used to go up on to the road, knitting all the way, to hear the church clock at Askrigg in Wensleydale strike the hour.

The Haverdale Beck cuts down the hillside and plunges into a wooded ravine with the farm of Summer Lodge deep in the gill at its head, the hamlet of Crackpot half way down, and Haverdale Mill at its foot. One of the two tributaries flows from the cave, Fairy Hole, and the other down Bloody Vale, supposedly the scene of a clash between Scots raiders and the men of the dale; battle-axes and pieces of armour have been found at Crackpot. Summer Lodge was the property of Bridlington Priory, occupied by the herdsmen of the canons perhaps only in summertime. Up behind this sheltered corner a ling-thatched barn is the survivor of five or six similar buildings for hay and stock.

The chimney of Haverdale Mill—most of the rest of the building is pulled down—speaks of another phase of Swaledale's industrial life—knitting. The Knowleses of Low Row built the mill in about 1835, and, besides yarn for knitting, carpets were made. But, hampered by the lack of water-power and the cost of carting coal for an engine from Tan Hill pits, the mill closed in about 1870.

All the way along it Whitaside gives superb views of the dale. Perhaps it is a grey afternoon with rain blowing up. From ragged cloud shafts of sunlight radiate down to the valley as if directed on to a stage. Every wet roof of barn or house is a pin-point of light, and a road gleams like white thread. The sun catches the swelling end of a hill that falls to the Swale. Beyond it the dale winds on.

But before going farther up let us briefly survey what is the theme of the story of Swaledale—the lead-mines.   Often in early times the theme is shot through with covetousness and greed, and often in the last century it embodies philanthropy and poverty. The lead-mines shaped the whole pattern of life of the dale for centuries.   Formerly there were very few yeomen families such as the Brodericks of Spring End and the Garths of Crackpot; and almost everyone else, living on small holdings, was connected with the mines.

At Draycott Hall at Fremington is an office that still contains the maps, plans, ledgers, and papers of the mines.   The hall is named after Anna Maria Draycott, who inherited the lead-mine royalties from the Duke of Wharton's sister, and who married the Earl of Pomfret, a major figure of eighteenth-century lead-mining in Swaledale.   Next, Peter Denys, a London lead merchant, who married one of the earl's daughters and thus acquired the royalties, carried on the story.

In the last century Draycott Hall was the home of Sir George Denys, who took a leading part in promoting the welfare of the industry as it declined.   In the garden is a monument to the past story of the mines—a lead figure of a bearded man, seated on pigs of lead, which personifies the planet Saturn, which to the old alchemists typified lead.

Apart from the Roman pigs of lead, which in any case are lost, early proof of mining in Swaledale is scant.   After the Norman Conquest records of leases, shipping, miners' rights, and lead merchants bring the story to monastic mining.   Rievaulx Abbey had mines at the head of the dale; and lead for the roofs of Bridlington Priory, that excelled even the renowned roofs of Jervaulx Abbey, no doubt came from Grinton.

In the seventeenth century the pace increased.   The lords of the manors, who owned the royalties, either leased ground or ran their own lead works; for example, the Whartons mined extensively and profitably at Old Gang, Blakethwaite, and Friarfold mines. The eighteenth century saw the climax of small workings: every lead-bearing area in the dale was tapped by shafts; partnerships of adventurers leased meers [1] of ground; and a share in a lead-mine was a popular investment for those with money.   By the end of the century 1,000 to 2,000 men were engaged in mining, and some

[1] A measure of ground of varying length in different districts.

6,000 tons of lead were raised annually.   Slowly the woods, burnt as fuel in the smelt mills, fell as before an advancing machine.

In the last century, after a time of desperate straits following the Napoleonic wars, the industry swelled out into the companies of Victorian times—the Old Gang, the A.D., the Hurst Mining Companies, to mention but a few.   Capital was sunk in expensive undertakings; levels were driven many miles into the hills; and the river and becks ran the colour of clay with the washings. From Lane End mine at the head of the dale to Hurst at the foot, spoil heaps strewed the hilltops and gills; and lead worth tens of thousands of pounds was raised each year.   Until in the 1880's the whole great gamble, pricked like a bubble by a slump in prices owing to imports of foreign lead, collapsed.

The liveliness of past centuries hovers in the wind where the mines are to be found on the wild and lonely hills of Swaledale. In the first half of the last century, when the population was more than treble that of to-day, hundreds of miners going to or coming from work trod hard the footpaths up the pastures.   Partnerships of eight or sixteen men took bargains at so much a bing (eight cwt of ore).   Work went on ceaselessly day and night in six-hour shifts.   On winter nights the lanterns of the men bobbed across the hillsides like moving stars.   Women and boys set peats to dry on the moor, or worked at 'kibbling,' sorting and washing the ore in the becks.   In every village lived one or more mining agents; and processions of carts shuttlecocked backwards and forwards on the dale roads.

Throughout the heyday of mining most of the lead was carried by pack-horses along jagger lanes to the port of Stockton, to which Hartforth and later Richmond were stages on the routes.   At Stockton agents shipped most lead to London, but part went to Holland, Sweden, Hamburg, and St Petersburg.   When the railway came to Richmond in 1846 the shipping ceased.   In times of bad trade lead piled up in the station yard, as it had once piled up on the wharves at Stockton.

Each day, winter and summer, the men walked from small holdings on the hillsides or from cottages in the villages, or they lived during the week at 'shops' near the mines.   They descended shafts by crude wooden ladders, perhaps carrying wooden props attached to their waist-belts.   Their groove clothes were seldom dry, and sometimes in winter froze on them as they returned home. The lives of smelters were shortened by the breathing of poisonous fumes. Yet the fresh air of Swaledale alleviated some of these evils.

Through good and bad times the miners worked hard and endured without complaint. House rents were low, but land, in great demand, was expensive. The men never tired of discussion of veins, pipes, and floats, or t'Owd Man, as their predecessors and their workings were called. With a naïve simplicity they threw themselves whole-heartedly into religious revivals. For amusement they organized horse-races and hound trails. They relished a day's poaching, played quoits and knur-and-spell, perhaps performed in a band composed of fellow miners, and on pay days drank, sang, and danced at night in the inns.

Throughout the centuries jubilation or despair punctuated the story of the mines. Gallons of ale were drunk to celebrate the striking of rich veins or the completion of ambitious schemes; and twice disputes over boundaries developed into prolonged and bitter trials at law. In 1697 and in 1707 the Whartons were engaged in lawsuits over the Grinton mines, and in the 1770's there was the tremendous boundary dispute between the Earl of Pomfret and Thomas Smith, the lord of the manor, over mines on Crackpot Hall Farm near Swinnergill at the head of the dale. This quarrel, which split the dale into factions, resulted in a victory for Thomas Smith, who died shortly afterwards. But the Earl of Pomfret, having dissipated his fortune, was imprisoned for debt in the Tower of London.

Many other dramas emerge from the past. For instance, one Good Friday in the last century a father and son, archers in the mines, were finishing some repair work at Brandy Bottle mine in Flinter Gill when the archway of the level fell in and trapped the son. The distracted father had to return for help, and met his wife near Gunnerside. She ran to the mine, entered the level, and knowing nothing of the way rushed in the dark and past dangerous places to where her son was lying buried. When rescuers arrived he was found to be dead.

Another tale relates how a miner, renting ground by the month, struck a rich pocket of lead. When the agent came round to inspect Thomas was afraid that the rent would be raised, so he sat on his find. In course of time he made enough money to buy a good farm. But all the old miners who could tell these tales have gone, and those who died recently only worked in the mines as boys.

The industry gradually faded out over the last twenty years of the nineteenth century. In any case all the easily accessible lead had been won, and that old enemy, water, had become more and more menacing. Families left for Durham coal-fields or Lancashire cotton mills. Some went to the lead-mines in Spain. The smelt mills, smithies, and mining shops, houses and cottages fell into ruin; the shafts ran in; at Reeth grass grew over the cobblestones where the market had been held. Gradually the people adjusted themselves to the life of a farming community.

3. HEALAUGH TO BIRKDALE

To JOURNEY into so narrow a valley as Swaledale is always something of an adventure. 'With each curve of the road there are new outlines to the hills, new becks and ravines to be discovered, new villages to surprise one over the brow of a hill,' wrote Ella Pontefract.

The dale road dips down to the river, runs up the hillside away from it, narrows to squeeze through villages, and twisting and turning across the high fells at length mounts to the watershed. Little is to be seen from it to remind us of past lead-mining days: many of the spoil heaps are grassed over, and in any case these are mostly to be found on the hilltops and in the gills; the miners' cottages have been restored as homes for people retired from towns, and farms and barns, once miners' small holdings, dot the green meadows; in winter an intense quiet prevails, gripping the dale like a hard frost.

Sometimes in early spring, with the sun facing us as we proceed, the dale lies submerged beneath a nebulous mist, softly blue, above which a wash of a deeper shade marks off the tops of the fells. A clear primrose light glances on to walls and the window-panes of isolated farmhouses; it catches a blade of grass here, a ripple of water there, and at evening turns to a pink glow on the hillsides. The valley, struggling from the rigours of winter, seems poised for the reawakening of spring.

After Reeth villages follow each other closely. First Healaugh with west of it Park Hall, a farmhouse on the site of the Whartons' hunting-lodge. Next come Feetham and Low Row that merge together along hilly greens. Feetham derives its name from the Old Norse *fit*, meaning meadow; Low Row means literally Low Row, from the fact that it was below the original route up the dale, which ran high on the hillside through Barf and Blades. At Feetham is the Punchbowl Hotel, once the Miners' Arms; and at Low Row are several large houses, such as Paradise and Gorton Lodge, once the homes of the Fryers and Gortons and later of the

259

Parkes and Knowles families: all connected with mining or the hosiery trade.

Here, when in 1761 John Wesley preached at Low Row and Blades and found 'an earnest, loving, and simple people,' the first seeds of Methodism were sown in the dale. Farther along the hillside was 'the new house adjoining Smarber Hall in Swaledale certified to be set apart for a public meeting house for Protestants,' built in 1691 by Philip Lord Wharton, the Dissenter, noted for his gifts of Bibles. Low Row Congregational church, built in 1809, took its place; but each year on the second Sunday in August a service is held in the open air at Smarber, where a low wall with seats built round it marks the site of the 'new house.'

We remember admiring the views from Smarber, elevated as it is above the valley, and being told by a realistic farmer's wife that views did not bring in money!

The road, clinging to the hillside, runs below Rowleth Wood, one of the few areas of natural woodland left in the dale, and dropping down into Gunnerside turns sharply at the bridge over the beck. Here are the King's Head Inn, the smithy, and in a cleft of the gill a bus garage that was originally the corn mill.

'At Gunnersett when t' grooves were going, ther'd be twenty or thirty young chaps on t' brig of a neet, there wer mar stir then,' an elderly dalesman once told us. To-day few people will usually be abroad; but if you chance to arrive at the village on a Monday in early July you may find a 'do' in progress, or a 'stir' as they say so much more effectively in Swaledale. Fifty or sixty people, sitting on forms on the bank of the by-road up the gill, watch the children compete in the sports of 'Midsummer Week,' an annual Methodist festival. As the large chapel below the bridge proclaims, the village is a centre of Methodism. After the mines closed, members of families who had left returned for 't'longest day' and 't'shortest day,' as the summer festival and a Christmas event were called. At the summer 'stir' a procession of children, headed by a band, used to wend its way on to the pastures to be given spice (gingerbread) and milk: the hillside was 'clad wi' people.'

Turn to a different scene. Look in at the smithy at Gunnerside eighty years ago. Supposing it is a gloomy winter's morning with hard-frozen snow on the road, David Calvert and his son, working at hearths on either side of the shop, are 'on sharping

Gunnerside

shoses' for many horses to prevent them slipping.   If we lingered we should see the smith write down in his daybook the names of the customers, most of whom are known by their by-names: Neddy Postman, Curly Jack, Kit Jock Kit.   So many large family clans lived in the dale—Aldersons, Rutters, Percivals, Calverts, Sunters—that individuals had to be distinguished by the addition of their parents' names, or by characteristics, or by their callings. David sometimes used his daybook as a diary, and on 20th October he noted that it was Gunnerside Fair Day.   This was a farmers' event for the sale of sheep and cattle, but also with stalls for spice, sweets, and toffee.

At the present day David Calvert's grandson is the smith at

Gunnerside. The door of the smithy is scored with the initials of mining companies and the hornburns of sheep made by branding irons, and forms a little record of past times.

Nowhere in the dales, unless it is in the neighbouring Hard Level Gill, are there to be seen more dramatic settings for the devastation wrought by lead-mining than in Gunnerside Gill. Both cleave majestic purple and black fells, slashed with patches of rushes, springy turf, tufted bents, and grey outcrops of limestone where slowly the scars of mining heal, and where now the tinkle of a peaty stream, the beating of sheep, the whistle of a shepherd to his dog, and the cries of moor birds alone break the silence.

For a walk up Gunnerside Gill take the green road, that half a mile west of the village turns off the pastures to run high up along the side of the gill. Soon below the track is Sir Francis level, named after Sir Francis Denys of Draycott Hall, and the last great level to be driven. Farther on, the gill on either side, shattered by hushing,[1] looks as if torn again and again by huge claws. In the hush on the west side a solitary juniper grows on a scar. Here is Lownathwaite mine, where the Earl of Pomfret was induced to grant too sweeping a lease, a mistake said to have caused his death; and Blakethwaite, from which one man in the last century raised lead worth £120,000. The ruins of Blakethwaite smelt mill, standing on a spit of land at a fork of deep heather-clad gullies, cry of desolation and of dramas played out long ago.

Westwards at the top of Botchergill lies Moss Dam, which by long races supplied water to Swinnergill on the one side and the mines in Gunnerside Gill on the other. When we were there one day in early May, black-headed gulls screamed as they rose from their nests, and sharp gusts of wind hinted at the bitter cold of other times of year in this exposed place.

To make a round and to reach the mining field of the Old Gang, cross the moor to Level House on Hard Level Gill. The ancient house, for long a ruin, once had 'an oven of hewn stone,' and here in 1692 lived Adam Barker, who buried his daughter in linen contrary to the current law. So past the Old Gang smelt mill and the Surrender mill of the A.D. Co. we reach a cross-roads and turn right for Feetham and so back to Gunnerside.

[1] A method of exposing lead ore by releasing water from a dam down a hillside.

Nowadays the dale road crosses the Swale at Gunnerside, but it used to continue up the north side of the valley and cross at Ivelet Bridge. This most lovely of hump-backed pack-horse bridges, spanning a rocky stretch of the river that matches it for beauty, has been left in a quiet backwater down a rough lane.

In 1832 Gunnerside Bridge was built—there had been a shaky wooden bridge before—and situated at a difficult crossing it fell three times in seven years. The first bridge stood forty-six years. But on 29th January 1883 it was severely damaged by a flood; on 26th July 1888 it was down again after a thunderstorm; and on 25th January 1890, only three months after it had been rebuilt, it was washed away once again.

If we take the old road we cross Gunnerside Pasture, the ancient cow close of the village, which is still run communally and has never been enclosed, and past isolated farms we reach Ivelet Gill and the shooting-lodge of Lord Peel, a prominent feature in this part of the dale. Below it in the group of a farm and five or six cottages that make up the hamlet of Ivelet is a head keeper's house, built in 1953 of local stone, and remarkable where for many years houses have been restored but seldom built.

On this side of the dale a cart-track leads on to Calvert Houses, a mile beyond Ivelet. A grand route for walkers, it was part of the Corpse Way and also formerly a well-used road continuing on the north bank of the Swale by Ivelet Side, Swinnergill, and East Stonesdale to the coal-pits at Tan Hill.

Calvert Houses, once the calves' houses, perches high up on a jutting shelf of land. Here the valley is so narrow that you can shout and almost be heard at the farm, Crow Trees, immediately opposite. Westwards the overlapping hills of the dale head— Muker Side, Kisdon, Great Shunnor Fell—draw nearer. When it lay on a busy road the hamlet boasted an inn, the Travellers' Rest, and many more dwellings than the three farmhouses and a cottage of the present day. In late Elizabethan times Richard, son of a Marmaduke Milner of Calvert Houses, settled in Leeds where he and his descendants prospered as merchants. William Milner was mayor in 1697, and his son was created a baronet.

From the valley bottom Oxnop Gill rises steeply in surging, swelling contours to the watershed between Swaledale and Wensleydale. Up it was once a busy route to Askrigg market; and later considerable traffic in goods fetched in carts used to ply between Askrigg station and Muker. For travellers and lead-miners there was an inn at Jenkin Gate, no longer a gate but a cattle grid on the west road. Five or six farmhouses dot the valley, and one or two barns were once houses. Hill Top, near the summit, braves the winds at 1,300 feet, and Rash Grange, at the foot of the gill, is a seventeenth-century house with a dated door-head, 'TC 1685.'

Low Oxnop, or Oxnop Hall, may well occupy the same site as the chief house of the monks of Rievaulx Abbey. The present farmhouse has mullioned windows with ornamental dripstones, a stone arched fire-place, and a stone dated 'EAI 1685.' Old houses, now converted into barns, adjoin it. Here dwelt George Kearton, one of those superhuman figures from the past, who once engaged an army of miners and plied them with gallons of ale, who fought wrestling contests at Tan Hill, who when he was a hundred followed the hounds in a pony chaise, and who died aged 125 in 1764.

In this grave sweet valley of the Swale meadows like the flowery meads of medieval paintings burgeon in early summer. Perhaps nowhere else in the dale does the yellow of buttercups splash the fields more boldly, or the pink of wood crane's-bill tinge them more deeply, or wayside bushes shower sprays of pink and white roses more freely than here round Gunnerside and Muker.

Soon the leafy lane, parting company with the Swale that skirts round the island hill of Kisdon, brings us to Muker. Seen across a bridge, the grey village makes an harmonious grouping on a terrace above the beck backed by abruptly rising meadow land. Muker church was built as a chapel of ease in Grinton parish in 1580; and starting in the eighteenth century a customary market was held in the village. It had a school founded in 1678; and to Muker School in the later years of the nineteenth century came Richard and Cherry Kearton, the naturalists, and Swaledale's most famous sons of recent years. If mining has gone, and with it the market, yet Muker still makes a centre for visitors and for the sheep-farming community of the dale head.

Up here the fells, stretching far-flung for miles, provide ideal ground for the Swaledale breed of sheep. A hardy, tough, horned sheep, able to live on exposed ground in all weathers except prolonged snow, the breed is distinguished by its black face with a grey nose, a thick, shaggy, but not coarse fleece, grey

Muker

mottled legs, and well-laid-back horns, those of the tups being large and curving. The Swaledale Sheep-Breeders' Association originally included the dale itself, Wensleydale, Teesdale, and part of Westmorland; and a system of marking pedigree stock on the horn, known as crowning, helps to maintain the quality of the breed. These sheep have increased in favour during the past few years, and registered flocks now graze the Pennines from the West Riding to Northumberland, the Lake District Fells, and the Cleveland Hills. At the autumn sales the best tups fetch big prices, £1,800 being the present record; and at Muker Show the value of a few sheep grouped together in a class may well be £1,000 or more.

At Thwaite, a mile west of Muker, the Buttertubs Pass from Wensleydale drops down to the village. Thwaite never seems to have quite recovered from the cloud-burst that caused so much damage in 1898. Here elderly people may tell you of going over the Buttertubs to Hawes market when there were no traps, not to mention motor-cars, and when the farm muck cart cleaned out and the bottom spread with rushes formed the means of transport; or they may describe the glories of Thwaite Fair—the stalls and the naphthaline flares at night—or show you a treasured fancy plate bought for a penny from a stall when they were children.

Talking to a Thwaite joiner one stormy winter's evening, we looked up at a grey implacable sky. 'It's snowing at Angram,' he remarked; and indeed as the road mounts the hill out of the village it seems to lead to even wilder regions—to Angram, Greenses, Aygill, Thorns, and Keld.

The few houses that make up Keld lie snugly round a little square off the main road. Change has come to the village recently: the Cathole Inn no longer greets you as it did until it was sold and converted into a house in the autumn of 1954; the following year the post office, for fifty-eight years kept by the Waggett family, was moved to the youth hostel that is housed in what was once the shooting-lodge at Keld Green. Beyond the village two stone houses, which, like the keeper's house at Ivelet, fit admirably into the scene, have been built by Lord Peel.

Truly these changes make little difference to Keld's magnificent setting of river scene, Pennine dale head, and wilderness of fells. It is the walker's ideal centre. You may breathe in great draughts of exhilarating air, and stride over the moors for miles without seeing either a house or a human being. You can scramble in the river gorge and see the waterfalls of Wainwath, Catrake, and Kisdon, or explore the side valleys of Stonesdale, Sleddale, Whitsundale, and Swinnergill, or after two or three hours' walking reach the summits of Great Shunnor Fell, High Seat, Nine Standards Rigg, or Water Crag.

For a short walk that to Swinnergill and Crackpot Hall (not to be confused with Crackpot near Low Row) is the most spectacular. The hall, so finely situated overlooking the Swale gorge, has been unoccupied since 1953 because of the distance from a road and because its foundations are shaken by mining subsidence. Near it was the home of the keeper of the deer of the Whartons, and Hall Out Pasture, enclosed in 1636 for the deer, was the scene of the Smith versus Pomfret lead-mining lawsuit.

From Keld the narrow road reaches Tailbrig and the Yorkshire-Westmorland boundary in seven glorious miles of wild moorland in an amphitheatre of giant fells. We reach Birkdale, a hamlet of scattered farms. Birkdale Tarn lies north of the road, and was dammed to supply water to Lane End mines. Look down from the road to the lonely ruins at the point where Great Sleddale and Birkdale Becks meet to become the Swale. By the roadside we pass Crook Seat, now a barn and once an inn; but there is no sign of Hollow Mill Cross that even a hundred and fifty years ago was only marked by a rough pile of stones on the right-hand side of the road at the summit.

Perhaps, as we have journeyed, it is winter with frozen waterfalls grotesquely swollen with ice like lava; or it is summer with the meadows encircling the farmhouses brilliantly green by contrast with the brown fells. Perhaps we have been to the top of High Seat or to see the well-built cairns of the Nine Standards, where the bleating of sheep and lambs, the cries of curlews, the soughing of wind through the rushes, and the gurgle of water in a sike alone disturb the silence.

ARKENGARTHDALE

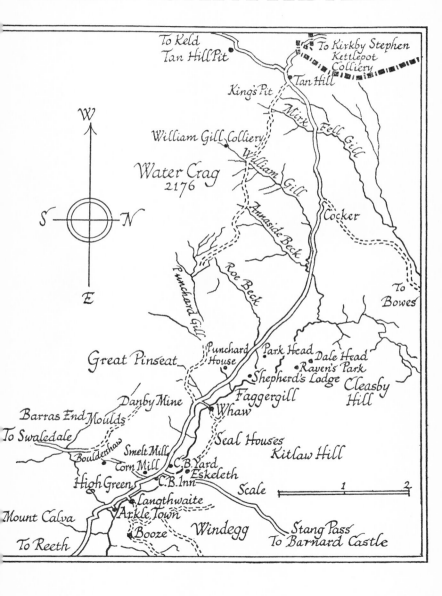

To Keld
Tan Hill Pit

To Kirkby Stephen
Kettlepot
Colliery

King's Pit

Tan Hill

Mirk

Fell Gill

W

William Gill Colliery

William Gill

Cocker

Water Crag
2176

S

N

Annaside Beck

E

Roe Beck

Punchard Gill

To
Bowes

Great Pinseat

Punchard
House

Park Head

Dale Head

Raven's Park

Shepherd's Lodge

Cleasby
Hill

Danby Mine

Faggergill

Barras End Moulds

Whaw

To Swaledale

Seal Houses

Kitlaw Hill

Bouldershaw

Smelt Mill

Corn Mill

C.B. Yard

Eskeleth

High Green

C.B. Inn

Scale

1

2

Langthwaite

Mount Calva

Arkle Town

Windegg

Stang Pass

To Reeth

Booze

To Barnard Castle

XIV

ARKENGARTHDALE

IDDEN away in the folds of the hills, Arkengarthdale
branches northwards off Swaledale at Reeth; and although
a turnpike to Tan Hill, Brough, and Kirkby Stephen ran
through it and a Roman road from Bainbridge to Barnard Castle
crossed it, these routes are now by-roads rather than highways.

Of all the Yorkshire dales, Arkengarthdale most preserves
memories of industry, scarred as it still is by the ravages of lead-
mining. It is a self-contained unit with its own church and
parish, chapel, manor-house, and school, and spaced along it are
the small village of Langthwaite and the hamlets of Arkle Town,
Booze, High Green, Eskeleth, Seal Houses, and Whaw. From
the heights of Water Crag at the head of the dale the Arkle Beck
hurries down some eleven miles before it joins the Swale near
Grinton. The atmosphere of this upland dale is clear, as if it
were always new-washed; larks sing above a green valley, and
curlews call over thousands of acres of moor.

Leaving Reeth the road traverses open common, shut in on the
east by the long cliff of Fremington Edge, mine-scarred and
partially wooded. In two miles, suddenly and without warning,
Arkengarthdale comes into view. We see not all the dale but
most of the three miles that are inhabited set out for our delight
like a picture with toy buildings painted by a child or a Sunday
painter.

On our left the deep cleft of Fore Gill and on our right Slei Gill
separate Arkengarthdale from Swaledale, or to be more specific
the townships of Reeth and Fremington from that of Arkengarthdale. Heather dapples the hills, and plantations of dark fir and
larch soften their bald outlines. High up on Great Pinseat across
Fore Gill the farmhouse called Bouldershaw catches the eye. In
the bottom the houses of Arkle Town, which was originally the
parish town with the church, face us; and on the hillside to the
right the few scattered farmhouses of Booze look down the valley.

271

Arkengarthdale

The dale road winds upwards through High Green, past the Methodist chapel, to Langthwaite, its houses thrown together next to a bridge under which a patch of water reflects the sky. Above the road is the new church and ahead the conical Kitlaw Hill, with almost on its summit the white-painted windows of a little farmhouse. As the dale turns the vista ends with a glimpse of moorland, token of the many miles of wild country at the head, and peeping out are the distant heights of Beldoo Hill on Stainmore and Mickle Fell in Teesdale.

Arkengarthdale, the dale of Archil's enclosure, is not included in the Domesday survey, but it was a forest of the Earls of Richmond mentioned before 1171. It became part of the Honour of Middleham in 1444, and was sold by Charles I to the citizens of London. In 1656 Dr John Bathurst, physician to Oliver Cromwell, bought it, and the connection with the dale of this family and its descendants by marriage lasted until 1912.

The story of this remote valley inhabited in the past by an independent and obstreperous people has often been turbulent. For long the villages and hamlets were no more than solitary cattle farms. In early centuries marauders frequently raided the forest, and in 1308 they burned the house of the Earl of Richmond at Arkengarth and killed the forester. In the seventeenth century the tenants quarrelled over rents with Dr Bathurst, who high-handedly threatened to transport them all to Ireland. From this era many local wills and inventories have survived, preserved amongst the records of the manor court that had right of probate. In the time of Charles I the forest was full of deer, and there were still 120 in the 1670's.

In 1657 Dr Bathurst founded a free school to have a school-master with a salary of £16 a year, and he also left funds for the binding out of apprentices, both of which charities still provide money for scholarships for the children of the dale. Although imperious, the doctor took a personal interest in his tenants; he sent tobacco from London for the miners and gave poor widows 1s. a quarter if they went to church when they were able.

Again as in Swaledale the theme of the story of the dale is the lead-mining industry, linked here with the mining of coal and the quarrying of chert. Although the old jingle dates them farther back:

> When Julius Caesar was a king
> Bowes Castle and Arkendale mines was a famous thing,

records begin in 1285, when the profits of the lord's mine in the dale and New Forest were £4.

Dr Bathurst worked many mines, as did his son and grandson, both called Charles Bathurst, after whom the C.B. Co. and the C.B. Inn were named. In the early nineteenth century the chief mining concern was under the direction of Frederick Hall, who, pleading the poverty of the miners, conducted a campaign for the raising of the price of lead. Later the Old Gang Co. and other lessees extensively developed the mines, of which Stang, Faggergill, Moulds, Windegg, and Danby were the most productive. Moulds was one of the most famous in the country, in Faggergill almost twenty-five miles of rail were laid, and in Stang level a miner could burn out a tallow candle before he reached his day's work.

In the last century the dale had at one time a population of 1,500. Besides the church as many as six Nonconformist chapels provided for the spiritual needs of the people. There were five inns and four beerhouses, including two inns at Whaw and two C.B. Inns, the present one and a second at Arkle Town. A small market was held once a month to coincide with the miners' pay day. Arkendale Rood Fair catered for the sale of farmers' stock, and a show for produce and stock was started in 1851. Even in 1890 120 pupils attended the school.

As at Grinton the church claimed a tithe on lead. Here it was levied only on all the ore that would not pass through an inch riddle, an implement that was kept at all the mines. After years of disputes a different arrangement was made in 1773. A strike of miners arose in 1873 over the maximum price to be paid to ore-getters. It lasted for twenty-two weeks and was remarkable in the history of mining here. It is remembered that during that time a few men and boys went to work in the lead-mines at Appletreewick in Wharfedale.

Slowly fading out the mines closed in 1902. Many people left or had already left to go to Durham, where the connection still remains rather than with the industrial West Riding or Lancashire. Nowadays the population is reduced to 300, and there are only two inns, one chapel, neither market, show, nor fair, and between ten and twenty children attending the school. Many cottages belong to townspeople; half the population of Langthwaite, for instance, consists of incomers. Yet for all this, a vigorous community of dalespeople is still to be found in this lovely little valley.

Leaving our vantage point we reach Arkle Town, a few houses down a lane off the main road. In the early eighteenth century one of these on the north side was the workhouse for the dale. A woman, Anne Raw, occupied the post of first governor and was paid 1s. a week; the poor knitted stockings for sale, and the house was warmed by peats bought at 8d. a cart-load. At the end of the lane once stood the church, where now in an ordinary field spangled with wild pansies are to be seen two table-tombs and a few headstones leaning at all angles, some almost sunk out of sight into the ground.

An elderly dalesman has told us a story relating to one of his fore-elders who lived at Arkle Town a hundred or more years ago. A lead-miner and a married man with three children, he one day walked the two miles to Danby mine, where he had half a mile to walk in the level, to work the early morning shift. He returned home and walked twelve miles to Middleham in Wensleydale to compete in sports in which he won the half-mile and mile races.

On past a shop and petrol pumps we 'go across the bridge,' as they say in the dale, to Langthwaite, its houses and the Red Lion Inn crushed into a small space at the foot of a steep hillside.

From it a pack-horse lane leads to Reeth on the east side of the Arkle and a rough road mounts to Booze, whose extraordinary name means the house by the curve. Booze consists of three farmhouses and a few holiday cottages.

Continuing up the dale we reach the Methodist chapel, closely linked with the story of the dale in the last hundred and fifty years. The large grey building was built in 1882 to replace an older chapel built in 1798, now used as a Sunday-school.

As in other remote places in the past, Methodism rather than the Church of England came to the help of the rough people of a mining community. Revivals occurred in Swaledale in the 1820's; but the greatest in Arkengarthdale started one Sunday morning in 1868 and continued for eleven weeks. Meetings lasted until one and two o'clock in the morning, and after that groups of young men gathered on the hillsides for prayer until daybreak. Amid emotional scenes whole families were converted and many people inspired to become local preachers.

A little beyond Langthwaite we reach the church, which is interesting as an example of a Regency building. It has a gallery, and from the interior you look through plain glass windows to the fells. The first church in the dale, at Arkle Town, was appropriated to Egglestone Abbey in Teesdale before 1292, and it was once a chapel of ease in the parish of Startforth, the parishioners having at times to walk ten miles there and ten miles back to the mother church.

Although they are not observed to-day, funeral customs are remembered. As the procession of mourners approached the church and the bell tolled out, a dirge was sung, each line being first announced by the clerk. It ran:

> Hark from the toll the dolesome sound,
> Thine ears attend the cry.
> Ye living men come view the ground
> Where ye must surely lie.

We were shown a worn wooden stamp with which a pattern whose central motif was a heart was impressed on funeral cakes.[1] The stamp was handed down from one woman to another. A woman would receive orders for perhaps a hundred or more cakes. They were cut in half, put together with the design outwards,

[1] For recipe, see Appendix C, page 311.

wrapped in white paper, sealed with black sealing-wax, and given to the mourners. Mrs W. H. Hutchinson of Old School House, who told us these details, remembered as a child running to meet her father returning from funerals to beg for this titbit.

After the church we reach the cross-roads of what was the Roman road, already mentioned in the chapter on Swaledale and now running across Arkengarthdale and over the Stang Pass to Barnard Castle. Here at this junction is the C.B. Inn, altered and renovated in recent years.

Here too, off the road at the foot of a copse of fir- and pine-trees, is the corn mill. The mill, at which the Hirds were millers for many years, had six pairs of stones and worked up to 1945. Before the First World War five sons with five horses ran it: one son stayed at home to grind, one went three times a week to Richmond for corn, and the rest delivered to farms. The water-wheel was taken down in 1955.

The road that we travel up the dale was formerly a busy route to the coal-pits at Tan Hill and a drovers' road for stock from the north being driven down to such fairs as Middleham and Askrigg Hill Fair. It was made into a turnpike from Tan Hill to Reeth in 1741, and it linked up with other turnpikes to Bowes and to Brough in Westmorland.

Long before the turnpike, pack-horse routes crossed the fells. One route took a more direct line to Tan Hill by turning off westwards just before Whaw Lane Head, crossing Little Punchard and Great Punchard Gills, and proceeding by Punchard Head, Annaside Edge, and William Gill to Tan Hill. Eastwards a pack-horse route led up Slei Gill eventually to join Jagger Lane through Hartforth and Melsonby to Darlington and Stockton. This route anciently originated as a salt track and was used later for the transport of lead. Evidently in the past evildoers fled this way for sanctuary at Durham Cathedral; to this day if children are naughty they will be threatened: 'Tha'll ha' ter gaen Darnton [Darlington] Trod.'

At the point where the Roman road drops down to the Arkle Beck to mount the long and steep Stang Pass running under Windegg much of interest is to be found. The first house on the right, Plantation House, was Lilly Jocks, an eighteenth-century inn for drovers, and in a field on the left is the little octagonal powder house for the lead-mines. Across the river, in well-kept gardens, is Scar House, built in 1855 on the site of the old manor-house.

Below it at the west side of a bridge over the Arkle is Old School House, perhaps the first site of the school founded by Dr Bathurst, which was replaced by a new school built in 1813 by George Brown, then lord of the manor, on the main road.

Wherever we cross the Arkle we find it framed in trees and burbling over a stony bed. It is the most musical of rivers as it tumbles over pebbles in little white-flecked rapids, and runs merrily from its birth on wild moors down the dale.

Across the Arkle is secluded Eskeleth, a few scattered cottages and a dilapidated chapel on the hillside, and below them Eskeleth Hall, until recently, when they were felled, backed by woods. The eighteenth-century hall faces down the valley towards Mount Calva, and in the past it was generally owned or occupied by lessees of the lead-mines. The chapel with three pointed windows was built in 1854 for the Barkerites, followers of George Barker who seceded from the Wesleyans. As a chapel it appears to have had a short life, for no one in the dale remembers it being used as a place of worship. Opposite it a building that is now two cottages was erected as a chapel for a similar group of people, the Kilhamites, but this was never actually used.

Returning to the main road and continuing up the dale we pass the centre of the lead-mining, on the left the ruins of the nine-teenth-century smelt mill with the arches over the hearths still standing, on the right the C.B. Yard and Terrace, once stores, offices, and a house for the manager, most of which have been converted into dwellings, and below them the remains of an eighteenth-century smelt mill. This, built as an octagon with a great roof and fine timber- and stone-work, fell into disrepair some twelve years ago, and has since been sold off piecemeal to builders. The second mill was built because at the expiration of a lease two companies disagreed. In the seventeenth century a smelt mill for the dale stood near Barras End on Blaeberry Gill at Foregill Gate where the Roman road crosses into Swaledale.

A little farther on is the platform where chert was loaded, and far away above us may be seen the chert quarry below the escarp-ment on the side of Great Pinseat near Danby mine. The hard flint-like stone was used for pottery-making, but owing to the importation of chert this small industry ceased in 1954.

From now on the road begins to leave cultivation and prepares to enter open moor. Across the valley lie the scattered habitations of Seal Houses dotted along the lower slopes of Kitlaw Hill. For centuries here and at Eskeleth lived the Peacocks, the most ancient and important family in the dale. One of them, John Peacock, who died in 1680, followed the trade of stockinger and travelled about the dales buying and selling stockings made of wool, carded, spun, and knitted by men as well as women.

High above Seal Houses is Kitlaw Hill Farm, whose white windows we saw from the distance. An elderly dalesman has told us a tragic story of his fore-elders who lived there. When his mother was a child, one of a family of four or five children, her mother died, and soon afterwards her father, clipping sheep, cut himself and died from blood-poisoning. Whilst he was ill a neighbour who was drunk came to visit him, and fell down the stairs, which had no banisters, and broke his neck. This man's wife, who had six children herself, brought up both families. The eldest parentless boy had left school and between them they managed to run Kitlaw.

Next down across a bridge over the river come the eight houses of Whaw, perhaps shining silver in the sunlight against a wood of fir and larch. These curious names—Whaw, Kitlaw, and Faggergill farther up—all speak of the Norse settlement of the dale. They mean respectively the enclosure near the fold where sheep are milked, the hill near the cow valley, and the sheep enclosure gill.

Sometimes enclosed, sometimes open, the road mounts across treeless moorland. Every now and then tracks strike off westwards to little derelict mines or isolated farmhouses. Looking down to where the road dips and turns to cross a gill stands Punchard House. This ancient farm was owned by William Conyers of Marske, who leased the lead-mines of the dale in the early sixteenth century. For the last ninety years owned by the Peacocks, it is a large well-known farm with a flock of some five hundred sheep. Forty years ago in Punchard Gill a great northern diver was shot.

Near Beck Crooks Bridge, at the junction of William Gill and Annaside Gill, the Arkle begins. Both gills rise on the huge wastes of Water Crag where the rare bird, the twite, nests. A signpost marks the rough road turning off to the right to Bowes

and Sleightholmedale.   We top the hill called Cocker, 1,529 feet;
and if it is a clear day see far ahead the Nine Standards on the
boundary of Swaledale and far beyond them Saddleback and
Skiddaw in the Lake District.   On our right stretch the featureless wastes of Stainmore, as desolate and awesome as any tract of
country in England.   At length, but not until we have almost
arrived, we see Tan Hill Inn, the highest inn in England, at 1,732
feet above sea level.

Tan Hill Inn and the roads that converge on it owe their origin
to the coal-pits round about.   To the west are Kettlepot and
Taylor Rigg, southwards on the road to Swaledale is Tan Hill, and
south-westwards are King's Pit and William Gill.   Coal was won
here in the thirteenth century: William Gill is a medieval name,
really William's Gill, and coal mined here warmed Richmond
Castle and in more recent times the castles of Lady Anne Clifford.

Such was the value of the pits that in the early years of the last
century King's Pit let for £450 a year.   At the end of the century
as many as fifty or sixty carts might be assembled on autumn days
at Tan Hill Pit to fetch coal for winter; and farmers, bringing
produce to sell on the way, came from Appleby and Kirkby
Stephen, Richmond and Bedale.   Tan Hill colliery, the last to be
worked, closed down about 1932.   Few signs are left of past
activity: an old building and shafts scattered all over the wild
boggy uplands where hawks hover and a solitary farmer shepherds
his sheep.

Although Tan Hill Inn has been modernized and the motor age
has robbed it of some loneliness, it still occupies a remote lofty
site four and a half miles from Keld in Swaledale, the nearest
village.   An eighteenth-century building, the inn was originally
King's Pit House, the ruinous building west of it was Tan Hill
House, and a third building stood just behind the inn.   Early in
the last century two of these buildings were inns; and Tan Hill
House was occupied by an old pitman and his wife and son until
about 1916.

For many years the Pounders were the innkeepers.   The story
goes of one of them appearing before the magistrates at Richmond
to apply for his yearly licence.   When he left the court he realized
that no hours had been stated, so he hastened back and was told:
'Mr Pounder, you have permission to keep open day and night.
Refuse no one at Tan Hill.'

From 1903 to 1945 the Peacock family kept the inn, and the wireless broadcasts of Susan, who died in 1937, made the place famous. Since they left, the inn has been modernized and its dales character diminished. Here the Swaledale Sheep Breeders' Association annually hold one of their shows.

From the rocks behind, called Summer House Hill, we can see round us the fells—Great Shunnor Fell, High Seat, and Nine Standards Rigg. On a clear day eastwards in the opposite direction drifts the smoke of Middlesbrough forty miles away. It represents modern industry that has left the dales untouched for our delight.

M. H.

J. I.

Askrigg, Jan. 1954–Jan. 1956.

APPENDICES

APPENDIX A

ABBEYS, CASTLES, AND CHURCHES

Bolton Priory

The Priory of St Mary at Bolton (by long usage erroneously called Bolton Abbey) belongs to the Duke of Devonshire, who allows the public free access. A house for Augustinian canons, it was founded in 1120 at Embsay, near Skipton, by Cecily Romilly, wife of William Meschin, lord of Skipton Castle; and their daughter, Alice, c. 1154, granted the Manor of Bolton to the canons, who moved there the following year. A community of a prior and fifteen canons, the priory was surrendered in 1539, and was then worth annually £389 4s. 5¾d. gross.

Apart from the church, few ruins of interest remain. The nave of the priory CHURCH, entered by the tower, still serves as the parish church, and the rest—transepts, choir, presbytery, and chancel—are the beautiful ruins facing the river, familiar to many people.

Originally aisleless, the CHURCH was repaired and lengthened c. 1180, when the crossing piers, the S. wall of the nave, and the N. and S. transepts, each with three chapels in their aisles, were built. The nave was completed c. 1240. Included in this were the magnificent W. front with its doorway, arcading, and lancet windows, and the upper part of the S. wall with a remarkable row of two-light windows on the inner side of which is a wall-passage. In c. 1330 the transepts were reconstructed, the N. aisle of the nave was rebuilt, and the chancel lengthened and rebuilt. The incomplete W. tower was begun in 1520 by the last prior, Richard Moone.

The ruined transepts and chancel show a diversity of architectural styles, and the 'stone-work and detail . . . are among the masterpieces of fourteenth-century art.' In particular note the wall-arcading (twelfth century) and the tracery of the Decorated windows, including the E. window.

Only the foundations of the CLOISTER remain, at a lower level than the church. Note in N.E. corner two fine Early English doorways. Similarly little is left of the octagonal CHAPTER-HOUSE; the doorway of this building has been removed to the GATEHOUSE, itself now part of Bolton Hall.

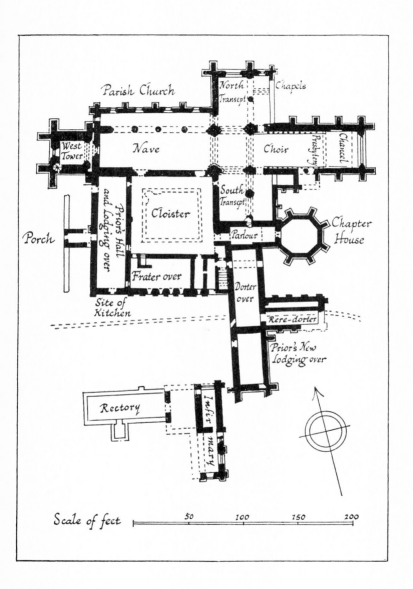

Parish Church

North Transept

Chapels

West Tower

Nave

Choir

Presbytery

Chancel

Prior's Hall and Lodging over

Cloister

South Transept

Porch

Parlour

Chapter House

Frater over

Dorter over

Site of Kitchen

Rere-dorter

Prior's New lodging over

Rectory

Infirmary

Scale of feet   50   100   150   200

JERVAULX ABBEY

The ruins of the abbey, owned by Mr W. L. Christie, lie in the grounds of Jervaulx Hall, and are open to the public.   The Abbey of St Mary, a Cistercian house, was founded in 1145 at Fors, near Dalegrange in Upper Wensleydale, by Acaris, ancestor of the FitzHugh family and a near relation of the Earl of Richmond.   In 1150 Fors was placed under Byland Abbey, and six years later, owing to the bleakness of the climate, the monastery was removed to its present site near East Witton, on land given by Earl Conan.   It was forfeited to the Crown in 1537; its gross annual value was £455 10s. 5d.

The extensive ruins are chiefly composed of the domestic buildings. Little of the once fine CHURCH, except foundations and bases of piers and responds, remains.   The CHURCH was completed in the early thirteenth century; it consisted of aisled presbytery, N. and S. transepts, and aisled nave.   Separated by two chapels and the rood-screen, the monks' and lay brothers' choirs occupied the latter.   Note at the foot of the high altar a mutilated figure of a recumbent knight representing Henry FitzHugh (d. 1387), and amongst other features a late twelfth-century door into the CLOISTER at the S. of W. bay of S. aisle.

The CLOISTER is not perfectly square.   The W. range is occupied by the CELLARIUM (200 feet long), with the lay brothers' dorter above.   On the S. of the CLOISTER little remains of the monks' FRATER, but connected by the WARMING ROOM their DORTER, with a row of thirteenth-century lancets, is the most prominent part of the ruins.   E. of the CLOISTER is the CHAPTER-HOUSE (early thirteenth century), once vaulted, and with twelfth-century central doorway, octagonal piers of a fossil limestone, with floriated capitals, and grave slabs of abbots.

To the E. run various ranges of buildings—the monks' REREDORTER, the INFIRMARY, and the MEAT KITCHEN (fifteenth century) with huge fire-places, ovens, sink, hatch, and refuse shute.

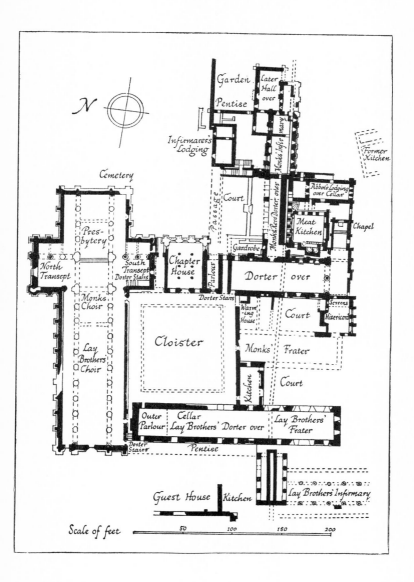

N

Garden

Later Hall over

Pentise

Infirmarer's Lodging

Former Kitchen

Cemetery

Court

Monk's Infirmary

Passage

Abbot's Lodging over Cellar

Pres-bytery

Monk's Rere-Dorter over

Meat Kitchen

Chapel

Gardrobe

North Transept

South Transept Dorter Stairs

Chapter House

Parlour

Dorter   over

Monks Choir

Dorter Stairs

Warm-ing House

Court

Screens

Misericord

Cloister

Monks'   Frater

Lay Brothers Choir

Kitchen

Court

Outer Parlour

Cellar   Lay Brothers' Dorter over

Lay Brothers' Frater

Dorter Stairs

Pentise

Guest House   Kitchen

Lay Brothers' Infirmary

Scale of feet   50   100   150   200

COVERHAM ABBEY

The site is in private grounds on the N. bank of the River Cover, one and a half miles S.W. of Middleham; access is by permission. The Abbey of St Mary de Caritate was a house of Premonstratensian canons, founded at Swainby, near Pickhill (near Thirsk), *c.* 1187, by Helewise, wife of Robert Fitzralph (builder of the keep at Middleham), with the assent of her son, Waleran. Her younger son, Ranulph, removed the house to Coverham, *c.* 1202. After partial destruction by the Scots in the fourteenth century the abbey was rebuilt. Rebels in the Pilgrimage of Grace collected here. The abbey was suppressed in 1536; there were then an abbot and sixteen brethren, and the gross annual value was £207 14*s.* 8*d.*

The remains, which are few, and chiefly of the CHURCH, are approached from Coverham Bridge under the arch of the INNER GATEHOUSE (*c.* 1500). The CHURCH consisted of aisled presbytery, N. and S. transepts, aisled nave, and probably a central tower. The chief remains above ground are three piers and two arches of the S. arcade of the nave (*c.* 1340), W. end of N. aisle with its doorway, and W. side of N. transept with two lancets (early thirteenth century). In the chancel, note the interesting grave slabs, one with cross fleury and a shield of the Fitzrandalls of Spennithorne. The CLOISTER, now a lawn and flower-beds, was S. of nave.

The present house (seventeenth century) was built by George Wray, and by the later inclusion of the GUEST HOUSE (sixteenth century) it has assumed its present proportions. Note: in the W. wall a large mullioned window with nine lights; in the E. wall two doorways, one with a black-letter inscription, 'Dn Gr. Abbas TMS Honfelde,' and over the other an inscription 'IHS,' letter 'A' for Abbot Askew, and the eagle of St John. Other fragments of masonry abound; some are built into a wall in the garden. Placed against a wall are two (once recumbent) figures of knights (mid thirteenth century), supposed to represent Ranulph Fitzrobert and his son; also there is an unidentified torso of a third effigy.

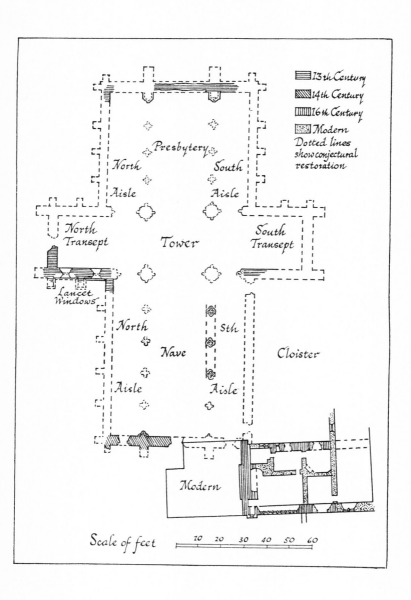

13th Century
14th Century
16th Century
Modern
Dotted lines
show conjectural
restoration

Presbytery

North

South

Aisle

Aisle

North
Transept

South
Transept

Tower

Lancet
Windows

North

Sth

Nave

Cloister

Aisle

Aisle

Modern

Scale of feet   10   20   30   40   50   60

EASBY ABBEY

The Abbey of St Agatha at Easby came under the charge of H.M. Office of Works in 1930. It was a house of canons regular of the Premonstratensian order, founded *c.* 1152 by Roald, Constable of Richmond Castle. In 1393, after the Scropes had acquired the patronage, Richard Scrope augmented the endowments. The abbey was surrendered in 1535, when its gross annual value was £188 16s. 2d. In 1886 the ruins were excavated by the Yorkshire Archaeological Society.

Owing to the nearness of the river and the parish church, the CLOISTER is irregular in shape and the position of some of the buildings does not conform to the usual plan. The fine early fourteenth-century GATE-HOUSE remains as a separate building, and the FRATER is approached first. The shell of the FRATER, almost complete, shows a sub-vault giving access to the outer court, cloister, and kitchen; and the upper floor, rebuilt *c.* 1300, was originally divided off at the E. end by screens, beyond which was the cellarer's office with loft over.

Of the CHURCH little remains: only parts of the lower walls of the chancel and transepts, fragments of the nave, and the fourteenth-century N. chapel. The chancel was enlarged *c.* 1340; and at the E. end of the choir tomb-recesses probably mark the burial-place of the Scropes.

N. of the church the INFIRMARY buildings (thirteenth century) stretch a considerable distance. They are comparatively complete with hall, chapel (built late fifteenth century), misericord, and cellar. N.W. of the hall are the buttery, pantry, and kitchen. The upper storey formed the ABBOT'S LODGING, comprising solar, hall, and chapel, with private access to the church.

Some of the woodwork from Easby was re-erected in neighbouring churches: the choir-stalls at St Mary's, Richmond, and the parclose screen, probably from the Scrope chantry, at Wensley.

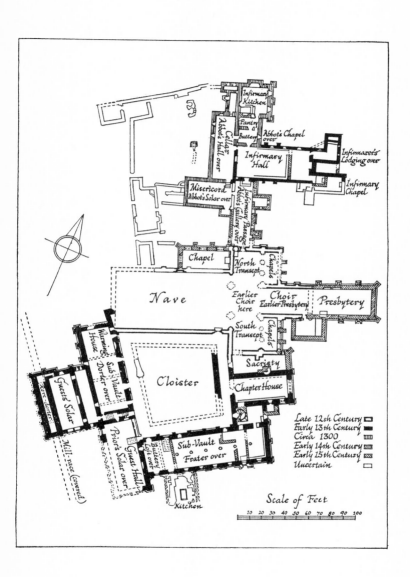

Infirmary
Kitchen

Pantry

Cellar
Abbot's Hall over

Buttery

Abbot's Chapel
over

Infirmary
Hall

Infirmarer's
Lodging over

Infirmary
Chapel

Misericord
Abbot's Solar over

Infirmary Passage
Abbot's Gallery over

Chapel

North
Transept

Chapel

Nave

Earlier
Choir
here

Choir
Earlier Presbytery

Presbytery

South
Transept

Chapels

Warming House

Sub-Vault
Dorter over

Sacristy

Guests' Solar

Cloister

Chapter House

Prior's Solar over

Guest Hall

Buttery
Cell over

Sub-Vault
Frater over

Mill-race (covered)

Kitchen

Late 12th Century
Early 13th Century
Circa 1300
Early 14th Century
Early 15th Century
Uncertain

Scale of Feet

10 20 30 40 50 60 70 80 90 100

Marrick Priory

The priory site adjoins a farmhouse on the N. bank of the Swale, reached by a farm road from Reeth or on foot by the nuns' stone stairs down through the woods from Marrick village, a mile away.   The Priory of St Andrew, a house for Benedictine nuns, was founded *c.* 1154 by Roger Aske, who endowed it with a hundred acres of land and the advowson of the parish church of Marrick.   Other gifts of land here and elsewhere followed.   Bear Park in Wensleydale was their most valuable property.   Although one of the smaller houses exempted from suppression, it was surrendered 17 November 1540; it then had a prioress and twelve nuns, and the gross annual value was £48 18*s.* 2*d.*

The parish CHURCH is still there, if in a neglected state.   Except for the tower it was pulled down and rebuilt in 1811; and old arches were used to form a chancel arch.   A chapel of ease in Marrick village, formerly a Roman Catholic church, bought in 1893, has replaced it.

Few ruins, apart from the CHURCH, remain.   The nuns, entering by the south door from a small CLOISTER, worshipped in the western half of the church, and the parishioners, entering by the north door, in the eastern end.   Some of the priory buildings are incorporated in the farmhouse; other remains may be picked out amongst the farm buildings, and the ruins of the old chancel, swathed in ivy, stand at the E. end of the church.   Note: fishponds between house and river.

Ellerton Priory

Across the river, a little E. from Marrick, is the tower of the Priory of St Mary, a small house of Cistercian nuns.   Little is known of its history, and medieval historians consider that it was founded by the Egglescliffe alias de Barden family.   It was surrendered in 1536, when its gross annual value was £15 14*s.* 8*d.*

The tower of the CHURCH, with a staircase to the top, dating from the fifteenth century, marks the site; and grave slabs of prioresses, Petronilla (d. 1251) and Ellen (d. 1268), also a third inscribed 'Hic jacet Wimerus P'sona,' are to be found inside the ruined walls of the nave.

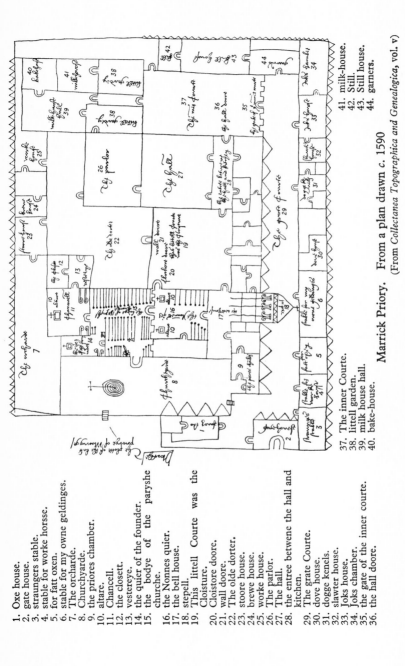

1. Oxe house.
2. gate house.
3. straungers stable.
4. stable for worke horsse.
5. for fatt oxen.
6. stable for my owne geldinges.
7. The orcharde.
8. Churchyarde.
9. the priores chamber.
10. altare.
11. Chancell.
12. the closett.
13. vestereye.
14. the quier of the founder.
15. the bodye of the paryshe
    churche.
16. the Nonnes quier.
17. the bell house.
18. stepell.
19. This littell Courte was the
    Cloisture,
20. Cloistore doore,
21. wall doore.
22. The olde dorter,
23. stoore house.
24. brewe house.
25. worke house.
26. The parlor.
27. The hall.
28. the entree betwene the hall and
    kitchen.
29. The grate Courte.
30. dove house.
31. dogge kenels.
32. slawter house.
33. Joks house,
34. Joks chamber.
35. the gate of the inner courte.
36. the hall doore.

37. The inner Courte.
38. littell garden.
39. milk house hall.
40. bake-house.

41. milk-house.
42. Still.
43. Still house.
44. garners.

Marrick Priory.   From a plan drawn c. 1590

(From Collectanea Topographica and Genealogica, vol. v)

Skipton Castle

In 1955 the castle was sold by Lord Hothfield to private purchasers. Parties are conducted round by a guide.

Of the first Norman fortress, erected by Robert Romilly, little remains except the Norman W. doorway through which the older part of the castle is reached. This stands on the site of the original KEEP, and with possibly the lower courses of the GATEHOUSE was erected by Robert Clifford in the fourteenth century. It was, however, much restored in the sixteenth century by the tenth Lord Clifford, the Shepherd Lord, and again *c.* 1659 by Lady Anne Clifford. The E. portion of the castle, the GREAT GALLERY terminating in the OCTAGON TOWER, was built *c.* 1536 by the first Earl of Cumberland for the reception of his daughter-in-law, Henry VIII's niece, Eleanor Brandon, and is now a private house.

The castle has suffered two sieges: as a stronghold for the king during the Pilgrimage of Grace, and during the Civil War when it surrendered to the Parliamentarians in 1645. It is an example of a fortified manor-house rather than a castle.

The GATEHOUSE, flanked by two fine drum-towers, was ruined in the Civil War siege, and dismantled in 1649. The upper part, rebuilt by Lady Anne, has an inscription in honour of her father, taken from Horace. On N. and S. sides of the parapet stone letters spell the Clifford motto, 'DESORMAIS' (Henceforth). Below it are the arms of Henry, fifth Earl of Cumberland. To the right of the archway is the SHELL HOUSE, decorated with shells traditionally said to have been brought back from one of his numerous voyages by George, third Earl of Cumberland, Lady Anne's father.

The old part of the castle is built round the CONDUIT COURT with round towers at the outer corners. A huge ancient yew-tree stands in the centre of the CONDUIT COURT, from which eight doorways lead to the interior, much of whose fourteenth-century masonry has been refaced. A dark apartment on the left, shown as the dungeon, may have been a cellar. The kitchen has a big fire-place at either end, stone ovens, and buttery and cellar off it. The GREAT HALL, where pictures and MSS. from the British Museum were stored in the Second World War, is fitted with an air-conditioning plant.

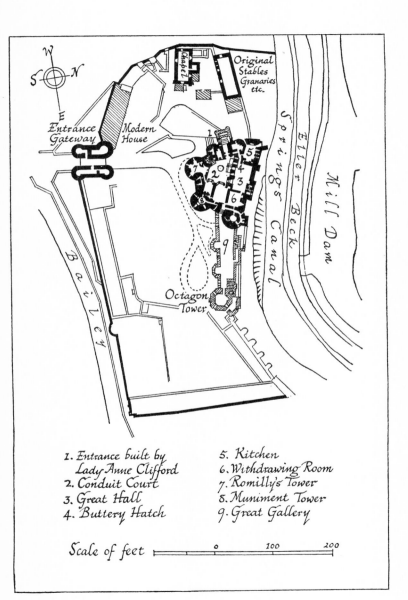

Scale of feet

1. Entrance built by
   Lady Anne Clifford
2. Conduit Court
3. Great Hall
4. Buttery Hatch
5. Kitchen
6. Withdrawing Room
7. Romilly's Tower
8. Muniment Tower
9. Great Gallery

MIDDLEHAM CASTLE

The castle came into the charge of H.M. Office of Works in 1925. The first motte and bailey fortress, built by the Norman, Ribald, stood on William's Hill in Sunskew Park; its occupation lasted about a hundred years. The present castle consists of a Norman KEEP and courtyard, enclosed by a curtain wall with corner towers, and surrounded by a moat. By marriage it came to the Nevilles of Raby Castle, and it was the headquarters of Warwick the Kingmaker. Five people were beheaded at Middleham in 1464. Following the Battle of Barnet it was given to Richard, Duke of Gloucester, afterwards Richard III, whose only son, Edward, was born and died at Middleham. The castle played no part in but was dismantled after the Civil War.

The main entrance was approached by a drawbridge across the moat to the GATEHOUSE at the N.E. corner. The latter is an early fourteenth-century three-storeyed building with gatehall and guard chamber on the ground floor. The rectangular KEEP, one of the largest in the country, was begun c. 1170 by Robert Fitzralph, and contains the principal living-rooms. A wall divides it into two, and the GREAT HALL is on the E. half of the first floor. From the S.E. angle a circular stair, from top to bottom, leads up to the parapets and down to the basement, where are kitchen, cellars, larders, and two wells. On the first floor of the KEEP in W. half is the SOLAR with a 'Chamber of Presence' to S.; the CHAPEL (late thirteenth century) is in the N.E. angle.

Ranges of buildings, which render the KEEP gloomy, occupy three sides of the curtain wall. In the S. range, with late thirteenth-century tower at S.E., are the BREWHOUSE, containing a horse-mill, and barrel-vaulted cellars, and over half the S. range is the LADY CHAMBER, once connected with the KEEP by a wooden gallery. At the S.W. is the ROUND or PRINCE'S TOWER.

The W. range contains the BAKEHOUSE on the ground floor of S. half, with the NURSERY above; the N.W. tower was added in the fourteenth century and heightened in the fifteenth century. The N. range contains AUDITOR'S KITCHEN and CHAMBER, and the GATEHOUSE. Note: groove for portcullis in the inner arch of the gatehall.

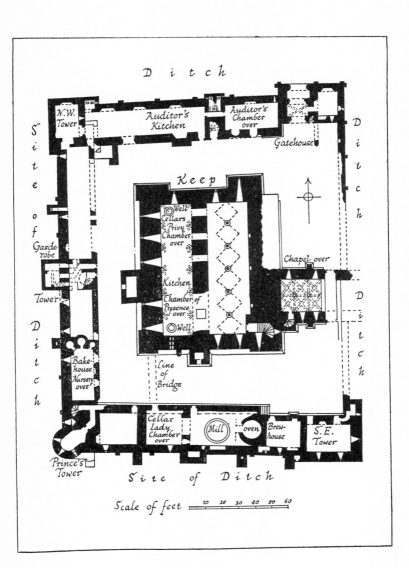

Ditch

N.W. Tower

Auditor's Kitchen

Auditor's Chamber over

Gatehouse

Site of Garderobe

Tower

Ditch

Keep

Well

Cellars

Privy Chamber over

Kitchen

Chamber of Presence over

Well

Chapel over

Ditch

Bakehouse Nursery over

Line of Bridge

Prince's Tower

Cellar lady Chamber over

Mill

oven

Brewhouse

S.E. Tower

Site of Ditch

Scale of feet   10   20   30   40   50   60

BOLTON CASTLE

Bolton Castle is owned by Lord Bolton, and is open to the public.   It
was built by Richard Scrope, first Lord Scrope, Chancellor of England,
who in 1379 obtained licence to crenellate his manor-house; some
details of its erection and construction are recorded by Leland.   From
13 July 1568 to 26 January 1569 Mary Queen of Scots was imprisoned
here.   Besieged by the Parliamentarian forces in 1645, the castle
capitulated, and was eventually dismantled.   The N.E. tower fell in a
storm in 1761, and in the early nineteenth century the S.W. tower and
W. curtain were roofed.

The castle, with square towers at the corners, and built round a
rectangular COURTYARD, is one of the most interesting of its period.
Originally only one entrance existed, at S. end of E. curtain; this with
a porter's lodge had a vaulted arch, and was guarded at each end by a
portcullis.   Other entrances, including the present one at the W. end,
are modern.   From the COURTYARD five doors, each with bar and portcullis, lead into the interior of the castle.   In the stone-vaulted ground
storey are: bakehouse, brewhouse, threshing floor, armourers' workshop, stables, store places, cellars, and the well, from which water could
be drawn up to the first floor.

The first floor of N. range consists of butteries, and the GREAT HALL.
Principal living-rooms adjoin the hall to the W. and run along W.
range.   The CHAPEL (1399), dedicated to St Anne, is on the second
floor of the S. range, and the N.E. tower contained the GREAT KITCHEN.

The second floor of the S.W. tower is traditionally MARY QUEEN OF
SCOTS'S ROOM, and from it a door leads to her bedchamber in the W.
range; but some authorities think it more likely that she occupied the
STATE APARTMENTS in the N.W. tower.   Nearly all the second floor of
the W. curtain is occupied by the SOLAR.   The GREAT CHAMBER, on the
first floor of the W. curtain, is now used as a museum for exhibits of
local interest.   Notice the DUNGEON in the basement of the N. turret,
the horse-mill in the ground floor of S.W. tower, and on the S. curtain
a secret chamber, seen by looking up from the entrance passage to the
guardroom.   Note: many masons' marks.

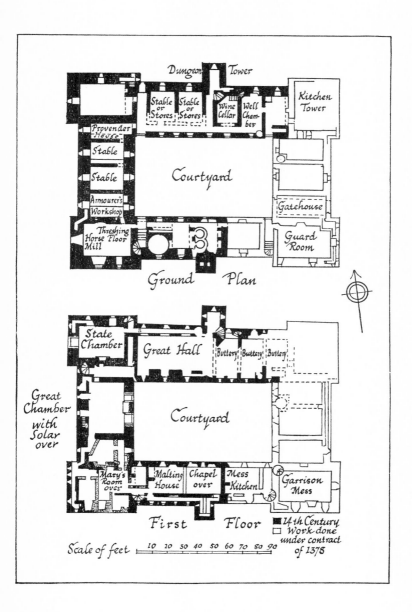

Dungeon Tower

Stable or Stores · Stable or Stores · Wine Cellar · Well Chamber

Kitchen Tower

Provender House

Stable

Stable

Armourer's Workshop

Threshing Horse Floor Mill

Courtyard

Gatehouse

Guard Room

Ground Plan

State Chamber · Great Hall · Buttery · Buttery · Buttery

Great Chamber with Solar over

Courtyard

Mary's Room over · Malting House · Chapel over · Mess Kitchen

Garrison Mess

First Floor

■ 14th Century
□ Work done under contract of 1378

Scale of feet ⊢ 10 20 30 40 50 60 70 80 90

RICHMOND CASTLE

The castle came into the charge of H.M. Office of Works in 1910. Situated on a lofty position above the River Swale, it consists of a massive KEEP and large triangular GREAT COURT surrounded by an extensive curtain wall with towers. The building, purely defensive in character, was begun in 1071 by Earl Alan Rufus as a protection against attack by English and Danes; and being naturally in a strong position was never a typical motte and bailey castle. King John came to Richmond three times; William the Lion, King of Scotland, was imprisoned in the castle; and David Bruce in 1346 and Charles I in 1646 were lodged there.

The main entrance is through the GATEHOUSE at the N. apex of the courtyard. Near it is the KEEP, 100 feet 6 inches high, from the top of which is a magnificent view. It was built by the fourth Earl Conan *c.* 1160–74 over the old gatehouse. In the ground floor is the stone vault (*c.* 1330), whose central pier is built over a well. The KEEP is reached from the vault by a stone stair, and, as was usual, has an entrance approached by stairs on the first floor.

Three rectangular towers, ROBIN HOOD TOWER, FALLEN TOWER, and GOLD HOLE TOWER, stood along the E. curtain wall, and along the W. wall was a fourth tower at the S.W. angle. N. of the latter stood the GREATER CHAPEL, mentioned in 1278, but the first chapel, dedicated to St Nicholas, was situated on the ground floor of ROBIN HOOD TOWER. To the late eleventh century belong the two-storeyed HALL, called after Scolland, sewer to the first earl, the living quarters, and the kitchen, all situated on the S.E. of the GREAT COURT. The COCKPIT, a second court, now laid out as a garden, may also date from the Norman period. Note the fine doorway into SCOLLAND'S HALL, and herring-bone masonry on the curtain wall between ROBIN HOOD TOWER and the COCKPIT wall, and near the tower at S.W. angle.

The castle was in want of repair in 1341 and a 'mere ruine' in Leland's day (*c.* 1540). In the nineteenth century a long barracks (now removed) occupied the W. side of the GREAT COURT.

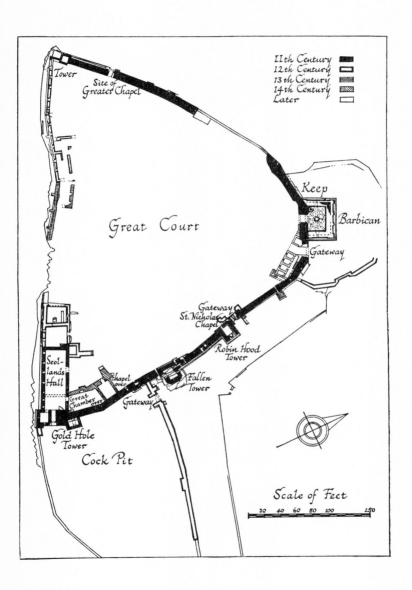

Tower

Site of
Greater Chapel

Great Court

11th Century
12th Century
13th Century
14th Century
Later

Keep

Barbican

Gateway

Gateway
St. Nicholas
Chapel

Robin Hood
Tower

Scot-
lands
Hall

Chapel
over

Great
Chamber over

Fallen
Tower

Gateway

Gold Hole
Tower

Cock Pit

Scale of Feet

20 40 60 80 100   150

CHURCHES

APPLETREEWICK (Wharfedale). St John the Baptist. Built in 1898 on site of two cottages. Improved 1933. Oak altar rails, reredos, and pulpit by Clarke of Burnsall, and pews and other woodwork by Thompson of Kilburn.

ARKENGARTHDALE. St Mary the Virgin. Rebuilt 1818–20 on new site, at cost of estate of George Brown (d. 1814). Gallery at W. end. Note: reredos and altar table (war memorial) by Thompson of Kilburn, and each side of sanctuary large wall tablets in black and fossil Dent marble to George Brown and Rev. John Gilpin (d. 1844), his son-in-law.

ARNCLIFFE (Littondale). St Oswald. First church *c.* 1100. Second church *c.* 1500 (of which only tower remains). Restored 1796, and again in 1841. Note: chancel window and screen erected to memory of Archdeacon Boyd (1835–81).

ASKRIGG (Wensleydale). St Oswald. Existed as chapel of ease under Aysgarth *c.* 1175. Restorations 1773 and 1853. S. aisle and tower fifteenth century. N. aisle, clerestory, and wooden roof sixteenth century. Piers of S. arcade (oldest architectural feature) octagonal. At E. end of S. aisle was chantry of St Anne, founded 1467 by James Metcalfe of Nappa Hall. Note: in W. window of N. aisle panel of fifteenth-century German glass, and tombstone of 'an honest attorney' on S.W. exterior wall.

AUSTWICK (W. Craven). The Epiphany. Built in 1841 and enlarged 1883. In Clapham parish until 1879. A church existed prior to 1650. Communion table made from oak from Lawkland Wood.

AYSGARTH (Wensleydale). St Andrew. Except for tower, rebuilt 1866. Note: S. of chancel, *c.* 1500 carved wooden screen, thirty-five feet in length, the finest work of its kind left in Yorkshire: before 1866 the screen divided chancel from body of church; magnificent pew-ends with poppy-heads made up into reading-desk; probably all work of Ripon carvers and either belonging to church or from Coverham Abbey, not brought from Jervaulx; N. of chancel, oak beam inscribed 'AS [Adam Sedbar] Abbas Anno Dñi 1536'; a small early font inscribed with a saltire (arms of either de Burghs or Nevilles).

BURNSALL (Wharfedale). St Wilfred. Coarse Perpendicular, but traces of early church. Rebuilt in the sixteenth century and tower added. Restored 1612 and 1859. Note: early Norman font with Anglo-Danish traditional sculpture round bowl; in W. end and N. chantry parts of eleven gravestones of Anglo-Danish period; and in N. chapel thirteenth-century alabaster carving of Adoration of Magi.

CARLTON (Coverdale). Chapel of ease under Coverham. Built 1855; restored 1875 and new schoolroom adjoining added.

CASTLE BOLTON (Wensleydale). St Oswald, *c.* 1325. No chancel arch, but corbels perhaps for rood-loft remain. Note: E. end, two niches; in chancel, triple sedilia; low-side window; N. of nave, bracket with black-letter inscription; font possibly fourteenth century; scratch dial on exterior of buttress of S. aisle.

CAUTLEY-WITH-DOWBIGGIN (near Sedbergh). St Mark. Modern with pleasant matching woodwork.

CHAPEL-LE-DALE. St Leonard. Formerly chapel of ease to Ingleton; date unknown. Separated in 1864 and 1869 restored. Note: memorial to workers on Settle–Carlisle railway.

CLAPHAM (W. Craven). St James. Probably a Saxon church here; known to date from *c.* 1170. Fourteenth-century tower. Present church, except tower, rebuilt 1814; restored 1899 and 1903. Note: old pewing fixed to aisle walls, wall tablets to Farrer family, and E. window medallions depicting Oliver, James, Thomas, and William Farrer.

CONISTON COLD (Upper Airedale). St Peter. Built 1846. Pleasant church with oak pews, pulpit, and reading-desk.

CONISTONE (Wharfedale). St Mary. Foundations said to be Saxon. Norman building restored 1846, architects Messrs Sharpe & Paley of Lancaster. Modern chancel arch and S. doorway in Norman style. Old arcade, of which two W. arches Norman and two E. probably Perpendicular. Note: memorials on wall and floor to Tennants of Chapel House and Wades of Kilnsey.

COVERHAM (Coverdale). Holy Trinity. Dates from *c.* 1250–75; *c.* 1350–75 S. aisle added. Fifteenth-century tower. Present building restored 1854 and 1878. Note: pre-Conquest stone as lintel to S. doorway.

COWGILL (Dent). St John. Built 1837 on site of old Presbyterian chapel. Note: marble wall tablet by George Nelson.

DENT (near Sedbergh). St Andrew. Blocked Early English N. doorway of early church. Present building Perpendicular. Clerestory and tower rebuilt eighteenth century. Church restored 1889–90. Note: floor of chancel, Dent marble bordered with limestone-marble from

Barrow; dated woodwork of pulpit and pews, and wall tablets to Dent families.

DOWNHOLME (Swaledale). St Michael. An aisleless Transition church *c.* 1170–80. In early thirteenth century, chancel arch with nail-head ornament rebuilt, and N. aisle added. Chancel rebuilt *c.* 1325–50. Several nineteenth-century restorations. Note: zigzag ornament on S. doorway, and on W. wall of porch tomb slab with incised cross and shears.

EASBY (Swaledale). St Agatha. Parish church before Easby Abbey was built. Originally an aisleless Norman building. Except for S. wall of chancel, rebuilt early thirteenth century. Later S.E. chapel added, and rebuilt again in Perpendicular period. Early fourteenth-century N. transept. Note: in chancel, beautiful thirteenth-century frescoes in terra-cotta and black; S. of chancel, trefoiled sedilia and piscina; N. of chancel, cast of Anglian cross (original at Victoria and Albert Museum); also N. of chancel, recessed arch, probably marks tomb of Richard Scrope (d. 1421); E. of S. aisle, two low-side windows; on nave arcade and S. wall, fragments of frescoes; elaborate Norman font; porch with two storeys, of which upper was priest's room.

GARGRAVE (Upper Airedale). St Andrew. Except Perpendicular tower, rebuilt 1852. Note: stained glass of E. window by Capronnier and well-designed wall tablet to J. W. Coulthurst.

GARSDALE (near Sedbergh). St John the Baptist. Dating at least from thirteenth century; rebuilt 1861 with bell-cote and lancet windows. Note: pulpit to memory of John Haygarth, F.R.S.

GIGGLESWICK (Ribblesdale). St Alkelda. Traces of Norman building; present edifice large Perpendicular church. Tower, nave, chancel arcades, and lower part of walls *c.* 1400. Restored and clerestory added end of fifteenth century. Many later alterations, particularly 1890–2. No chancel arch. Once three chantries: in S. aisle of chancel, Carr, later Dawson, Chapel, now restored as war memorial, and perhaps site of Chantry of the Rood, founded by James Carr for furthering education—the origin of the grammar-school; at E. end of N. aisle, the Tempest Chantry; at N. side also, possible site of Stainford Chantry. Note: seventeenth-century woodwork, especially pulpit carved with names and badges of twelve tribes of Israel; E. of N. aisle recumbent figure of knight in plate armour said to be of Sir Richard Tempest (d. 1488), and headless effigies, possibly of his wives.

GRINTON (Swaledale). St Andrew. Of original early Norman aisleless church only N. jamb of chancel arch and window above tower arch remain. Twelfth-century tower arch. Fifteenth-century arcade. Sixteenth-century chapel and vaulted sacristy N. of chancel. Sixteenth-century tower reconstructed. Restored 1896. To S. is Blackburn Chapel with in S.W. corner a squint giving view of altar from church-yard. To N. is Swale Chapel. Note: on N. pier of chancel arch, remains of rood-loft stair; circular Norman font.

HALTON GILL (Littondale). St John the Baptist. Mentioned by Harrison (1577). Rebuilt 1636 and restored 1848. Simple building with wide chancel arch. Adjoining is school, originally vicarage.

HARDRAW (Wensleydale). St Mary the Virgin and St John the Baptist. Existed as chapel of ease in parish of Aysgarth *c.* 1600. Present church erected 1800 by Earl of Wharncliffe, replacing eighteenth-century building. Note: interior walls of unplastered Stags Fell stone.

HAWES (Wensleydale). St Margaret. In existence as chapel of ease in parish of Aysgarth *c.* 1480. Rebuilt on new site 1851. Large-scale plan for restoration begun 1930. Note: much good new memorial woodwork, partly dated 1932–9, architect L. Hicks, woodworkers Messrs Wood, partly 1946, architect G. E. Charlewood, woodworkers Messrs Bramley, all of Newcastle.

HORSEHOUSE (Coverdale). St Botolph. Agreement made 9 April 1530 between the canons of Coverham Abbey and fifty-two heads of local families that chapel here, apparently newly erected, should be served by one of the canons. Marked on Saxton's map (1577). With exception of tower, rebuilt 1867.

HORTON-IN-RIBBLESDALE. St Oswald. Norman church with no chancel arch dating from *c.* 1100. Restored 1400, 1823, and 1879. Perpendicular tower, porch, and windows. Arcades run through from W. to E. end, with in chancel pointed arches and in nave circular. Note: large Norman font, much decorated with chevron pattern; Norman S. doorway with zigzag carving; fragments of old glass in W. window, one showing a bishops' head, said to be Thomas à Becket's; E. and W. of churchyard are lich-gates.

HOWGILL (near Sedbergh.) Holy Trinity. Aisleless building with small gallery. Original chapel and school founded in 1685 by John Robinson. Rebuilt on new site and consecrated 1838. Note: in a case, pitch-pipe formerly used in church.

HUBBERHOLME (Wharfedale). St Michael and All Angels. At one period referred to as St Leonard's. A Transition church, to which period belong tower arch and S. doorway. N. arcade 1500. S. arcade crude local work of same date or rather earlier. Restored 1863 by Ewan Christian of London, and electricity installed and roof releaded in 1955. Chief object of interest is the rood-loft: Percy badge is carved on it in two places and it bears the inscription 'Anno Dom MDLVIII hoc opus erat Willmi Jake carpet.' Morning is best time to see this. Note: Transition font with Perpendicular base; pews by Thompson of Kilburn; porch is much older than date on it (1696).

INGLETON (W. Craven). St Mary the Virgin. Tower (fifteenth century), but no trace of early church. Rebuilt several times, including 1743 and 1886. Note: 'Vinegar Bible,' and richly carved Norman font with reliefs of the life of Christ.

KETTLEWELL (Wharfedale). St Mary. Aisleless Norman church pulled down and present church built 1820, restored 1885. Some beams from old church are at Buckden House. Note: Transition font.

KIRKBY MALHAM (Malhamdale). St Michael the Archangel. Wholly Perpendicular with good tower, built on site of older church. No chancel arch. Clerestories run whole length of church. Note: on three W. piers of arcades and on S. wall, niches which until Reformation held figures of saints; over the third pier from W. in N. arcade is carved 'IHS' surmounted by a crown; in Lambert Chapel, S. of chancel, monuments to that family; seventeenth-century pewing; old altar rails; fourteenth-century oak chest; Transition font; in vestry, framed copy of Oliver Cromwell's signature from the registers.

LANGCLIFFE (Ribblesdale). St John the Evangelist. An aisleless building erected 1851.

LEYBURN (Wensleydale). St Matthew. Built 1868 as a chapel of ease in Wensley parish. Separated in 1956. Lectern, prayer-desk, and pulpit by Thompson of Kilburn.

LINTON-IN-CRAVEN. St Michael and All Angels. Dates from *c.* 1150. Enlarged and almost rebuilt in Decorated period. Restored 1861. Chancel arch and two arches of N. arcade Transition. Some Decorated windows. W. window Flamboyant. Bell-turret possibly thirteenth century, moved to present position in fourteenth century. Note: in sanctuary, pre-Reformation stone altar with symbolic five crosses; hanging on pillar of S. arcade, rare ninth- or tenth-century crucifix; S. side of S. aisle, two cinquefoiled niches; good Norman font.

LONG PRESTON (Ribblesdale). St Mary. A church here mentioned in Domesday Book. Present building mostly Decorated.

Chancel rebuilt 1868. Church reseated, gallery removed, and Hammerton Chapel restored in 1924. Note: S. of sanctuary, Hammerton tomb slab bearing inscription and heraldry; crude hexagonal font with canopy dated 1726; fine Jacobean pulpit; carved oak settle and chair.

LUNDS (Wensleydale). Existed as chapel of ease in parish of Aysgarth *c.* 1600. Small barn-like building in large churchyard half a mile off road.

MARSKE (Swaledale). St Edmund. Traces of Norman work in nave wall. N. arcade is Early English. Church considerably altered in seventeenth century, and restored in 1830 and 1889. Note: Norman S. doorway; crude octagonal font, dated 1663 and with initials 'THM' (Timothy and Margaret Hutton); on exterior, Hutton shield over porch; at W. end is blocked twelfth-century doorway.

MELBECKS (Swaledale). Holy Trinity. Built 1840 and restored 1886. Library in vestry contains several Wharton Bibles.

MIDDLEHAM (Wensleydale). SS. Mary and Alkelda. A church existed here in twelfth century. Present building dates from *c.* 1280. Restored in 1878. Prevailing style is Decorated. E. window Reticulated. Clerestory, tower, and aisle windows Perpendicular. In 1478 Richard, Duke of Gloucester, made church collegiate; it was suppressed in 1856. Charles Kingsley was a titular canon. Note: on N. wall, tomb slab with rebus of Robert Thornton, 22nd abbot of Jervaulx (d. 1533); in W. window of N. aisle, fragment of fifteenth-century glass representing martyrdom of St Alkelda; one of S. windows (1934) dedicated to memory of Richard III. Exterior: in E. wall, fragment of Saxon knotwork; on N. wall, Norman chevron; above S. doorway, rough carving of Crucifixion.

MUKER (Swaledale). St Mary the Virgin. Original ling-thatched church (1580), built as chapel of ease under Grinton, remained until 1761 when it was enlarged and reroofed. Restored again 1890, when musicians' gallery was removed. Exterior: at E. end, three carved stones; tombstones with quaint inscriptions.

PRESTON - UNDER - SCAR (Wensleydale). St Margaret. Built 1862 as a chapel of ease under Wensley. Altar-piece by Muriel Metcalfe.

REDMIRE (Wensleydale). St Mary the Virgin. The aisleless twelfth-century church with Early English lancets was restored 1894. Roof and E. window Perpendicular, the latter having fragments of glass with shields of Nevilles and Scropes of Bolton. Note: on N. wall of nave, projecting corbel to carry rood-beam; octagonal Early English font; simple S. doorway with zigzag moulding. Exterior: S. of chancel, blocked, square, low-side window, near it a scratch dial.

RICHMOND (Swaledale). Holy Trinity. In centre of market-place and dates from *c*. 1150. Original parish church of town. Rebuilt several times. Was used as refuge during the plague; the N. aisle once a court-room for assize and consistory courts, and the ringing chamber was a warden's post in the last war. In 1740 S. aisle was pulled down and replaced by arcade, houses, and shops. Next, nave and N. aisle restored but church shortened and cut off from tower, round which were built shops and later offices. Some of these buildings have gone. Note: Early English S. doorway with contemporary ironwork.

RICHMOND (Swaledale). The parish church of St Mary. Church existed twelfth century, but in 1858–9 it was practically rebuilt. W. bays of S. and N. arcades date from *c*. 1150 and *c*. 1190 respectively. Late twelfth-century or early thirteenth-century N. doorway. Mid-fifteenth-century vaulted N. porch and W. tower. At E. end of S. aisle memorial chapel of Green Howards. Note: in chancel, magnificent stalls from Easby Abbey; S. of sanctuary, elaborate monument to Sir Timothy Hutton, his wife and children; much woodwork by Thompson of Kilburn; memorials to Christopher Clarkson, historian (d. 1835) and George Cuitt, artist (d. 1818). Churchyard: on N. side the Plague Stone, marking burials, and S.W. of porch, below sedilia in churchyard wall, tombstone of Robert Willance.

RYLSTONE (near Skipton). St Peter. The church was entirely rebuilt 1854, and parish carved out of Burnsall 1876.

SEDBERGH (Lune valley). St Andrew. Traces of Norman work in two blocked windows above tower arch, W. arches of N. arcade, and inner doorway of N. porch. Arcades run whole length of church. S. arcade, whose W. respond is a clustered pier, and N. arcade, beyond the double respond, are Early English. Perpendicular windows and tower. Note: old pews and alms box; unusual memorials. Exterior: interesting finial decorations and curious faces terminating dripstones of windows; lich-gate.

SETTLE (Ribblesdale). Holy Ascension. Built 1838, architect Thomas Rickman of Liverpool. Church has a gallery and stands N. and S. In porch, wall tablet to workmen of Settle–Carlisle railway.

SKIPTON (Airedale). Holy Trinity. Mentioned in 1120. Early church formed part of endowment of Embsay Priory. Present building Decorated, enlarged in Perpendicular period. Inscription on N.E.

pinnacle records repairs by Lady Anne Clifford (1655). Building consists of seven bays with aisles through to end. To Decorated period belong: three W. bays with four-clustered shafts, and a window at E. end of N. aisle. Four E. bays are perhaps Perpendicular. Note: left of entrance part of fresco representing Death; in S. wall Decorated trefoil-headed sedilia; Transition font with Jacobean cover; fine Perpendicular chancel screen (1533); in sanctuary—elevated to allow for Clifford vault—three magnificent Clifford tombs.

SPENNITHORNE (Wensleydale). St Michael the Archangel. A church here mentioned in Domesday Book. Of Norman church three arches of N. arcade remain. W. arch of N. arcade, and S. arcade, added in Early English period. In the fourteenth century W. tower built, aisles widened, chancel rebuilt and lengthened, and vestry added. Church restored in the seventeenth century, eighteenth century, and 1872. Note: S. of chancel, sedilia (fourteenth century); altar rails commemorating coronation of Elizabeth II made from local oak by Arthur James; pair of oak candlesticks by Rev. J. N. Jory; reredos by Thompson of Kilburn; in vestry, Anglo-Danish grave slab, stone altar, part of roof-beam from Jervaulx, and bassoon; screen (thirteenth century) at W. end of nave said to have come from Jervaulx; at E. end of N. aisle, altar-tomb probably of John Fitzrandall (d. 1517); W. end of S. aisle, wall painting (sixteenth century) representing Time and Death. Exterior: figures on tower parapet, and many gargoyles and grotesque heads.

STAINFORTH (Ribblesdale). St Peter. Built 1842. Attractive white and blue colour scheme.

STALLING BUSK (near Semerwater). St Matthew. Entirely modern, built 1908 to replace church, now ruined, near lake. This old church built by James Lobley 1603, ruinous in Civil War, rebuilt 1722.

THORNTON-IN-LONSDALE (W. Craven). St Oswald. Of Norman church only tower remains. Chancel, nave, and side chapel rebuilt 1870, with three Norman arches incorporated. Burnt down during a blizzard on night of 25 February 1933, and present church (1935) a replica of 1870 church, including Norman arches at N.W. of nave. Pleasant pink sandstone of interior came from Tebay and green roofing slates from Coniston. Note: Redmayne Chapel with memorials to this old local family.

WENSLEY (Wensleydale). Holy Trinity. Present church dates from 1240; chancel arch and capitals, bases of two nave arcades, and S. chancel wall are of this date. Aisles rebuilt *c.* 1330; vestry with priest's lodging above, and N. and S. porches, are fifteenth century, and tower and W. end of aisles were rebuilt in the eighteenth century. Note: plate tracery in E. window; triple sedilia with detached columns and dogtooth ornament; low-side window; magnificent Flemish brass (fourteenth century) to Simon of Wensley, rector 1361–94; chancel screen (fifteenth century); chancel stalls with poppy-heads (1527), work of Ripon carvers; Bolton family pew, enclosed at back by beautiful parclose screen (sixteenth century) brought from Scrope chantry at Easby Abbey; over pew are colours of Loyal Dales Volunteers; N. wall of N. aisle, a slab with figures of Henry and Richard Scrope (sixteenth century), two small late ninth-century cross-slabs, and portion of medieval wall painting; easternmost pillars have mural paintings; pulpit dated 1760 and interesting font (1662).

WITTON, EAST (Wensleydale). St John the Evangelist. New church that replaced old church of St Ella at Lowthorpe S.E. of E. Witton. Plaque on W. wall records that in 1809 Earl of Ailesbury built new church to commemorate jubilee of George III. Architect was Henry Hake Seward. Completed in 1812, it was altered in 1872, when G. Fowler Jones was architect. Pulpit by Thompson of Kilburn.

WITTON, WEST (Wensleydale). St Bartholomew. Church mentioned in 1281, but except for tower (sixteenth century) present building was largely built in 1875. Note: in vestry, Anglian cross; two old bells, the larger an 'alphabet' bell, the smaller very ancient.

APPENDIX B
POPULATION TABLES

WEST RIDING	1801	1851	1881	1891	1931	1951
AIRTON	139	225	203	212	192	171
APPLETREEWICK	244	305	281	229	191	225
ARNCLIFFE	241	165	147	137	98	81
AUSTWICK	478	561	473	422	423	465
BARDEN	191	208	391	173	125	111
BOLTON ABBEY	120	109	142	169	193	163
BUCKDEN	280	374	297	239	222	203
BURNSALL WITH THORPE	289	253	188	155	121	154
CALTON	98	75	59	75	51	109
CLAPHAM CUM NEWBY	847	914	676	712	601	607
CONISTON COLD	342	289	337	392	182	154
CONISTONE WITH KILNSEY	182	178	179	116	138	127
CRACOE	191	159	127	91	128	127
DENT	1,773	1,630	1,209	1,113	925	786
ESHTON	84	84	64	76	70	55
FLASBY WITH WINTERBURN	120	124	128	163	94	117
GARGRAVE	728	1,214	1,287	1,296	1,232	1,417
GARSDALE	571	709	602	535	410	326
GIGGLESWICK	556	855	976	1,015	786	862
GRASSINGTON	763	1,138	617	480	1,076	1,151
HALTON GILL	139	77	86	77	79	76
HANLITH	81	36	34	26	43	39
HARTLINGTON	105	76	82	61	73	57
HAWKSWICK	69	57	51	45	43	50
HEBDEN	341	460	313	209	289	252
HELLIFIELD	237	279	424	601	1,026	1,045
HETTON	172	155	142	146	97	80
HORTON-IN-RIBBLESDALE	570	464	526	666	726	710
INGLETON	1,106	1,391	1,625	1,568	2,227	1,892
KETTLEWELL WITH STARBOTTON	634	607	378	313	330	304
KIRKBY MALHAM	167	139	145	107	103	55
LANGCLIFFE	260	601	683	681	540	501
LAWKLAND	368	379	301	307	225	235
LINTON	186	352	127	117	244	409
LITTON	114	114	78	61	65	59
LONG PRESTON	573	590	706	734	646	610
MALHAM	262	188	148	163	126	171
MALHAM MOOR	98	92	126	118	99	120
OTTERBURN	26	54	39	47	60	53
RYLSTONE	177	123	130	136	122	120
SCOSTHROP	90	75	67	80	59	56
SEDBERGH	1,639	2,235	2,268	2,374	2,234	2,330

WEST RIDING	1801	1851	1881	1891	1931	1951
SETTLE	1,136	1,976	2,213	2,253	2,455	2,297
SKIPTON	2,305	5,044	9,091	10,376	12,461	13,207
STAINFORTH	203	225	207	203	211	239
THORNTON-IN-LONSDALE	—	412	320	295	299	260
THRESHFIELD	201	271	167	119	380	375

NORTH RIDING	1801	1851	1881	1891	1931	1951
ABBOTSIDE, HIGH	559	588	493	412	330	285
ABBOTSIDE, LOW	235	161	130	143	140	120
AGGLETHORPE WITH COVERHAM	156	204	110	102	142	146
ARKENGARTHDALE	1,186	1,283	999	761	345	304
ASKRIGG	761	633	624	552	488	414
AYSGARTH	268	253	370	235	299	259
BAINBRIDGE	785	814	683	595	562	488
BISHOPDALE	84	77	87	91	61	34
BURTON CUM WALDEN	446	483	444	409	367	284
CALDBERGH WITH SCRAFTON, EAST	73	96	72	75	43	56
CARLTON HIGHDALE	328	388	247	204	181	165
CARLTON TOWN	236	274	252	199	209	184
CARPERBY CUM THORESBY	280	342	244	232	242	210
CASTLE BOLTON	242	240	169	149	121	118
DOWNHOLME	114	129	112	73	74	77
EASBY	85	114	123	147	119	126
ELLERTON ABBEY	79	58	44	48	21	30
GRINTON	518	598	377	280	279	225
HAWES	1,223	1,708	1,890	1,615	1,406	1,196
LEYBURN	446	800	972	982	1,440	1,281
MARRICK	474	555	307	246	146	137
MARSKE	239	244	268	222	180	133
MELBECKS	1,274	1,661	1,165	600	402	388
MELMERBY	106	120	110	102	74	72
MIDDLEHAM	728	966	818	732	651	644
MUKER	1,119	1,321	837	615	502	416
NEWBIGGIN	121	130	104	101	77	67
NEW FOREST	68	67	49	36	53	21
PRESTON-UNDER-SCAR	260	407	362	298	248	206
REDMIRE	320	373	347	243	229	203
REETH	1,128	1,344	988	667	616	588
RICHMOND [1]	2,861	4,106	4,502	4,216	4,769	6,166
SCRAFTON, WEST	107	139	106	106	73	62
THORALBY	313	288	216	218	160	123
WALBURN	40	33	30	30	31	31
WENSLEY	237	285	322	261	212	207
WITTON, EAST, WITHIN	388	325	240	249	227	243
WITTON, EAST, WITHOUT	294	285	236	222	131	79
WITTON, WEST	446	550	550	404	377	355

[1] Municipal borough.

APPENDIX C

SOME REGIONAL RECIPES

ORIGINAL AND OLD-FASHIONED ARKENGARTHDALE RECIPES

(Mrs W. H. Hutchinson of Arkengarthdale)

1. CHEESECAKES:

Pastry: $3\frac{1}{2}$ lb. flour, 2 lb. butter, $\frac{1}{2}$ lb. lard, salt.   Do not add water or baking-powder.

Filling: 7 pints milk with 1 small teaspoon rennet made into curd. $1\frac{1}{2}$ lb. castor sugar, $1\frac{1}{2}$ lb. currants, $\frac{1}{4}$ lb. lemon peel cut very small, 4 eggs or more if required for a soft consistency, 2 tablespoons cream, 2 or 3 oz. melted butter, mixed spices.   To make curd (previous night) heat milk to blood heat and add rennet.   Keep warm, stand an hour, break down, remove whey gently, and leave hung up in cloth all night to drain.   Mix in remainder of ingredients for filling, make up as small tarts and bake in very hot oven.

2. FUNERAL CAKES:

12 lb. flour, 10 lb. butter, 9 lb. sifted sugar, 3 teaspoons baking-powder, 1 small teaspoon carbonate of soda, a few caraway-seeds.

Mix all together, weigh 5 oz. to a cake, press out with a stamp. Makes a hundred cakes.

3. LOVEFEAST LOAF:

$\frac{1}{4}$ stone flour, 1 lb. butter, $\frac{3}{4}$ lb. lard, 2 lb. sugar, 2 lb. currants, $\frac{1}{4}$ lb. lemon peel, 2 eggs, 2 oz. yeast, 2 teaspoons baking-powder, 1 teaspoon carbonate of soda, salt, mixed spices, milk to mix.   Makes four large loaves.

4. MELL CAKES (BANNOCKS):

2 lb. flour, 14 oz. lard, 8 oz. currants, 2 teaspoons baking-powder, salt.

Make into a stiff dough and roll into rounds the size of a breakfast plate.   When cooked and whilst hot split and butter generously. Sift sugar on each and pile one on top of another.

311

5. Secret Cakes:

3½ lb. flour, 1 lb. butter, ¾ lb. lard, salt, a little baking-powder. Filling: 1½ lb. currants, ½ lb. sugar, 2 oz. lemon peel, 1 oz. butter.

Wash currants, then stew gently with other ingredients and a little water. Roll out pastry and cut out size of a cheese plate. Pinch well the dampened edges.

6. Yule Cake:

3½ lb. flour, 1 lb. currants, 1 lb. raisins, 1 lb. sugar, 12 oz. lard, 2 eggs, 4 oz. yeast, mixed spices, peel, salt.

Lay in with hot milk, set to prove, then put into tins and put to rise again. Bake in moderate oven. Makes four loaves.

Farmhouse Wensleydale Cheese Recipe
(Miss C. Bell of Askrigg)

It is difficult to write down a recipe for Wensleydale cheese. So much depended on the skill of the maker, who worked from long experience and individual judgment, never wholly from a set recipe.

1. Skim off cream, and heat milk and cream separately to 85° F.
2. Mix cream with milk (never overheat cream).
3. Add cheese rennet (1 dessertspoon to 20 gallons of milk).
4. In next ten minutes give an occasional gentle stir.
5. Leave an hour to curdle.
6. Cut down *very gently* with knife or breaker (metal object like a tennis racket) into pieces about size of fingers.
7. Again let it stand for half an hour.
8. Either cut it again or use breaker.
9. Stir gently round and round and round.
10. Ladle off whey and make sure no 'slips' (curds as in 6) are left.
11. Let it sink gradually to the bottom.
12. Strain it by putting cheese strainering (loosely woven cloth) over curd and letting whey come through it; ladle off.
13. When dry enough put into lead-bowl or hang up in strainering, to let all whey run out.
14. Leave for about four hours.
15. Break into small pieces, place cheese calico over vat, put curd in this, place in cheese vats, and put sinker (lid) on.
16. Press, gradually at first, for twenty-four hours.

17. Pickle in brine a day or two, small cheeses a shorter time than large ones. (Brine is correct strength if an egg will float in it.)
18. Bandage with calico to preserve shape.
19. Keep downstairs until wet has run off. Turn them twice a day.
20. Take up to shelves of cheese room. Turn every day.

Utensils required: cheese kettle, cheese vats, breaker, sieve, strainering, calico, cheese press.

In six months' time you should have blue Wensleydale cheeses. To be perfect they must be made from rich milk of young cows fed on sweet herbage of dales meadows.

Stamp for impressing design on funeral cakes

APPENDIX D

A SHORT LIST OF DIALECT WORDS COLLECTED IN SWALEDALE AND WENSLEYDALE

Ah light seea, I understand so.
Alawand, I'll warrant.
Alopod, I'll uphold.
Amang hands, in the midst of other work. We're thrang wi t'hay an' howing turnips amang hands.
Anthers, perchance. I walked anthers I got a ride.

Bat and breead, when mowing the 'bat' is the distance the mower advances, and the 'breead' the breadth of his cut.
Belk, to belch.
Bensil, to thrash.
Bettermer, better. Bettermer folk.
Boose, a stall in a cow-shed.
Bumblekites, blackberries.

Caingy, bad-tempered dog or person.
Catarz, cat-haws. Hawthorn berries.
Cheg, to chew. He were chegging away.
Choops, fruit of the wild rose. Hips.
Clag, to stick.
Clashy, stormy and wet. Varra clashy weather.
Clumpst, cold. My feet are fairly clumpst.
Creel, a wood and rope farming implement for carrying hay on a man's shoulders.
Cu frae, origin. Come from. Whar's ta cu frae?

Dasher, comb with large teeth for combing hair.
Dashery, housework. Thou's gitten dashery done.
Daunton, mid-morning snack.
Dazzened, cold, starved.
Deg, to sprinkle water. See 'at clooas is degged.
Donnot, naughty child.
Dowly, lonely, dreary.
Dree, slow, tedious.

Fansome, pretty, handsome. A child with winning ways. A fansome lile thing.
Feckend, most, a majority.

Feeding storm, one storm following another.
Flay crah, a scarecrow.
Flish, a blister.
Flite, to scold.   Ah gave him a good fliting.
Floudby, cold and wild.   A floudby day.
Foob, to puff, bubble up.   It's foobed up.

Geeavlock, gavelock, crowbar.
Geg or *gag o' t'ee*, judging by the eye, instead of measuring.
Glave, shivery, cold.   A glave sort o' neet.
Glep, to glance.   Ah just glep't in.
Glishy, gleaming.   T'sun's varra glishy.
Glop, gloppen, to stare open-mouthed.
Grosky, greening up of vegetation.
Gussy, growing.   A gussy sort of day.

Hankled, confused, disordered.   Garn's (yarn's) fair hankled up.
Hapsha rapsha, haphazard.
Heck, back door of a cart.
Huggins, hips.   A part of the body.
Hullet, owl.

In bank, downhill.

Jadder or *jather*, vibrate.   His teeth jaddered again.
Jemmers, hinges.
Jike, to squeak.   T'watter was so hard, it fair jiked on yer face.

Kep, to catch.   T'lad kepped t'bull grandly.
Kitlin, young cat.
Kittle, to itch.   He kittles all ower him.
Kizzened, withered, wizzened.
Knacky, clever, handy.   He's a knacky chap.
Kysty, fastidious.   Oor Jim, he's a kysty lile chap.

Lander, a wooden trough, especially gutter on eaves of house.
Leea, a scythe for mowing grass.
Leetening, a rally in one ill.   A bit of leetening.
Let weet, never informed anyone.
Lish, agile.   He's as lish as ivver he were.
Loun, sheltered, quiet.   It's a varra loun day.
Low, a flame.   Cooals is lowing.

Maffly, muddled, not so well.   Ah'se varra maffly to-day.
Mannerly, good.   She's a gey mannerly body.   We've a mannerly crop
   of hay.   A mannerly day.
Marra to bran, spit and image.
Mense, decorate, improve.

Mouth hold, a good long drink.
Muffatees, knitted cuffs.
Murl, to crumble.   Plaister were that dry, it fair murled away.

Nazzart, rascal.   Thou lile nazzart.
Neeaf, fist.   He's a neeaf like a ham.
Nephezel, thrifty or greedy.
Nowl, to toll.   Wheea's t'bell nowling for?

Oxters, under the arm-pits.

Packy, cloudy.   Clouds is varra packy taneet.
Panable, pleasing to the eye.
Pash, a sudden heavy shower.   It's been a heavy pash o' rain.
Pleean, to complain.   He pleeaned badly to me.
Pretha, pray thee.   Preliminary phrase to any remark.

Reach teea, invitation.   Reach teea, there's plenty to yet [eat].
Reckle, to stir the fire.   Reckle t'fire up.
Reeasted, meaning either jibbed, of a horse, or rancid as applied to bacon.
Rowk, untidy, all upset, disordered.

Same, lard.   Gaa tet shop an' bring a pund o' same.
Sarra, to serve.   Gaa an' sarra t'hens.
Scale, to disperse, scatter.   He's scaling t'coo claps.   Send us a bottle
   o' medicine to scale it [a complaint] away.
Sewerlie, surely.
Sikelike, suchlike.
Sile, milk strainer.
Sitha, sista, see there.   Look sista he's gaen ter kill 'issel.
Skellet, a small iron pan.
Slape and promise, slipshod and half done.
Slockened, to slake the thirst.   Ah've gitten a good drink an' ah'm
   slockened.
Sluff, to shed, or a berry skin.
Smed up, steam or frost on windows.
Smoot, a hole in a wall.   Smoot-hole.
Snirp, to scorch.   T'meat's gitten all snirped up i' t'oven.
Snizy, raw, cold.   A snizy day.
Sooker steeane, large flag over fire with opening for smoke.
Speean, to wean.   It's aboot time that barn [child] was speeaned.
Squab, langsettle.   A long bench usually near the hearth.
Steck, shy, jib.   T'horse takes steck an' weeant stir.
Steg, old gander.
Stiddy, anvil.
Stilter, to stagger.
Strickle, scythe sharpener.
Strinkle, to scatter.

Tarrant or *testril*, a bad child.   Lile tarrant.
T'eean with t'uther, the one with the other.   T'eean side wit t'uther
    side.   T'eean way wit t'uther.
Teeave, to paddle.   He went teeavan away through all t'snaw.
Teng, to sting.   A wasp's just tenged lile chap.
Thibel, a stick for stirring porridge.
Tied, obliged.   Ah'se tied to gang [forced to go].
Trunnel or *trinel*, wheelbarrow wheel.
Twankey, large, bulky.
Twitchbell, earwig.

Ware, to spend.   He wared his brass on't.
Wark, ache.   Ah'm nearly killed wi' backwark.   (Similarly 'toothwark.')
Weeak, to cry with fright.   When t'schulemaister hit him wi' t'cane he
    fair weeaked.
Welder, many.
Wemmle, to overturn.   Pan wemmled ower.
Weng, leather shoe-lace.
Whemmed, moved.   Ah wasn't a bit whemmed.
Whyah, well, yes, used in several senses.   Whyah ah'll be gitten doon
    heeame.
Womel, angry.
Wummel, A boring tool.

Yal, ale.
Yan, one.
Yow, ewe.

SELECTED BIBLIOGRAPHY

Victoria County History of Yorkshire, vols. i, ii, and iii, and *North Riding,* vol. i

Volumes of the Y.A.S.J. and Y.A.S. Record Series

'Guide of Model of Ingleborough,' *Memoirs of the Geological Survey*

'The Geology of Ingleborough,' *Memoirs of the Geological Survey*

The *Dalesman,* and *Dalesman* Pocket Books

Early Yorkshire Charters, vols. i, iv, and v

T. D. WHITAKER: *History of Richmondshire; History of Craven*

H. SPEIGHT: *Craven and the North-West Yorkshire Highlands; Romantic Richmondshire*

T. WHELLAN & CO.: *York and the North Riding,* vol. i

Directories (1822, 1823, 1838, 1840, 1867, 1890)

ELLA PONTEFRACT AND MARIE HARTLEY: *Wharfedale; Wensleydale;* and *Swaledale*

THOMAS BRAYSHAW AND RALPH M. ROBINSON: *The Ancient Parish of Giggleswick*

FREDERICK WILLIAMS: *The Midland Railway*

A. RAISTRICK: *Malham and Malham Moor*

A. RAISTRICK: 'Iron Age Settlements in West Yorkshire.' Y.A.S.J., vol. xxxiv

W. H. DAWSON: *The History of Skipton*

J. W. MORKILL: *Kirkby Malhamdale*

R. BALDERSTONE: *Ingleton Bygone and Present*

F. RILEY: *Dentdale and Garsdale*

JOHN J. BRIGG: *The King's Highway in Craven*

LORD FARRER: *Some Farrer Memorials*

W. THOMPSON: *Sedbergh, Garsdale, and Dent*

J. FAIRFAX-BLAKEBOROUGH: *Northern Turf History,* vols. i and ii

INDEX